Contemporary Perspectives on Language and Cultural Diversity in Early Childhood Education

A volume in
Contemporary Perspectives in Early Childhood Education
Olivia N. Saracho and Bernard Spodek, *Series Editors*

Contemporary Perspectives in Early Childhood Education

Olivia Saracho and Bernard Spodek, *Series Editors*

Contemporary Perspectives on Mathematics in Early Childhood Education
Edited by Olivia Saracho and Bernard Spodek

Contemporary Perspectives on Science and Technology in Early Childhood Education
Edited by Olivia Saracho and Bernard Spodek

Contemporary Perspectives on Social Learning in Early Childhood Education
Edited by Olivia Saracho and Bernard Spodek

Contemporary Perspectives on Socialization and Social Development in Early Childhood Education
Edited by Olivia Saracho and Bernard Spodek

Contemporary Perspectives on Language Policy and Literacy Instruction in Early Childhood Education
Edited by Olivia Saracho and Bernard Spodek

Contemporary Perspectives on Families, Communities and Schools for Young Children
Edited by Olivia Saracho and Bernard Spodek

International Perspectives on Research in Early Childhood Education
Edited by Olivia Saracho and Bernard Spodek

Studying Teachers in Early Childhood Settings
Edited by Olivia Saracho and Bernard Spodek

Contemporary Perspectives on Play in Early Childhood Education
Edited by Olivia Saracho and Bernard Spodek

Contemporary Perspectives on Early Childhood Curriculum
Edited by Olivia Saracho and Bernard Spodek

Contemporary Perspectives on Literacy in Early Childhood Education
Edited by Olivia Saracho and Bernard Spodek

Contemporary Perspectives on Early Childhood Ed Personnel: Preparation, Practice and Professionalism
Edited by Olivia Saracho and Bernard Spodek

Contemporary Perspectives on Language and Cultural Diversity in Early Childhood Education

Edited by

Olivia N. Saracho
University of Maryland

Bernard Spodek
University of Illinois

IAP
INFORMATION AGE PUBLISHING, INC.
Charlotte, NC • www.infoagepub.com

KH

Library of Congress Cataloging-in-Publication Data

Contemporary perspectives on language and cultural diversity in early childhood education / edited by Olivia N. Saracho, Bernard Spodek.
p. cm. – (Contemporary perspectives in early childhood education)
Includes bibliographical references.
ISBN 978-1-60752-416-8 (pbk.) – ISBN 978-1-60752-417-5 (hardcover) – ISBN 978-1-60752-418-2 (e-book)
1. Language arts (Early childhood) 2. Reading (Early childhood) 3. Early childhood education–Activity programs. I. Saracho, Olivia N. II. Spodek, Bernard.
LB1139.5.L35C64 2010
372.6–dc22
2009053672

Printed in the United States of America

10/28/13

Editorial Advisory Board

Consulting Editors

CONTENTS

PART II

LINGUISTICALLY AND CULTURALLY DIVERSE FAMILIES AND COMMUNITIES

PART III

TEACHERS OF LINGUISTICALLY AND CULTURALLY DIVERSE CHILDREN

PART IV

CONCLUSION

CHAPTER 1

LINGUISTICALLY AND CULTURALLY DIVERSE CHILDREN

Their Educational Dilemmas

Olivia N. Saracho and Bernard Spodek

Over the past three decades, the foreign-born population in the United States has tripled, reaching 35 million people in 2005. Gollnick and Chinn (2008) report that the total population is growing at an annual rate of two million people; almost half of that expansion is from the immigrant population. The United States Census Bureau (2003) estimates that by 2030 approximately 40% of children will be new immigrants to the United States and that most of them will be non-English speakers who speak their native language in their home.

Over the last 15 years, the number of culturally and linguistically diverse children under five years of age in the United States has increased from 26% to 45% (United States Census Bureau, 1990, 2005). Increasingly more such children are being educated and cared for in early childhood settings. The enrollment of preschool linguistically and culturally diverse children

Language and Cultural Diversity in Early Childhood Education, pages 1–17

has doubled from 20% in 1990 to approximately 40% in 2000 (United States Census Bureau, 1990, 2000). Immigrants' ethnic backgrounds have shifted from predominantly white Europeans to Latinos and Asians. This has increased the ethnic diversity in the United States population, particularly among young children. The United States Department of Education (2007) estimates that by the year 2020, more than two thirds of the public school population in the United States will consist of children of African-American, Asian-American, Latino, or Native-American backgrounds.

During the last 10 to 15 years, immigrants have also shifted their destinations within the United States. Immigrant families continue to be highly concentrated in "traditional gateway" states, such as California; but an increasing dispersion of immigrants has developed in new areas, including many small communities (Dinan, 2006). Many communities, which are not entering locations for immigration, find that the children of immigrants have become the fastest-growing element in their child population. Some immigrant families have a mixed-status—the parents are noncitizens, but the children are citizens. These immigrant parents differ in their educational profiles, their English-language fluency, and their economic status. The United States is considered among the most culturally, ethnically, racially, and linguistically diverse countries in the world. Its children in early childhood settings continue to become increasingly culturally and linguistically diverse.

In the open-ended American society, the education system provides opportunities for social mobility. Our nation has also used schools to communicate society's values to children of different cultures and languages. Language and culture are the predominant elements in the children's lives. Culture defines their distinctive experiences, whereas language assists them to communicate their culture in society (Saracho, & Spodek, 1995).

During the 1990s, early childhood researchers became aware of the need to explore ways to offer programs and services that responded to the needs and preferences of young children from diverse cultural and linguistic families (Tabors, 1998). Researchers found that each group may respond to a different teaching method. They recommend that early childhood teachers use a range of strategies in working with young children from varied cultural and linguistic backgrounds. Most early childhood teachers are members of a cultural group that differs from this diverse population (Saluja, Early, & Clifford, 2002). They also lack experiences in working with linguistically and culturally different children (Hollins & Guzman, 2005), and may have difficulty discussing race (Gay & Howard, 2000).

Early childhood teacher preparation programs differ in the degree to which they provide appropriate knowledge to their enrollees, which would allow them to work effectively with young children from diverse backgrounds (Early &Winton, 2001). Lim, Maxwell, Able-Boone, and Zimmer

(2009) found that the Bachelor's degree programs from the 2003/2004 Integrated Postsecondary Education Data System showed the absence of full-time faculty from culturally diverse backgrounds. This limits the required coursework they offer that focuses on working with children and families from culturally diverse backgrounds. However, the National Council for Accreditation of Teacher Education accreditation requires coursework that focuses on working with bilingual children and English language learners. It is important that professionals develop a groundwork of knowledge and practical strategies to meet children's needs, especially those who are from linguistically and culturally diverse backgrounds.

SOCIAL JUSTICE AS CULTURAL DIVERSITY

Earlier definitions of cultural diversity were related to race/ethnicity, age, gender, sexual orientation, class, religion, or geography. Recently, social justice has become a component of cultural diversity, in an effort to describe the different groups' experiences. Social justice is associated with recognizing the appropriate and equitable distribution of resources, advocacy, and empowerment (Vera & Speight, 2003), but it later evolved to include other positionalities, such as race, ethnicity, gender, age, sexual orientation, religion, geography/region (Bryan, 2007; Smith, Foley, & Chaney, 2008). Multiculturalism, cultural diversity, and social justice became integrated through the concern for people with similar situations and marginalizations (Warren & Constantine, 2007). In addition, social justice is directed toward an understanding of the individuals' circumstances and the conditions that weaken their lives and cause them to become marginalized (Vera & Speigh, 2003). Robinson-Wood (2009) states that "how it is done and to what extent it is done in relation to social justice, describes a social justice framework" (p. 284). Harley, Alston, Turner-Whittaker (2008) examined the movement that integrated cultural diversity and social justice to provide a model for curriculum development.

Historically, cultural differences among people reflected the sociopolitical climate of the time, anthropological development, deficit models' points of view, and, presently, the value in diversity (Lee, Blando, Mizelle, & Orozco, 2007). For more than a decade, scholars accepted the concern for extending the characteristics of social justice (Goodlad & Riddell, 2005) to involve both visible and invisible uniqueness (Harley, Jolivette, McCormick, & Tice, 2002; Robinson-Wood, 2009), as well as to include cultural diversity. Explicitly, cultural diversity would be defined to include race, ethnicity (Smart & Smart, 1995), sexual orientation (Harley, Hall, & Savage, 2000), language (Leal-Idrogo, 1995; Smart & Smart, 1995), gender (Chung & Rubin, 2008), age (Kampfe, Harley, Wadsworth, & Smith, 2007), geography

(Harley, 2006; Harley, Bishop, & Wilson, 2002), religion (McCarthy, 1995; Morrison-Orton, 2004), and meeting points of these multiple elements (Harley et al., 2002; Robinson-Wood, 2009; Sue & Capodilupo, 2008). It is important that early childhood professionals understand and accept these elements and incorporate the knowledge of them into a just practice.

ACADEMIC PATHS REFORMS

Recent findings suggest that young children's learning experiences are critical to their learning development, which has attracted the attention of researchers, scholars, and policy makers. Interest has focused on the early childhood policy and practice that can help improve the academic paths of children in poverty, who are considered to be at high risk for early school drop out, poor academic performance, and behavior problems (Lim, Maxwell, Able-Booneb, & Zimmer, 2009). Many of these children are from linguistically and culturally diverse families. The purpose of this volume is to review and summarize the current state of knowledge related to linguistically and culturally diverse children. We have attempted to expand cultural diversity to include social justice, which we hope will be helpful in providing effective teacher preparation programs and high quality programs for linguistically and culturally diverse children.

Schools need to offer young children opportunities that support their home language, if it is other than English, and to use their native language to promote their learning. Saracho and Spodek (1983) describe the penalties that children have faced in the school during past generations. Parents and teachers would tell children from homes where both the language and culture were obviously different from that of mainstream America to disregard the life that they have learned to value. Young children immediately learned that to succeed in school, they had to follow the ideal that was offered by their mainstreamed "American" teacher. Their instructions were, "Speak the way the teacher speaks, not the way we speak at home!" "Learn to behave like a 'real American'!" (Saracho & Spodek, 1983, p. viii) "You must overlook and suppress everything else."

ENGLISH LANGUAGE LEARNERS

Presently, one out of seven children in the United States is in the group of children who are considered English language learners (ELLs) whose native language differs from the school's English language. In the early 1970s, studies on ELLs emerged, and researchers continue to be interested in this population. They are examining the ELLs' educational performance and identifying the characteristics of effective schools for ELLs. Also, the political debate over bilingual education (i.e., providing instruction in the students' native language) has instigated researchers to evaluate the effectiveness of bilingual education in comparison with other ways of teaching English. This has produced a large collection of studies on the education of ELLs, including basic instructional methods and characteristics of effective programs (August & Hakuta, 1998). The first three chapters in this volume review and analyze studies on ELLs. The first two focus on language, while the third reviews the importance of listening in second language acquisition.

In the chapter, "The Politics of Language and Educational Practices: Promoting Truly Diverse Child Care Settings," Judith K. Bernhard and Veronica Pacini-Ketchabaw review the significance of language in the early years with a particular focus on language maintenance and bilingualism in North American early schooling. The analysis of the common phenomenon of quick home language loss among children in child care centers is focused on the power relations among teachers, families, children, and the society at large. Young children and families often receive subtle messages from educators that convey to them that their home language is not as valuable as English. Bernhard and Pacini-Ketchabaw recommend innovative instructional practices to challenge the common phenomenon of loss of children's first language and culture and to foster cultural and linguistic diversity. These recommendations point toward the need of addressing the politics of language loss.

The United States has long been a nation of incredible cultural and linguistic diversity. This trend of ethnic and racial population diversification continues most rapidly among its young and school-age children. In 2005, 25% of the birth cohort in the United States, some one million newborns, was Hispanic, with over 70% born to mothers whose primary language was Spanish and of immigrant "origins." Academic achievement gaps for this Hispanic population, especially those coming to school not speaking English, are present at the beginning of kindergarten and become more solidified from the third through the eighth grades; this population has a significantly lower rate of finishing high school and attending college. Moreover, today's population continues to have deep concerns with regard to the quality of education, and the public has acted at the federal and state levels to mount educational policies directed at these achievement gaps. Many of these specific reform initiatives have been aimed at Hispanic students for several decades. These reforms have generated some movement at the policy, practice, and achievement levels.

New, innovative policies and educational practices, such as early education, dual language programs, and family-centered interventions, are examples of new thinking with regard to this population. Since language is a key element in the young Hispanics' cognitive development and early learning, in "Language Development and Early Education of Young Hispanic Children in the United States," Eugene E. García and Bryant Jensen discuss topics (e.g., bilingualism and second language learning) that relate to questions of language use and practice. They review and discuss studies on the relevant characteristics of Hispanic children in terms of proportional representation and provide, where possible, descriptions of Hispanic samples of children. Although many studies have described the cultural context in which young Hispanics use and develop language, few have made the conceptual and methodological links necessary to understand how home and school contexts (including differences between contexts) influence early literacy and learning outcomes. To fill this major gap in the literature, García and Jensen discuss this issue at greater length in the final section of their chapter. In addition to research on language and literacy development, they review the literature on school program effectiveness, including dual-language programs, research on assessment, English acquisition, cross-linguistic transfer, and directions for future research and practice. Most of the studies discussed focus on the school-age young Hispanic children whose ages range from five to eight years of age, with a few studies on Hispanics in ages between infancy and four years of age. Their chapter is organized thematically to respond to the following questions:

- What is the range of linguistic proficiency of young Hispanic children in the United States?
- How do linguistic properties between Spanish and English relate and develop for young Hispanic children?
- What relationship does social context have with the language and literacy development of young Hispanic children in the United States?
- What schooling program options are available to young Hispanic children learning English, and what does the evidence show in terms of programmatic features that promote literacy, academic achievement, and "academic" English proficiency?

García and Jensen conclude with a summary of critical issues related to the linguistic development and early education of young Hispanic children in the United States. In accordance with the literature reviewed, they offer a set of recommendations for future research endeavors.

In the last 15 years, the United States has experienced a demographic shift that has dramatically increased the racial, ethnic, cultural, and linguistic diversity among young children and families who are enrolled in early childhood programs. The increasing number of Latino dual language learners (DLLs) constitutes a challenge and an opportunity for the provision of high quality early care and education. Furthermore, many of the widely used indicators of program quality would benefit from further addition of elements related to serving young diverse learners. In "Language and Literacy Development in Latino Dual Language Learners: Promising Instructional Practices," Dina C. Castro, Ellen Peisner-Feinberg, Virginia Buysse, and Cristina Gillanders review current research and identify knowledge gaps and future research directions related to instructional practices to promote language and literacy development in Latino DLLs. The studies they reviewed suggest that implementing specific instructional accommodations is beneficial to meeting the educational needs of Latino DLLs. However, additional research is needed to add to the knowledge about specific instructional approaches that are effective in promoting language and literacy in young Latino DLLs.

Studies estimate that students spend between 50% and 75% of their time in school listening to the teacher, other students, or audio media (International Listening Association, 2008; Smith, 2008). The importance of listening skills is amplified in second language contexts, where students lack an understanding of the language (McKay, 2008; National Capital Language Resource Center, 2008). Since listening is important in the children's academic success, effective listening skills and strategies need to be considered with young ELLs (Jalongo, 2008). Thus, listening becomes of critical importance for these children, because listening is the first language ability that is developed in children without hearing impairments. Furthermore, ELLs, to a large extent, rely on listening in the early stages of language acquisition in both their first language and in other languages that they learn. Developmental stages in second language acquisition indicate that "silent" is the beginning stage, because ELLs usually are silent for a period of time before they make an effort to compose any utterances in their second language (Ellis, 2007). In "Young English Language Learners as Listeners: Theoretical Perspectives, Research Strands, and Implications for Instruction," Mary Renck Jalongo and Nan Li discuss the particular significance that listening has for young ELLs, because it is foundational to the other language arts of speaking, reading, and writing. They begin their chapter with an overview of demographic data on ELLs in the United States. Next, they use Stephen Krashen's theory of second language acquisition to analyze three strands in the literature:

- Studies of the listening environment
- Investigations of vocabulary development in young ELLs
- Research on the oracy/literacy connection

Jalongo and Li conclude their chapter with the implications of the research by focusing on the types of programs, instructional practices, and teacher behaviors that promote the language development of young children.

LINGUISTICALLY AND CULTURALLY DIVERSE FAMILIES AND COMMUNITIES

Young children and their families reflect an increasing diversity of language and culture. Early childhood programs are responsible for offering a friendly environment that respects the diversity in the children's and families' language and culture; encourages children's relationship to their families and community; and promotes the families' social factors in the children's development, including their child rearing practices, family roles, sociolinguistic patterns, historical, political, and economic systems, as well as the individual's family socialization and behavior patterns. Young children and their families depict society's language and cultural diversity. The National Association for the Education of Young Children (NAEYC, 2005) stresses the need to provide young children with an environment that respects diversity, fosters their relationship with their families and community, and protects the children's home languages and cultural identities. The children's language and cultural differences need to be acknowledged, understood, respected, and accepted (Saracho & Martínez-Hancock, 2005). Since children and families represent different cultures, the next four chapters focus on families, communities, and their cultures. In "The Interface of the American Family and Culture," Olivia N. Saracho provides a brief overview about culture and how it affects young children and their families. In the first section, she describes several definitions of culture and its relationship to children and families. She then describes the importance of family support and the culture of several families, focusing on the cultural values of immigrant families, Hispanic American Families, Mexican American families, American Indian Families, and economically challenged families. She concludes with educational implications in using the children's language and culture as an asset to their learning. She also provides some recommendations for educators and researchers.

Research suggests that young children of indigenous backgrounds can benefit from early childhood education programs that treat culture as a framework, as opposed to an ingredient. The process of creating programs grounded in cultural values requires a deep rethinking of the assumptions inherent in early childhood education programs designed to serve indigenous groups. The concept of developmentally appropriate practice has long served as the criterion for discussions of early childhood education, bringing with it universalistic assumptions about the appropriate way to teach young children and the standard form of learning. As a result, these discussions have ignored the children's cultural and linguistic backgrounds. This has lead research in early childhood education to be based on the assumptions of *differences* instead of *deficits* (Castagno & Brayboy, 2008; Osborne,

1996). Thus, it is essential that research in early childhood education be conducted to address issues of diversity in culture and language.

Four theoretical perspectives relating to globalization and education are world culture, world systems, postcolonial, and culturalist. However, current global trends have been criticized for failure to support educational alternatives that will preserve local languages and cultures, ensure progressive educational practices that will protect the poor against the rich, and protect the environment and human rights. Therefore, they seem to promote educational practices that deny the place of local cultures and languages (Spring, 2008), as well as the United States' endorsement for universal preschool, which is likely to reduce the available alternatives to families of diverse backgrounds (Sarsona, Goo, Kawakami, & Au, 2008). The exception transpires in situations, such as that of Hawai'i, where state legislation supports several early childhood efforts, including home visits, family care, parent-participation preschools, and center-based preschools. In "Culture as Framework versus Ingredient in Early Childhood Education: A Native Hawaiian Perspective," C. Kanoelani Nāone and Kathryn Au describe Keiki Steps, a parent-participation preschool program designed for Native Hawaiian communities that is built on the cultural values of family, community, and close ties to the land. In their chapter, Nāone and Au maintain the importance of building early childhood education programs for indigenous students on the foundation of indigenous perspectives, using the Native Hawaiian perspective as their example. They believe that traditional Hawaiian educational values and methods should be adopted for the education of Native Hawaiian students, including the very youngest. In their view, it is not enough to infuse culture into education; culturally based values and methods need to drive how education is delivered. A proper honoring of the family, community, land, and indigenous language have the potential to revitalize education for young Native Hawaiian children, and, in the process, offer program innovations beneficial to teachers and students of many ethnic groups in Hawai'i and around the globe. Nāone and Au begin by defining what they mean by an indigenous perspective, with a specific application to Native Hawaiians. They provide a conceptual overview of culture as a framework versus culture as an ingredient, and an overview of culturally responsive instruction. They introduce Keiki Steps, a parent-participation preschool (also referred to as a family–child interaction learning program) for Native Hawaiian children, as an example of a program that uses Hawaiian culture as its framework. To make clear how Keiki Steps has been shaped by Hawaiian culture, they discuss two key values that should inform early childhood programs designed for Native Hawaiian children: *'ohana* (family) and *kaiāulu* (community).

One of the consequences of globalization is the increasing movement of people around the world. Migration is usually by choice or because of matters related to war and persecution that generate refugees and asylum-seekers. The transitional displacement of people in the early twenty-first century has meant that 200 million people have moved away from their country of birth (Global Commission on International Migration, 2005). Australia, Canada, and the United States are the "three major receiving nations for transnational migrants" (Adams & Kirova, 2006, p. 199). They have long histories of immigration. In 2009, the estimated net migration rate for the United States is 4.32 migrants per 1000 of the population; for Canada, the rate is 5.63 per 1000 of the population, and for Australia, the rate is 6.23 per 1000 of the population (Central Intelligence Agency [CIA], 2009). In addition, these nations accept quotas of refugees from refugee camps.

According to the United States Census Bureau (2000), almost 46 million people (18 % of the population) spoke a different language from English, and, of these, 29 million (about 60 percent) spoke Spanish (Nieto & Bode, 2008) as their first language. Such diversity is manifested in public school enrolments in the United States. From 1990 to 2000, the school-age population (ages 5–17 years) increased 17 percent, while the percentage of English language learners increased 46 percent (Nieto & Bode, 2008). According to Nieto and Bode (2008), immigration is one of the "most contentious issues" (p. 7) in the United States. Transnational migration brings demographic changes that produce challenges for education and social services. While there is a growing body of literature about educational concerns associated with migrant and refugee children, young migrant and refugee children are often not included in this research, because it concentrates on secondary and primary schooling. In "Migrant and Refugee Children, Their Families, and Early Childhood Education," Susan Grieshaber and Melinda G. Miller review the literature that relates to young migrant and refugee children, their families, and early childhood education. More specifically, they synthesize the state of knowledge relating to curriculum, parents, and teacher education. Following the analysis of recent research, Grieshaber and Miller conclude with some suggestions for researchers, policy makers, and practitioners.

Even as the population of school children becomes more diverse in sociocultural and linguistic experience, the curricular trend is toward more regulated, uniform literacy programs for young children; within such programs, child writing is an individual act dependent on skill mastery. Moreover, the increased emphasis on literacy has engulfed times and spaces once allotted to dramatic and constructive play, including drawing. As a response to such trends, in "The Cultural and Symbolic 'Begats' of Child Composing: Textual Play and Community Membership," Anne Haas Dyson considers child composing as, itself, a form of symbolic play on paper. Drawing on the theoretical and empirical literature, she focuses on two critical "begats" of young school children's writing: experience manipulating, or playing with, the symbolic stuff—the voices and images—of their everyday lives; and a community of peers within which and for which children compose. In the process, Dyson illustrates that, far from uniform, children's diverse experiences as cultural beings inform the ways in which they make sense of and take some control over the written medium.

TEACHERS OF LINGUISTICALLY AND CULTURALLY DIVERSE CHILDREN

Early childhood teachers and children need to restore oral storytelling to an audible, respected position on early childhood classrooms stages. In "Teachers Telling Stories: Inviting Children into Imaginative and Diverse Worlds," Celia Genishi, Cara Furman, Julianne P. Wurm, Molly Cain, Laura Osterman, Aya Takemura, and Wei-Yee Angela Tsang describe the current pressure on practitioners to emphasize literacy and, more specifically, early reading skills in prekindergarten and kindergarten curriculum. Storytelling in early childhood classrooms means listening to the relative loudness of read-alouds of picture books and lessons about letters and sounds. The children's experiences in schools and early childhood centers are limited to exposure to commercially published books and instruction in reading. The curriculum is defined in relation to literacy, while children are narrowly defined as "readers." Genishi and Dyson (2009) discuss in detail that the focus for diverse young learners should be to provide them with opportunities to speak, move, listen, dramatize, experiment with drawing and writing, and play, which have been fading, as well as the broad goal of communicative flexibility.

In their chapter, Genishi and her colleagues focus on storytelling in early childhood classrooms. Their purpose is to invite—or re-invite—early childhood educators into a literacy practice based on talk, that is, the oral telling of stories with powers that are independent of the printed word. They begin by briefly describing the educational context in many contemporary classrooms for children whose ages range from three to eight years, with an increasing focus on literacy and early reading and decreasing attention to child-oriented events and activities, such as storytelling and play. Next Genishi and her colleagues review and analyze the literature related to the teachers and children's storytelling, since both types are interrelated and are important in the early childhood education curriculum. Finally, within the framework of a master's-level course on language and literacy for prospective early childhood teachers, they introduce their own stories about their experiences as storytellers in the classroom. They conclude the chapter with their thoughts on the impact of stories on their own practices and their potential impact on prospective teachers of young children.

Children in early childhood programs have become progressively more diverse. For example, in 2005, this population consisted of 33 percent of the United States residents and there was an increase in the ratio of diverse students born outside of the United States (KewalRamani, Gilbertson, Fox, & Provasnik, 2007). Although the United States has always been a country that has embraced many cultures and identities, the diversity definition, fundamental categories for specific groups, and children's experiences have been quickly expanding. For example, the extensive range of families (e.g., extended, sole parent, gay, step families) who are raising children (Dau, 2001) and the categories that the individuals use to identify their ethnicity or gender (e.g., bi-racial, transgendered) continue to develop. Simultaneously, the technologies that connect individuals beyond geography and physical space have modified learning. Children are involved in multi-literacies (e.g., blogs, websites, social networking sites), and have access to all types of knowledge. These diversities challenge teachers in important ways:

- Teachers differ from the children they teach. Most of the early childhood teachers are White, female, monolingual, and middle class (Goodwin, 2002; Hyun, 1996). Their limited cultural knowledge challenges the teachers, who have difficulty responding to the numerous backgrounds of their young students (Hyun, 1996).
- Some early childhood teachers have difficulty responding to all diversity groups. For example, Robinson (2002) surveyed and interviewed a large group of teaching staff in several diversity areas (e.g., gender, gay and lesbian issues, multiculturalism, bilingualism and biculturalism, and indigenous issues) and found that teachers felt that lesbian and gay issues were the least related to their work with young children.
- There is a wide discrepancy between the children's experiences prior to attending school and the available resources that will prepare them for an effective school education. On the other hand, many young children have limited or no access to these resources.

Effective early childhood educators need to individualize instruction and respond to their students in equitable ways. Equity means that current social and institutional structures need to be examined in order to determine which are the favorite perspectives and to enthusiastically apply this knowledge to provide children with equal access to their education. To perform impartial instructional strategies requires that teachers understand the way power and institutional oppression work in insinuating ways in their classroom interactions, because the teachers' actions unknowingly continue to be based on bias and stereotypes. Thus, equity instruction goes beyond teaching strategies and includes the teachers' tool kit, consisting of a professional philosophy about injustice and bias, a knowledge base that communicates such beliefs, and a variety of techniques that act upon and integrate these views to achieve equity (Katz 1995; Ryan & Hornbeck, 2007).

In their chapter, "Preparing Early Childhood Teachers to Enact Social Justice Pedagogies," Sharon Ryan and Nora Hyland review the research on early childhood teacher preparation and diversity as a way of rethinking how to prepare teachers to enact social justice or more equity oriented pedagogies. They begin by drawing on work in the K-12 sector to tease out the differences between terms used to describe what has often been labeled "multicultural" (Ramsey, 2006) with the aim of reasoning through shifts in the field from "beyond heroes and holidays" to more equity-focused pedagogies. Then Ryan and Hyland review the empirical research that examines the preparation of preservice teachers in order to address issues of diversity and how this research does or does not prepare teachers to conceptualize and address issues of inequity. They conclude their chapter with an argument for the development of a strategic research agenda that will lead to the reinvention of content and pedagogical approaches in early childhood teacher preparation. Their aim in asserting this research agenda is to ensure that diversity, difference, and social justice are viewed as foundational for all early childhood educators, no matter where they work and whom they teach.

The enduring challenge based on the American assumption that all are created equal and that all children deserve an equal chance to learn, to work, to contribute, and to prosper (Raudenbush, 2009, p. 169) continues to be of the foremost concern in the United States. Inequality continues to be a dominant concern, although many modifications have occurred. In the final chapter, "Classroom Diversification: A Strategic Future Perspective for Equal Rights," Olivia N. Saracho and Bernard Spodek discuss the way the presence of ethnic minority groups composed of immigrants and native populations threatens society. It assumes that the logic of the national and the multicultural are incompatible. In addition, society perceives immigrants and ethnic minorities to be realistic and symbolic threats. Public arguments on immigrants and ethnic minorities emphasize the alleged threat to national identity and culture. Those opposed to these groups perceive that that national interests, beliefs, and values are threatened by newcomers and minorities; therefore, they are against multiculturalism and minority rights. Saracho and Spodek encourage multicultural recognition and the support of equal rights for all members (e.g., immigrants and ethnic minorities) of society. They conclude with recommendations for educational research and practice.

REFERENCES

Adams, L. D. & Kirova, A. (2006). Introduction to Part IV: Far from home with fluctuating hopes. In L. D. Adams & A. Kirova (Eds.), *Global migration and education: Schools, children, and families* (pp. 199-202). Mahwah, NJ: Erlbaum.

August, D., & Hakuta, K. (Eds.). (1998). *Educating language-minority children.* Washington, DC: National Academy Press.

Bryan, W. V. (2007). *Multicultural aspects of disabilities:A guide to understanding and assisting minorities in the rehabilitation process.* Springfield, IL: Charles C.Thomas.

Castagno, A., & Brayboy, B. (2008). Culturally responsive schooling for indigenous youth: A review of the literature. *Review of Educational Research, 78*(4), 941–993.

Central Intelligence Agency (CIA). (2009). The world factbook. Retrieved on June 7, 2009, from https://www.cia.gov/library/publications/the-world-factbook/geos/ca.html

Chung, W., & Rubin, S. E. (2008). Women with disabilities: Special issues in rehabilitation. In S. E. Rubin & R. T. Rossler (Eds.), *Foundations of the vocational rehabilitation process* (6th ed., pp. 459– 482). Austin, TX: Pro Ed.

Dau, E. (2001). Exploring families: The diversity and the issues. In E. Dau (Ed.), *The anti-bias approach in early childhood* (2nd ed.; pp. 115–133). Frenchs Forest, Australia: Pearson Education.

Dinan, K. A. (2006). *Young children in immigrant families: The role of philanthropy.* New York: National Center for Children in Poverty, Columbia University Mailman School of Public Health. Retrieved on August 11, 2009, from http://www.nccp.org/publications/pdf/text_661.pdf

Early, D. M., & Winton, P. J. (2001). Preparing the workforce: Early childhood teacher preparation at 2- and 4-year institutions of higher education. *Early Childhood Research Quarterly, 16,* 285–306.

Ellis, R. (2007). Educational settings and second language learning. *Asian EFL Journal, 9*(4), Article 1. Retrieved on August 11, 2009, from http://www.asian-efl-journal.com/Dec_2007_re.php

Gay, G., & Howard, T. C. (2000). Multicultural teacher education for the 21st century. *The Teacher Educator, 36,* 1–16.

Genishi, C., & Dyson, A. H. (2009). *Children, language, and literacy: Diverse learners in diverse times.* New York: Teachers College Press and Washington, DC: National Association for the Education of Young Children.

Global Commission on International Migration. (2005). *Final report: Migration in an interconnected world: New directions for action.* Retrieved on March 5, 2009, from http://www.gcim.org/en/finalreport.html

Gollnick, D. M., & Chinn, P. C. (2008). *Multicultural education in a pluralistic society* (8th ed.). Upper Saddle River, NJ: Merrill Prentice Hall.

Goodlad, R., & Riddell, S. (2005). Introduction: Disabled people and social justice. *Social Policy &Society,4,* 43–44.

Goodwin, A. L. (2002). Teacher preparation and the education of immigrant children. *Education and Urban Society, 34,* 156–172.

Harley, D. A. (2006). Indigenous healing practices among rural elderly African Americans. *International Journal of Disability, Development and Education, 53,* 433–452.

Harley, D. A., Alston, R. J., Turner-Whittaker, T. (2008). Social justice and cultural diversify issues. *Rehabilitation Education, 22*(3/4), 237–248.

Harley, D. A., Bishop, M., & Wilson, K. B. (2002). Rural rehabilitation: Old problems in a new day. *Journal of Rehabilitation Administration, 26,* 5–13.

Harley, D. A., Hall, M., & Savage, T. A. (2000). Working with gay and lesbian consumers with disabilities: Helping practitioners understand another frontier of diversity. *Journal of Applied Rehabilitation Counseling, 31,* 4–11.

Harley, D. A., Jolivette, K., McCormick, K., & Tice, K. (2002). Race, class and gender: A constellation of *positionalities* with implications for counseling. *Journal of Multicultural Counseling and Development, 30,* 216–238.

Hollins, E., & Guzman, M. T. (2005). Research on preparing teachers for diverse populations. In M. Cochran-Smith & K. M. Zeichner (Eds.), *Studying teacher education: The report of the AERA Panel on research and teacher education* (pp. 477–548). Mahwah, NJ: Erlbaum.

Hyun, E. (1996). New directions in early childhood teacher preparation: Developmentally and culturally appropriate practice. *Journal of Early Childhood Teacher Education, 17,* 7–19.

International Listening Association (ILA). (2008). Facts on listening. Retrieved on August 11, 2009, from http://www.listen.org/Templates/fact_time_spent.htm#time

Jalongo, M. R. (2008). *Learning to listen, listen to learn: Building essential skills in young children.* Washington, DC: National Association for the Education of Young Children.

Kampfe, C. M., Harley, D. A., Wadsworth, J. S., & Smith, S. M. (2007). Methods and materials for infusing aging issues into the rehabilitation curriculum. *Rehabilitation Education, 21,* 107–116.

Katz, L. (1995). *Talks with Teachers of Young Children.* Norwood , NJ: Ablex.

KewalRamani, A., Gilbertson, L., Fox, M. A., & Provasnik, S. (2007). *Status and trends in the education of racial and ethnic minorities.* Washington, DC: National Center for Educational Statistics.

Leal-Idrogo, A. (1995). Further thoughts "the use of interpreters and translators in delivery of rehabilitation services." *Journal of Rehabilitation, 61,* 21–23.

Lee, W. M. L., Blando, J. A., Mizelle, N. D., & Orozco, G. L. (2007). *Introduction to multicultural counseling for helping professionals* (2nd ed.). New York: Routledge.

Lim, C., Maxwell, K. L., Able-Boone, H., & Zimmer, C. R. (2009). Cultural and linguistic diversity in early childhood teacher preparation: The impact of contextual characteristics on coursework and practica. *Early Childhood Research Quarterly, 24*(2), 64–76.

McCarthy, H. (1995). Integrating spirituality into rehabilitation in a technocratic society. *Rehabilitation Education, 9,* 87–95.

McKay, D. R. (2008). Career planning: Here is why you need good listening skills. Retrieved on August 11, 2009, from http://careerplanning.about.com/cs/miscskills/listening_skill.htm

Morrison-Orton, D. J. (2004). How rehabilitation professionals define the concepts of spirituality and religion when working with individuals with disabilities. *Journal of Social Work in Disability & Rehabilitation, 3,* 37–55.

National Association for the Education of Young Children. (2005). NAEYC Position Paper: *where we stand summary: Many languages, many cultures: Respecting and responding to diversity.* Retrieved on July 8, 2009, from http://208.118.177.216/about/positions/pdf/diversity.pdf

National Capital Language Resource Center (NCLRC). (2008). *The essentials of language teaching: Teaching listening.* Retrieved on August 11, 2009, from http://www.nclrc.org/essentiall/listening/liindex.htm.

Nieto, S. & Bode, P. (2008). Affirming diversity: The sociopolitical context of multicultural education. (5th ed.). Boston, MA: Pearson.

Osborne, A. B. (1996). Practice into theory into practice: Culturally relevant pedagogy for students we have marginalized and normalized. *Anthropology & Education Quarterly, 27*(3), 285–314.

Ramsey, P. G. (2006). Early childhood multicultural education. In B. Spodek, & O. Saracho (Eds.), *Handbook of research on the education of young children* (2nd ed., pp. 279–301). Mahwah, NJ: Lawrence Erlbaum.

Raudenbush, S. W. (2009). The *Brown* legacy and the O'Connor challenge: Transforming schools in the images of children's potential. *Educational Researcher, 38*:(3), 169–180.

Robinson, K. H. (2002). Making the invisible visible: Gay and lesbian issues in early childhood education. *Contemporary Issues in Early Childhood, 3*, 415–434.

Robinson-Wood, T. L. (2009). *The convergence of race, ethnicity, and gender: Multiple identities in counseling* (3rd ed.). Upper Saddle River, NJ: Pearson.

Ryan, S., & Hornbeck, A. (2007). Pedagogy. In R. S. New and M. Cochran (Eds.), *Early Childhood Education: An International Encyclopedia.* Westport, CT: Praeger.

Saluja, G., Early, D.M., & Clifford, R.M. (2002). Demographic characteristics of early childhood teachers and structural elements of early care and education in the United States. *Early Childhood Research and Practice, 4*(1), 1–19.

Saracho, O. N., & Martínez-Hancock, F. (2005). Mexican American families: Cultural and linguistic influences. In O. N. Saracho & B. Spodek (Eds.), *Contemporary perspectives on families, communities, and schools for young children* (pp. 203–224). Greenwich, CT: Information Age.

Saracho, O.N., & Spodek, B. (Eds.) (1983). *Understanding the multicultural experience in early childhood education.* Washington, DC: National Association for the Education of Young Children.

Saracho, O.N., & Spodek, B. (1995). The future challenge of linguistic and cultural diversity in the schools. In E. E. García, B. McLaughlin, B. Spodek, & O. N. Saracho, O. N. (Eds). *Meeting the challenge and cultural diversity in early childhood education,* (pp. 170–173). New York: Teachers College Press.

Sarsona, M., Goo, S., Kawakami, A., & Au, K. (2008). Equity issues in a parent-participation preschool program for Native Hawaiian children In C. Genishi & A. Goodwin (Eds.), *Diversities in early childhood education: Rethinking and doing* (pp. 151–165). New York: Routledge.

Smart, J. F., & Smart, D. W. (1995). Ethnic minorities and rehabilitation: Point counterpoint—The use of translators/interpreters in rehabilitation. *Journal of Rehabilitation, 61*, 14–20.

Smith, C. (2008). How can parents model good listening skills? Retrieved on August 11, 2009, from http://www.rusd.k12.ca.us/parents/listening.html.

Smith, L., Foley, P. F., & Chaney, M. P. (2008). Addressing classism, ableism, and heterosexism in counselor education. *Journal of Counseling & Development, 86,* 303–309.

Spring, J. (2008). Research on globalization and education. *Review of Educational Research, 78*(2), 330–363.

Sue, D. W., & Capodilupo, C. M. (2008). Racial, gender, and sexual orientation microaggression: Implications for counseling and psychotherapy. In D. W. Sue & D. Sue (Eds.), *Counseling the culturally diverse: Theory and practice* (5th ed., pp. 105–130). Hoboken, NJ: Wiley & Sons.

Tabors, P. O. (1998). What early childhood educators need to know: Developing effective programs for linguistically and culturally diverse children and families. *Young Children, 53*(6), 20–26.

United States Census Bureau (1990). *U.S. Census 1990.* Retrieved on August 11, 2009, from http://www.census.gov

United States Census Bureau. (2000). *U.S. Census 2000.* Retrieved on August 11, 2009, from http://www.census.gov

United States Census Bureau. (2003). Language use and English-speaking ability: 2000. Census 2000 Brief. Issued October 2003. Washington, DC: Author. Retrieved on August 11, 2009, from www.census.gov/prod/cen2000/doc/sf3.pdf

United States Census Bureau. (2005). *American Community Survey 2005.* Retrieved on August 11, 2009, from http://www.census.gov

United States Department of Education. (2007). *The condition of education.*Washington, DC: National Center for Education Statistics.

Vera, E. M., & Speight, S. L. (2003). Multicultural competence, social justice, and counseling psychology: Expanding our roles. *The Counseling Psychologist, 31,* 253–272.

Warren, A. K., & Constantine, M. G. (2007). Social justice issues. In M. Constantine (Ed.), *Clinical practice with people of color* (pp. 231–242). New York: Teachers College Press.

PART I

ENGLISH LANGUAGE LEARNERS

CHAPTER 2

THE POLITICS OF LANGUAGE AND EDUCATIONAL PRACTICES

Promoting Truly Diverse Child Care Settings

Judith K. Bernhard and Veronica Pacini-Ketchabaw

ABSTRACT

This chapter emerges from more than a decade of research in common educational practices, as experienced by diverse families in the early childhood system. In particular, we write this piece because we are concerned that many of the issues around language loss that we have been writing about since the late 1990s are still relevant today. Language and the politics of language, especially, continue to affect many early childhood education classrooms in the 21st century. In North America, it is known that the vast majority of immigrant and English language learners will lose basic competence in their first language by the time they reach high school. Nonetheless, we have found there is much that can be done to improve the retention of their first lan-

Language and Cultural Diversity in Early Childhood Education, pages 21–41

guage and culture. As our years of study indicate, there is no need to despair over a loss that is probably not as inevitable as some may believe.

In this chapter, we argue that the phenomenon of language loss has a multitude of causes. Among them is the politicization of language within the context of early childhood education. Classroom instructional practice is also a factor, as is the situation that immigrant family members commonly find themselves in during their immigration and settlement process. The purpose of the chapter is to show how losses of first language and culture can be challenged in classrooms and schools.

We begin with a brief review of key findings from the literature on, first, the relationship between language and culture and, second, language maintenance and bilingualism in North American early childhood settings. We then address the ways in which power relations among teachers, families, and children affect language loss and the disappearance of language diversity. We also take a brief look at the subtle messages that teachers often inadvertently transmit to their students—messages that convey to students that their home language is not as valuable as English. The second part of the chapter proceeds with a description of innovative classroom practices intended to foster first language preservation, family involvement, and cultural and linguistic diversity. A list of recommendations for educators and families is given at the end of the chapter.

THE SIGNIFICANCE OF LANGUAGE IN THE EARLY YEARS

Language and Culture

Cultural values and beliefs are transmitted through language (Ochs, 1986), which, in turn, is the main mediator of cultural knowledge construction (Vygotsky, 1978). Peters and Boggs (1986) argued that modes of speaking become characteristic of each particular culture. Cultural values are implicit in features that are part of language, although individuals are not always aware of this particular feature. Indeed, children learn language by using interactional routines, "a sequence of exchanges in which one speaker's utterance, accompanied by appropriate nonverbal behaviour, calls for one of a limited set of responses by one or more other participants" (Peters & Boggs, 1986, p. 81).

Ochs and Schieffelin (1984) showed that the acquisition of language and sociocultural knowledge are linked processes. They found that language socialization differed across three distinct societies where different patterns used towards infants' language were observed "adapting situation to the child and adapting the child to situations" (p. 304). More recent research regarding the language socialization of children conducted in Latino communities has highlighted the loose associations family members draw between language and cultural identity (Schecter, Sharken-Taboada, & Bayley, 1996; Schecter & Bayley, 1997). Although Schecter and Bayley (1997) observed that families with a Mexican background were differently committed to the actual use of Spanish as a vehicle for affirming cultural identity, they also found that an overwhelming number of families awarded a central and important role to their home language in the formation of that identity.

Language Maintenance and Bilingualism in Early Schooling

The challenges of acquiring a second language in the classroom while, at the same time, trying to maintain the ability to have meaningful conversations with family members can have a profound effect on children's attachment. The pushes and pulls of this situation can seriously compromise children's sense of security and the ability to know that their expressed needs will be met. The situation is further complicated, given that the children involved may need to be able to make themselves understood in different and perhaps even contradictory ways for both their families and their educators at the very moment in their lives when they are learning to regulate their emotions and act in socially acceptable ways.

One of our earlier studies (Bernhard, Lefebvre, Murphy Kilbride, Chud, & Lange, 1998) investigated the language socialization of children in various immigrant communities in Canada. It highlighted how the educational system tends to operate under an assimilative approach, contributing to the eventual loss of children's home language. In this pan-Canadian study on childcare centers, it was found that, in some cases, 80% of the children in a particular language group were in centers where there was not even one person who shared their language.

A second and third study, conducted with Latin American parents (Bernhard, Freire, Torres, & Nirdosh, 1998; Pacini-Ketchabaw, Bernhard, & Freire, 2001), indicated that elementary school-age children tend to lose their mother tongue during the "normal processes" of institutional functioning of Canadian schools. Although the parents who participated saw Spanish-language maintenance as a way to foster family unity, Latino identity, and professional advancement, the strong assimilative messages received from the schools resulted in their doubting the desirability of openly speaking Spanish at home. Many of the parents became convinced that, in order to get ahead, their children needed to become quickly immersed in English. They did not realize, however, that acting on this belief too strongly often meant that the first language would be lost in a very short time.

Numerous other studies have shown the alarming rate of home language loss in the first years of schooling, particularly when children do not have a chance to practice their home language. Not only do children lose the valuable social and cognitive benefits associated with bilingualism, they also face the disastrous consequences of not being able to talk to their parents and grandparents or receive necessary feedback and guidance from them on various aspects of life, ranging from sexual activity to academic decisions and other normative behavior (Chumak-Horbatsch, 2008; Gonzalez-Mena & Bhavnagri, 1997; Park & Sarkar, 2007). Wong-Fillmore's (1991) well-known study of 1000 families living in the United States outlined how loss of home language negatively affects communication between children and their families. The findings indicate the necessity for schools to proactively recognize and build on the family's cultural capital, including their home language.

Studies have been conducted that review the links between cognitive development and bilingualism. The three areas within cognitive development that have been positively linked to balanced bilingualism include metalinguistic awareness, concept formation, and analogical reasoning. Research has shown metalinguistic awareness to be an important element in intellectual development (Hakuta, 1986) and schooling participation (Lindfors, 1991). Metalinguistic awareness involves the ability to objectify language, focusing on the form, rather than the meaning, of the sentences. Bilingual children outperform monolingual children on awareness of language features such as component sounds, word-meaning correspondence, rules of grammar, semantics, and ambiguity (Lee, 1996). Bilingual children also display superior performance on concept formation tasks (Bain, 1974; Liedtke & Nelson, 1968). Lastly, analogical reasoning has been found to have developmental importance in cognition; children with strong bilingual proficiency were found to display stronger analogical reasoning ability (Díaz, 1985).

A number of researchers have pointed out the rarity of additive, as opposed to subtractive, bilingualism (Cummins, 2000; Genesee, 1987; Swain & Lapkin, 1982). According to Cummins (2000, p. 37), additive bilingualism refers to "the form of bilingualism that results when students add a second language to their intellectual tool-kit while continuing to develop conceptually and academically in their first language." In the North American context, several studies (e.g., Bernhard, Chud, Lefebvre, & Lange, 1996; Chumak-Horbatsch, 2008; Pacini-Ketchabaw, Bernhard, & Freire, 2001; Schecter, Sharken-Taboada, & Bayley, 1996; Wong-Fillmore, 1991) reveal that proficient bilingualism is still rare among children of immigrants.

Although an additive approach is desired and sometimes possible, parents more often experience schools as unsupportive or oblivious to mother tongue retention issues. Because the second language, rather than the home language, is the one that receives most emphasis, the child's cultural and linguistic identity takes on a new and unfamiliar shape right before the parents' eyes. Although parental intentions and practices are good indicators for later language usage by their children (Siren, 1991), parental cultural strength, residence in ethnic neighborhoods, and language usage at home are also significant factors. In simple terms, a number of minority language communities are likely, within a generation, to have no young adult speakers of the language.

The findings just reviewed document first language loss, as well as its negative effects on identity. The circumstances that contribute to these outcomes are complex and shifting. In the next sections of the chapter, we look at this complex set of factors.

THE POLITICS OF LANGUAGE

Globalization, with its unequal flow of people from south to north, has increasingly challenged the assumption of a monoculture (Luke & Grieshaber, 2004). It is no longer possible to assume that classrooms in the global north can or will share a single language, culture, or ethnicity. Similarly, migration pathways are complex, such that many immigrant families live multilocal, transnational lives. Thus, the entire premise of acculturation is being questioned as immigrant families operate in a number of social fields and often have obligations across two or more nation states. The redefinition of migrants also implies a renewed understanding of what counts as knowledge and how social relations are differentially valued.

In spite of this context, if one looks at schools today, it can be said that mainstream practices around literacy and, indeed, mainstream ideas regarding what counts as literacy, reflect dominant societal values (MacNaughton, 2005). Dominant discourses are reflected in daily practices and are formulated by ideas that have become recognized as what counts as natural and normal.

A number of studies have addressed issues of language through a framework that considers power relations (Corson, 2000; Cummins, 2000; Bernhard et al., 1998). Many of these studies focus on the misconceptions regarding the inherent superiority of the English language and how these views often result in situating minority languages as repressed languages. This attitude is only possible because the history of the dominant group is seen as superior. Meaning and history often negate the cultural capital of linguistic minorities.

Recent writings on the role that language ideologies play in the production and re-production of social differences offer important insights (Blackledge, 2003; Blommaert, 1999; Blackledge & Pavlenko, 2002; Schieffelin, Woolard, & Kroskrity, 1998). Blackledge and Pavlenko (2002, p. 123) have pointed out, for example, that "language ideologies are about more than individual speakers' attitudes to their languages, or speakers using languages in particular ways. Rather, they include the values, practices and beliefs associated with language use by speakers, and the discourse which constructs values and beliefs at state, institutional, national and global levels." In his theory of language and power, Pierre Bourdieu postulated that forms of knowledge function as resources or *symbolic power*, differentially valued in various social fields. An essential element addressed by Blackledge and Pavlenko (2002), as they draw on the work of Pierre Bourdieu, is *symbolic power*:

> Bourdieu's model of symbolic value of one language or language variety above others rests on his notion that a symbolically dominated group is complicit in the misrecognition, or valorization, of that language or variety. The official language or standard variety becomes the language of hegemonic institutions because the dominant and the subordinated group both misrecognise it as a superior language. (Blackledge & Pavlenko, 2002, p. 124)

Despite prevalent discourses of diversity and inclusion, minority children's cultural capital is rarely considered as a valuable form of knowledge. Early childhood educators' understandings of children's language development are mediated by a discourse of monolingualism, in that they consider English as the natural and legitimate language for young children (Pacini-Ketchabaw & Armstrong de Almeida, 2006). The knowledge and resources of families that represent the child's cultural capital (Bourdieu, 1994) are typically ignored as vital funds of knowledge. Moll and his team (González, Moll, & Amanti, 2003) have inspired many researchers to show the numerous ways that educators can tap the "funds of knowledge" that are possessed by diverse families.

Attention to the politics of language, namely, the perceived superiority of English, provides insights into interesting struggles around bilingualism and multilingualism. For example, we might ponder why bilingualism and multilingualism are overvalued in the business world and undervalued in educational institutions. Scholars writing on the politics of language (Lin & Martin, 2005; May, 2001) might suggest that, in order to engage with this dilemma, we are to problematize the idea of languages, particularly English, as neutral. In other words, we are to question that bilingualism or multilingualism begins from equally valued languages. Beginning from the premise that languages are not neutral and are always already embedded in power relations, then we can ask the following questions that can take us deeper into our inquiry: Who benefits when children's home languages are supported in educational systems and who benefits when bilingualism and multilingualism are used to expand imperial power through capital? What roles do bilingualism and multilingualism play in sustaining globalization and international networks of capital? What role does English play in sustaining these relations? What positions of prestige are maintained through bilingualism and multilingualism in the business world?

DEVELOPMENTALISM AND LANGUAGE

Language development is a part of child development discourses. Textbooks on child development assume a "universal" child (Bernhard, 1995, 2003). Sections on language development treat bilingualism and multilingualism as non-necessary additions to "normal" language development. In their pre-service education, early childhood educators typically rely on developmentally appropriate practices, learn how to support normal language development, and acquire a "sensitivity" to the issue of bilingualism and multilingualism. The field of child development has constructed a "true" child that allows us to make sense of what children are, what they should be, and what they need in order to fit into a specific ideal (Burman, 2008). This "universal," "true" child is a monolingual child.

The common theme among these discourses is subtle, but important. Even though the maintenance of minority languages is not "discouraged," it is assumed to be an impediment to success. The context has been termed by Cummins (2000) as the "default option," in which diverse family knowledge and cultural capital is divorced from what actually happens in the classroom, underpinning pedagogies focused on monolingual, English curriculum. In these cases, *normality* is usually defined as speaking English.

These ideological and discursive ideas manifest themselves in different, and subtle, ways in early childhood education practices. For example, educators say that diversity of language is "tolerated." However, in fact, linguistic diversity is often undervalued or ignored. Teachers often wonder if the home language contributes to children's underachievement. Therefore, they tend to focus on what children do not know (e.g., English), as opposed to what they do bring to the classroom. Teachers have expressed the concern that there are too many languages represented in their classrooms and that they cannot be experts on every one of these languages.

To illustrate these points, here are two conversations that one of the authors of this chapter had with early childhood educators within the context of her research. Both of the quotes come from educators working with immigrant children in a mid-sized city in western Canada, where immigrant children form a very small proportion of the population. Rather than situating language within political contexts, these educators view language as only a milestone in children's lives:

Participant 1: Children are the same all over the world. No matter what. They have the same development levels; they are interested in similar things. They learn . . .

Interviewer: Like what? What do you mean when you say they are interested in similar things?

Participant 1: They all like puppy dogs, and they all play with cars, and they all like dolls, and there's not much difference. When they hurt, they cry. When they're scared, they cry. Yeah, I haven't found a lot of difference between the children that are or are not Canadian born. I mean their language is different. Their food tastes are different. But they are still all the same [. . .]

Participant 2: We had two of the families for a while tried . . . one of the grandparents ended up staying in the classroom. Sometimes we do that with the English speaking kids . . . But it ended up not working out because the grandparents spoke only their own language and so the children were still speaking only in their own language. And they were kind of, you know, thrown into the deep end of the pool where they had to listen to me. They went to the grandparent to have their shoes tied or have their lunch opened or have their nose wiped and I wasn't bonding with the children. They weren't relying on me and they weren't learning any English, so in the end we had to cut those ties too. (Pacini-Ketchabaw & Armstrong de Almeida, 2006, pp. 326–327)

One can see here that teachers' attitudes will likely affect how students perceive their own background, how they are empowered or disempowered as they interact with educators. One can say generally that their interactions are mediated by the role that teachers assume in relation to language incorporation, community participation, pedagogy, and assessment. Teachers may unwittingly contribute to students' feelings of shame about their cultural and linguistic background.

We found that educators do not overtly discuss language issues or ask parents about their goals and wishes regarding their children's language acquisition. In fact, during our interviews, educators indicated attitudinal support for first language maintenance. However, when we investigated their actions, we found a gap between their attitudes of support and any appreciable actions. This is not to say that they were actively discouraging home language maintenance. However, they were not taking any opportunities to encourage home languages, either. It is important to stress that we are not discussing an individual failing. No particular act has necessarily been committed, nor was anything ordinarily required omitted. We are talking about the pressures generated by institutions that are felt by certain groups, despite the goodwill and ordinary efforts of individual teachers.

Educators sometimes give parents subtle, but powerful messages about their home languages and the superiority of English, as we will illustrate below. But it is crucial to note that messages are conveyed to the children irrespective of the teacher's talk; sometimes examination of a transcript shows no clue of the impact on the student. Following is an example of a mother who expressed the concern of the home language as inferior. This mother—who emigrated from Colombia to Toronto—participated in a study focused on the lived experiences of Latin American parents raising their children in their mother tongue:

> One day I told the teacher that I like speaking in Spanish with my daughter because I wanted her to learn both languages. The teacher answered me that I should speak in English and not in Spanish. She told me that she thought that I should speak to my daughter in English. I didn't do what she suggested because for me that was to slow her down in learning Spanish. I told this to the teacher. And she told me again that she thought that I should speak to her [my daughter] in English. The teacher always said that it would be best if I spoke in English to my daughter. (Pacini-Ketchabaw, Bernhard, & Freire, 2001, p. 18)

This mother's experience suggests that the school personnel did not attach any particular value to her home language. The message that she received was that her knowledge and cultural capital were marginal to what was being taught at school. Even when educators explicitly recognize parents as partners in their children's education, they may not see a way to involve them in meaningful ways or to access their expertise.

Overall, we found in our research that families' intentions and desires to maintain their mother tongue became overwhelmingly difficult to attain as they received little encouragement from dominant institutions. Practitioners' influence on parents' decisions and actions regarding their children's learning is enormous. For some of the mothers participating in our studies, feelings of insecurity, and sometimes guilt, led them to abandon the use of their mother tongue with their children. As a result, the mother tongue was lost. In the next section we describe some noteworthy and promising exceptions to the scenarios above.

CLASSROOM PRACTICES THAT PROMOTE FIRST LANGUAGE MAINTENANCE AND RETENTION OF HOME CULTURE

In most large metropolitan cities in North America, today's early childhood education classrooms reflect the globalizing conditions of our time. Classrooms have become spaces where various cultures, languages, "racial" backgrounds, and ethnicities meet. In this context, schools that are making efforts to move away from being mainly sites of social and cultural reproduction to become sites of social transformation and linguistic cultural diversity are inspiring (Blackledge, 2000). There are many impressive initiatives designed for young children that use heritage language and community knowledge as the basis for adapting curricula to better meet the needs of linguistically diverse populations.

The growing body of family literacy programs is one example of alternative pedagogical frameworks that, rather than focusing on the value of monolingual English families, see the value of diverse forms of cultural capital (Ada, 1988; Ada & Campoy, 2003). Another set of studies has reported the value of using dual-language resources such as story books, audio tapings of stories and songs, videos of storytelling and CD-ROMs of interactive activities (Edwards, 1998; Goldenberg, Reese, & Gallimore, 1992; Schecter & Cummins, 2003). These resources have been used not only in classrooms, but are also sent home to encourage parental involvement in children's literacy, as well as to foster confidence in parents whose mastery is in the home language. A third approach is to invite parents to participate in the classroom to tell stories or encourage children to tell stories in the home language, using props and dramatic play to enact them (Blackledge, 2000; Edwards, 1998). Chow and Cummins (2003) encourage teachers to greet children and sing songs in multiple languages, as well as encourage students to respond to questions in the classroom by using both languages.

Allocating sufficient resources to hire bilingual staff also contributes to creating a non-tokenistic environment for home language maintenance. While it may be impossible to hire a person proficient in every language represented by the children in a school or center, having an appropriate cross-section of effective bilingual teachers, assistants, and interpreters is an important commitment to multi-language children (Bernhard, Lefebvre, Chud, & Lange, 1995; Blackledge, 2000; Edwards, 1998). Such an approach is also likely to diminish parents' perceptions of the school or center as unapproachable.

This section has suggested that deficit-based programs can be contrasted with empowering programs designed from a perspective based on strengths. Empowering programs start with the assumption that children are born with the desire to learn, and that parents want to help and have much to contribute to their children's education. It is up to educators to find ways to tap into the accumulated knowledge that families have acquired over the course of their lives. These meaningful life experiences—these "funds of knowledge," to use a term coined by Luis Moll—can be successfully applied in early childhood classrooms.

The remainder of the chapter presents an overview of two specific approaches that, we believe, create openings for transformation and for addressing the political nuances of language issues in early childhood education.

The Early Authors Program

The conscientization theories of Paulo Freire (1973) were a main underlying framework of our work with the Early Authors Program (EAP) and the Authors in the Classroom programs described in this section. Freire, who worked to empower oppressed communities in Brazil, believed that the interaction between teacher and student did not occur in a vacuum, but rather in an elaborate social context in which the pupils did not passively reproduce the information presented to them. By empowering students and using cultural references, he tapped into sources of strength and ideals. For example, when Freire worked with peasants to teach them to read, he found that, in order to be effective, the learning opportunity needed to be experiential and emotionally engaging. His teaching involved discussion and dialogue, rather than repetition and memorization. The process of becoming conscious of their place in the system was labeled *conscienticization.* Freire's methods were outlined in *The Pedagogy of Hope* (2004), a book that has inspired educators worldwide to encourage their students to read the "world through the word."

The Authors in the Classroom Program was developed to improve the possibility of more equitable outcomes for all children. Originated by Ada and Campoy (2003), it was implemented at the early education level in under the name, Early Authors Program (see Bernhard, Cummins, Campoy, Ada, Winsler, & Bleiker, 2006; Bernhard, Winsler, Bleiker, Ginieniewicz, & Madigan, 2008; Taylor, Bernhard, Garg, & Cummins, 2008).

The Early Authors Program was first implemented in Miami-Dade County in one of the poorest areas of the US. This was a large-scale 12-month early literacy intervention for 3–5 year old children. It involved 32 child care settings, 16 family child care providers, 74 center-based care providers, 1179 children, and 800 families. The Early Authors Program aimed to promote early bilingual literacy in preschool children by having the adults and children create bilingual books. Each center was provided with a digital camera, color printer, computer, and laminating equipment. A total of 3,286 books were written by children, parents, and educators in both English and the home languages of the children, usually Spanish or Haitian-Creole. The books were based on family histories, the children's lives, and the children's interests. The children, their friends, relatives, and pets were often the main characters in their stories. One assumption of the program was that if children reared in economically and socially disadvantaged situations were going to grow up to become leaders of their communities, they needed to be treated as protagonists of their own lives at the moment their personality was developing.

The children and adults created the dual language books and read them together. They took pictures that became the illustrations for some of the books. Family photographs were also scanned and used to illustrate the books. Children's drawings were also incorporated into their books. Lamination made the books durable enough to withstand repeated use. Copies of the books were placed in the classroom libraries and other copies were taken home by the children and added to their family libraries. In addition, copies of the books were displayed in an exhibition at the local children's museum.

The Early Authors Program used a pre-test/post-test experimental design, in which the children in the program were randomly selected from the larger group of consenting families in the classrooms or centers. Similarly, children in the control group were randomly selected from the larger group of centers that were serving the same population of families in the same neighborhoods as the experimental group.

Program leaders used the term *identity texts* to describe the literature created by the children and their educators and parents. The children's identities were incorporated into the stories, increasing their pride in themselves and their families. The books served as mirrors in which the children's identities were reflected. Reading these very meaningful books engaged the children and developed "affective bonds to literacy." Moreover, the process was geared toward the acquisition of a strong sense of self-worth and pride in cultural identity. In terms of identity and self-esteem, one of the literacy specialists whose language and cultural heritage was English said:

> I think making their own books [allowed them] to see themselves in the books and to talk about themselves. And, I think there was a lot of pride when the book was finished... When they got their final book, they shared it with the class and they just beamed. They were so excited to show their book and they felt so proud. (Learning Specialist #5, p. 1)

The process of self-authoring books aimed not only at enrichment of children's outcomes, but also at the strengthening of links between and among children, their families, and educators. Classroom observations and parent interviews suggest that, in the process of transcribing these compositions in English and in the home languages, the relationship between educators and family members was reframed, in that parental knowledge became a form of academic capital.

There were also important academic outcomes. The Early Authors Program used a rigorous experimental design and the children's development was carefully assessed using standardized instruments. One of the measures used was the LAP-D (Nehring et al., 1992), a norm-referenced, standardized developmental assessment instrument that yields raw scores, standard scores, age-equivalents, and national percentile scores in four domains (three were used here): language (two subscales—*naming* and *comprehension*), cognition (two subscales—*counting* and *matching*), and fine motor (two subscales—*object manipulation* and fine *motor writing*). The LAP-D has been shown to have good internal consistency reliability (.76 to .92) and reasonable construct validity (in terms of correlations with other standard assessments of developmental competencies). Another of the pre–post instruments was the PLS-R (Zimmerman et al., 2002), a measure of a child's expressive (expressive communication scale) and receptive (auditory comprehension scale) language skills. This instrument was administered either in English or Spanish, depending on the child's dominant language, according to the child's teacher. The skills tapped by he PLS-4 at all ages are important precursors for literacy development (Armbruster et al., 2001). The test–retest stability coefficients for the PLS-R range between .82 and .95 for the two subscale scores, and .90 to .97 for the total language score.

The children in the experimental group made considerably greater gains between the pre-test and the post-test than the children in the control group. More specifically, 3- and 4-year-old children who participated in the Early Authors Program intervention showed greater gains than control children in language and literacy development, according to all measures—the PLS-R and the LAP-D (expressive and receptive language). Children receiving the Earl Authors Program intervention not only made greater gains in their absolute levels of language skill, but they also maintained or gained in their position nationally, compared to controls, in terms of either percentile scores (in the case of the LAP-D) or developmental-age-relative-to-chronological-age scores (PLS-R), both based on national norms for their age groups. (For specific scores, see Bernhard, Winsler, Bleiker, Ginieniewicz, & Madigan, 2008.)

The qualitative data provided additional information on the effects of the program. Educators reported that the children "love to interact and look at each other's books." Subsequently, they noted a growing interest in their own and other children's books. One language specialist who spoke both English and Spanish said:

> On a number of occasions when I went to visit the center, they wanted to have their own books read to them versus a traditional book.... The book was about them and they wanted to hear what the story was about, and they wanted to look at the pictures in the book because they could relate to it, it had meaning.... But the part I liked best was when they went back and looked at their photos and could explain what they were doing in the photos, and it made sense because it tied right into the "I can."... Basically, they wrote their own books. The "I can" book they wrote themselves. (Learning Specialist #7, p. 1)

The teachers who worked in the program provided feedback indicating that they were encouraged by moving away from a "banking" model of education to more of a "problem-posing" model (Freire, 1973). A statement made by a literacy specialist of Hispanic heritage who is bilingual in

Spanish and English identified her understanding of the impact that such a program had for the teachers, parents, and children involved:

> I think that the program was absolutely an amazing experience, and I was honored and privileged to be a part of it. I see its value, and I really hope that the outcomes of what we feel have been very successful really show as a success... because I see the success in the parents, I see it in the teachers, I see it in the students. I think it was a wonderful experience and I'm glad I was a part of it.... I feel that the growth on the emotional end of the Early Authors Program is huge with parents, caregivers, students, the literacy specialists themselves. I think that that's where the value lies. It might show in the academic and I hope it does. But again, because the philosophy is a two-part philosophy [emotional and academic], an assessment is not going to show all of the growth that really has taken place. (Learning Specialist #13, p. 14)

The Early Authors Program was a novel project in both its genre and approach. Although transformative literacy projects had been used before in other settings, the Miami-Dade project implemented the program on a new scale and with an age group not previously served. As the evaluation results show, there were gains in a number of important areas. Yet, the program was not without its difficulties and limitations. For example, there are possible researcher and new intervention effects. The presence of researchers made it impossible to determine, in the present design, how much of the effect was due to the inherent characteristics of the program and, thus, makes unclear the degree to which the present results could be replicated in a normal classroom with a typically lower level of support. This problem of transition from research to successful widespread adoption in educational settings is well-known in the empirical literature. It is important to continue implementation and evaluation efforts to determine where improvements can be made and to understand why certain aspects of the program were more successful than others.

The Early Authors Program provides early childhood educators with one starting point for tapping into families' funds of knowledge and for acknowledging family and community cultural capital. The authors hope that this experience will inspire other versions of Early Authors, and, thus, involve children and parents in producing and reading dual-language books. This seems to be a promising way of helping children in childcare centers retain their home languages, develop positive identities, and create an affective bond to literacy that has the potential to last a lifetime.

Pedagogical Narrations

Another practice that has great potential to make education more inclusive of cultural and linguistic diversity is *pedagogical narrations*, a curriculum tool with political possibilities that can be used to unpack language ideologies (e.g., Pacini-Ketchabaw & Berikoff, 2008). The term *pedagogical narrations* refers to the process of a teacher's observing, recording, and, individually and collectively with colleagues, interpreting a series of related ordinary moments selected from classroom practice, including children's conversations, children's own work, and teachers' dialogues with children. The process is ongoing and cyclical, and it is based on the art of critical reflection on the part of a community of learners that includes educators, children, and their families.

While the term *pedagogical narrations* is used in parts of Canada, this process is called *pedagogical documentation* in the city of Reggio Emilia, Italy and in Sweden (Dahlberg, Moss, & Pence, 1999; Rinaldi, 2006), *learning stories* in New Zealand (Carr, 2001), and *action research* in parts of Australia (MacNaughton, 2003). Pedagogical narrations are used as a tool to make children's learning visible and reflect upon the educator's practices. What is of interest within the context of this chapter is the critical reflective aspect of pedagogical narrations, as it allows educators to become aware of and disrupt hegemonies of language.

The approach to pedagogical narrations assumes children's competence and strengths. Educators are taught to notice children and to observe what they are interested in and how they are learning. After careful observations, educators recognize what the children in their classrooms are up to, what are they trying to do, and what are they interested in. Following this approach, educators do not impose their ideas on their students. Rather, they truly recognize children's ideas as valuable and important contributions to the classroom. Fleet (2006) describes how, by incorporating a pedagogical narrations approach, a student teacher allowed a child-initiated project to take place in her classroom. The student teacher was thus able to engage in more meaningful ways with ELL children who had often been "overlooked." The student teacher observed:

> Some of the children did not enjoy participating in social/group activities (may have been a result of their language difficulties or frustrations). These children were often overlooked by teachers and peers. Implementing a child-initiated project which had an active social group focus could develop and extend children's verbal and non-verbal language, participation in social learning situations, sharing and negotiation skills, team work, cooperation, self-esteem, confidence, self help skills, and primarily the co-construction of knowledge. (Fleet, 2006, p. 228)

Pedagogical narration has been recommended by Dahlberg, Moss, and Pence (1999, p. 145), who argue that it is "a vital tool for the creation of a reflective and democratic pedagogical practice," a tool for questioning dominant ideas and taking responsibility for making meanings and decisions in the field of early childhood. Through pedagogical narrations, educators do not formulate in advance specific goals for children's projects or activities, nor do they follow preset themes. Their objectives are flexible and adapted to the interests of the children. Within this framework, early childhood educators see themselves as observers and researchers, and the pedagogical documentation they create as a component of their research. They make careful observations and document their observations with notes, pictures, audiotapes, videotapes, diaries, and other narrative forms.

But more importantly, educators also engage in an in-depth interpretation of the observations gathered in their practices. It is through this process of interpretation that they often come to question the universalistic developmental theories of early childhood. Teachers become aware of some of their implicit assumptions about children by becoming exposed to diverse cultures in a genuine way. Through these and similar interventions, educators come to consider the perspectives of others and enrich their understanding of diverse children's background and cultural capital. Educators learn to ask different questions and consider multiple perspectives on what is observed in the classroom.

When dealing with language issues, some of the questions that should be considered when reviewing ordinary moments of practice might include:

- What are the origins of my assumptions about this child's language learning?
- What authority do my understandings about language learning have?
- How much do my understandings of children's language learning rely on developmental truths?
- To what extend do my understandings of children's language learning reinforce a developmental regime of truth?
- How are the children included/excluded based on language issues?
- What languages represented in this classroom have I silenced?
- Whose experiences of language are not recorded? Whose perspective is missing?
- What have I not seen or understood about language relationships in this ordinary moment? And what have been the struggles between different ideas, practices and relationships of languages over time, for instance, in how we organize the classroom or how we plan for learning?
- How does language diversity appear in what children do in the classroom and in what I do? And how does its absence affect my understandings and actions? (Adapted from MacNaughton, 2005, pp. 41, 151)

Pedagogical narrations can be employed to uncover the hidden meanings of language practices in order to consider alternative discourses. Language practices are often taken for granted and are rarely contested or resisted by researchers, practitioners, families, or children themselves. Through pedagogical narrations, it is possible to adopt a critical and self-aware approach to language practices by critically evaluating and acting on our omissions/silences/unjust practices by re-imagining and re-inventing equitable practices, recognizing that language practices and choices involve social and political issues.

CONCLUSION

As this chapter has argued, losses of first language and culture—which some people believe are an inevitable part of the immigration process—can, in fact, be challenged in classrooms and schools. The wider social picture cannot be ignored. It is desirable that there be changes in society's attitudes toward diversity on a number of fronts, including work-related environments. We are not trying to induce guilt in the majority society; we are attempting to recommend specific practices that will, in fact, be for the benefit of everyone. The primary purpose underlying all of these practices is to draw upon, rather than shun, the cultural and linguistic capital possessed by immigrant families and communities.

This chapter has reviewed some ways in which educators can begin to make a difference and tap the funds of knowledge of *all* families and communities connected to their students. Early childhood educators need to become aware of the ways in which monolingual and monocultural approaches are unwittingly promoted. Furthermore, educators would do well to give immigrant children and families a greater role in the education process and demonstrate in concrete terms that teachers and schools believe that children and their families posses cultural capital and valued knowledge, experiences, and skills. With programs such as the Early Authors Program and the pedagogical narrations approach mentioned above, educators can begin to build a more just and diverse society, beginning in their own classrooms.

Recommendations

- Early childhood educators would do well to familiarize themselves with issues regarding language, particularly their own involvement in the social relations of language issues.

- Families would benefit if early childhood educators were to have a greater understanding of bilingual issues and to successfully communicate to families the benefits of bilingualism, as well as the value of maintaining home culture and language.
- Families can encourage educators to take a proactive attitude toward children's languages by organizing projects focused on home languages, acknowledging children's linguistic accomplishments, and generally taking a proactive stance toward working with schools to maintain minority languages (e.g., Edwards, 1998).
- Families would do well to form community groups that meet outside the centers in which problems can be shared and common approaches can be developed. Based on their participation in such groups, families can do more to communicate their views about home language maintenance to school personnel. A goal of families' groups should be to give the families hope for achieving their goals and a belief that interactions with early childhood educators can be successful.

REFERENCES

Ada, F. (1988). The Pajaro Valley experience: Working with Spanish-speaking parents to develop children's reading and writing skills in the home through the use of children's literature. In T. Skutnabb-Kangas and J. Cummins (Eds.), *Minority education: From shame to struggle.* Clevedon: Multilingual Matters.

Ada, A., & Campoy, I. F. (2003). *Authors in the classroom: A transformative education process.* Boston: Allyn & Bacon.

Armbruster, B. B., Lehr, F., & Osborn, J. (2001). *Put reading first: The research building blocks for teaching children to read.* Washington, DC: Partnership for Reading.

Bain, B. (1974). Bilingualism and cognition: Toward a general theory. In S.T. Carey (Ed.), *Bilingualism, biculturalism, and education: Proceedings from the Conference at College Universitaire Saint Jean* (pp. 119–128). Edmonton: University of Alberta.

Bernhard, J. K. (1995). Child development, cultural diversity, and the professional training of early childhood educators. *Canadian Journal of Education, 20*(4), 415–436.

Bernhard, J. K. (2003). Toward a 21st century developmental theory: Principles to account for diversity in children's lives. *Race, Gender, and Class, 9*(4), 45–60.

Bernhard, J. K., Chud, G., Lefebvre, M. L., & Lange, R. (1996). Linguistic match between children and caregivers. *Canadian Journal of Research in Early Childhood Education, 5*(2), 5–18.

Bernhard, J. K., Cummins, J., Campoy, I., F., Ada, A., Winsler, A., & Bleiker, C. (2006). Identity texts and literacy development among preschool English Language Learners. *Teachers College Record, 108*(11), 2380–2405.

Bernhard, J. K., Freire, M., Torres, F., & Nirdosh, S. (1998). Latin Americans in a Canadian primary school: Perspectives of parents, teachers, and children on cultural identity and academic achievement. *Journal of Regional Studies, 19*(3), 217–236.

Bernhard, J. K., Lefebvre, M. L., Murphy Kilbride, K., Chud, G., & Lange, R. (1998). Troubled relationships in early childhood education: Parent teacher interactions in ethnoculturally diverse settings. *Early Education and Development, 9*(1), 5–28.

Bernhard, J. K., Lefebvre, M. L., Chud, G., & Lange, R. (1995). *Paths to equity: Cultural, linguistic and racial diversity in Canadian early childhood education.* Toronto: York Lanes Press.

Bernhard, J. K., Winsler, A., Bleiker, C., Ginieniewicz, J., & Madigan, A. (2008). Read my story: Promoting early literacy among diverse, urban, preschool children in poverty with the Early Authors Program. *Journal of Education for Students Placed at Risk, 13*(1), 76–105.

Blackledge, A. (2000). *Literacy, power and social justice.* Staffordshire, UK: Trentham Books.

Blackledge, A. (2003). Imagining a monocultural community: Racialization of cultural practice in education discourse. *Journal of Language, Identity, and Education, 2*(4), 331–347.

Blackledge, A., & Pavlenko, A. (2002). Introduction. *Multilingual, 21,* 121–140.

Blommaert, J. (1999). *Language ideological debates.* Berlin: Mouton de Gruyter.

Bourdieu, P. (1994). Social space and symbolic power. In *The polity reader in social theory* (pp. 111–120). Cambridge, MA: Polity Press.

Burman, E. (2008). *Deconstructing developmental psychology* (2nd edition). NY: Routledge.

Carr, M. (2001). *Assessment in early childhood settings: Learning stories.* London: Paul Chapman Publishing.

Chow, P., & Cummins, J. (2003). Valuing multilingual and multicultural approaches to learning. In S. Schecter and J. Cummins (Eds.), *Multilingual education in practice: Using diversity as a resource* (pp. 32–55). Portsmouth, NH: Heinemann.

Chumak-Horbatsch, R. (2008). Early bilingualism: Children of immigrants in English-language group care. *Psychology of Language and Communication, 12*(1), 3–27.

Corson, D. (2000). *Language diversity and education.* NY: Erlbaum.

Cummins, J. (2000). Language, power, and pedagogy: Bilingual children in the crossfire. Buffalo, NY: Multilingual Matters.

Dahlberg, G., Moss, P., & Pence, A. R. (1999). *Beyond quality in early childhood education and care postmodern perspectives.* London; Philadelphia, PA: Falmer.

Díaz, R. M. (1985). The intellectual power of bilingualism. In *Second language learning by young children* (pp. 68–84). Sacramento, CA: Advisory Committee for Child Development Programs.

Edwards, V. (1998). *The power of Babel: Teaching and learning in multilingual classrooms.* Staffordshire: Trentham Books.

Fleet, A. (2006). Interrogating diversity. In J. Robertson, A. Fleet and C. Patterson (Eds.), *Insights: Behind early childhood pedagogical documentation* (pp. 225–245). Baulkham Hills, NSW: Pademelon.

Freire, P. (1973). *The pedagogy of the oppressed.* New York: Seabury Press.

Freire, P. (2004). *Pedagogy of hope: Reliving pedagogy of the oppressed.* New York: Continuum International Publishing Group.

Genesee, F. (1987). *Learning through two languages: Studies of immersion and bilingual education.* Cambridge, MA: Newbury House.

Goldenberg, C., Reese, L., & Gallimore, R. (1992). Effects of literacy materials from school on Latino children's home experiences and early reading achievement. *American Journal of Education, 100,* 497–536.

González, N., Moll, L. C. & Amanti C. (2003). *Funds of knowledge: Theorizing practice in households, communities, and classrooms.* Mahwah, NJ: Erlbaum Associates.

Gonzalez-Mena, J., & Bhavnagri, N. P. (1997). The cultural context of infant caregiving. *Childhood Education*(Fall), 2–8.

Hakuta, K. (1986). *Cognitive development of bilingual children.* Center for Language Education and Research, LA: University of California at Los Angeles.

Lee, P. (1996). Cognitive development in bilingual children: A case for bilingual instruction in early childhood education. *Bilingual Research Journal, 20*(3 & 4), 499–522.

Liedtke, W.W., & Nelson, L. D. (1968). Concept formation and bilingualism. *Alberta Journal of Educational Research, 14,* 225–232.

Lin, A., & Martin, P. W. (2005). *Decolonisation, globalisation. Language-in-education policy and practice.* Clevedon: Multilingual Matters.

Lindfors, J.W. (1991). *Children's language and learning.* Needham Heights, MA: Allyn & Bacon.

Luke, A., & Grieshaber, S. (2004). New adventures in the politics of literacy: An introduction. *Journal of Early Childhood Literacy, 4*(1), 5–9.

MacNaughton, G. (2003). *Shaping early childhood: Learners, curriculum and contexts.* Maidenhead: Open University Press.

MacNaughton, G. (2005). *Doing Foucault in early childhood studies: Applying poststructural ideas.* NY: Routledge.

May, S. (2001). *Language and minority rights. Ethnicity, nationalism, and the politics of language.* New York: Longman.

Nehring, A. D., Nehring, E. F., Bruni, J. R., & Randolph, P. L. (1992). *Learning Accomplishment Profile—Diagnostic Standardized Assessment.* Lewisville, NC: Kaplan Press.

Ochs, E. (1986). Introduction. In B. Schieffelin, & E. Ochs (Eds.), *Language socialization across cultures* (pp. 1–13). Cambridge, MA: Cambridge University Press.

Ochs, E., & Schieffelin, B. (1984). Language acquisition and socialization: Threee developmental stories and their implications. In R. Schweder, & R. Levine (Eds.), *Essays on mind, self and emotion* (pp. 276–319). Cambridge, MA: Cambridge University Press.

Pacini-Ketchabaw, V., & Armstrong de Almeida, A. (2006). Language discourses and ideologies at the heart of early childhood education. *The International Journal of Bilingual Education and Bilingualism, 9*(3) 2006, 310–341.

Pacini-Ketchabaw, V. & Berikoff, A. (2008). The politics of difference and diversity: From young children's violence to creative power expressions. *Contemporary Issues in Early Childhood, 9*(3), 256–264.

Pacini-Ketchabaw, V., Bernhard, J., & Freire, M. (2001). Struggling to preserve home language: The experiences of Latino students and families in the Canadian school system. *Bilingual Research Journal, 25*(1), 1–31.

Park, S., M., & Sarkar, M. (2007). Parents' attitudes toward heritage language maintenance for their children and their efforts to help their children maintain the heritage language: A case study of Korean-Canadian immigrants. *Language, Culture and Curriculum, 20*(3), 223– 235.

Peters, A., & Boggs, S. (1986). Interactional routines as cultural influences upon language acquisition. In B. Schieffelin, & E. Ochs (Eds.), *Language socialization across cultures* (pp. 80–96). Cambridge, MA: Cambridge University Press.

Rinaldi, C. (2006). *In dialogue with Reggio Emilia: Listening, researching and learning.* NY: Routledge.

Schecter, S., & Cummins, J. (Eds.) (2003). *Multilingual education in practice: Using diversity as a resource.* Portsmouth, NH: Heinemann.

Schecter, S., & Bayley, R. (1997). Language socialization practices and cultural identity: Case study of Mexican-descent families in California and Texas. *TESOL Quarterly, 31*(3), 513–541.

Schecter, S., Sharken-Taboada, D., & Bayley, R. (1996). Bilingual by choice: Latino parents' rationales and strategies for raising children with two languages. *The Bilingual Research Journal, 20*(2), 261–281.

Schieffelin, B., Woolard, K., & Kroskrity, P. (1998). *Language ideologies: Practice and theory.* NY: Oxford University Press.

Siren, U. (1991) *Minority language transmission in Early Childhood: Parental intention and language use.* Stockholm: Institute of International Education Stockholm University.

Swain, M. A., & Lapkin, S. (1982). *Evaluating bilingual education.* Clevedon: Multilingual Matters.

Taylor, L. Bernhard, J. K., Garg, S., & Cummins, J. (2008). Affirming plural belonging: Building on students' family-based plural and linguistic capital through a multiliteracies curriculum. *Journal of Early Childhood Literacy, 8*(3), 269–295.

Vygotsky, L. S. (1978). *Mind in society: The development of higher psychological processes.* Cambridge, MA: Cambridge University Press.

Wong-Fillmore, L. (1991). When learning a second language means losing the first. *Early Childhood Research Quarterly, 6,* 323–346.

Zimmerman, I. L., Steiner, V. G., & Evatt Pond, R. (2002). *Preschool Language Scale (PLS-R)* (4th ed.). San Antonio, TX: The Psychological Corporation.

CHAPTER 3

LANGUAGE DEVELOPMENT AND EARLY EDUCATION OF YOUNG HISPANIC CHILDREN IN THE UNITED STATES

Eugene E. García and Bryant Jensen

ABSTRACT

Young Hispanic (or Latino) children (ages 0–8) are currently the largest and fastest-growing ethnic minority population in the US (Collins & Ribeiro, 2004; Hernandez, 2006; Hernandez, Denton, & Macartney, 2007). As educational programs, policies, and practices move forward—especially those targeting the youngest groups of children—it is important that *relevance* and *appropriateness* continue to be resonating themes. But what can be concluded about a large population of children with diverse language and educational experiences at home and in school? What can be ascertained from the empirical literature, theory, extant programs and policies associated with language and early learning for young Hispanics? And what are the home and school factors important to differences in early cognitive development and educational well-being? The intent of this paper is to explore these questions in a system-

Language and Cultural Diversity in Early Childhood Education, pages 43–64

atic fashion, relying on current evidence vis-à-vis theory and practice, and to present avenues of future research.

Because language is a central feature to the cognitive development and early learning for young Hispanics (García, Jensen, & Cuellar, 2006), topics explored in this paper are linked to questions of language use and practice. Bilingualism, second language learning, and related issues, therefore, appear and reappear throughout this synthesis. We recognize that not all Hispanic children are English language learners. Many are raised in English-only homes. Moreover, Hispanic children represent various racial groups, national origins, social classes, geographical locations, and immigrant generations. While we are aware of the incredible diversity found within this group, there are general trends, patterns, and themes significant to young Hispanics, as a whole. Such are important to understand as efforts are made to improve educational opportunities for young Hispanics. To avoid gross generalizations, we discuss key characteristics of Hispanic children in terms of proportional representation and provide, where possible, descriptions of Hispanic samples of children in the studies reviewed. As in most reviews, the evidence must be weighed, critiqued, and understood in its proper context where applications are made to individuals or small groups.

A review of this sort is more likely to be read by academicians and researchers. In some cases, policymakers and practitioners will read it. Our hope is that, by discussing replicated research findings, inconsistencies (where they exist), and further needs in educational and related research, this review will allow us to move forward—that our work will continue to build on the current knowledge base.

Important to mention early in this paper is that language and its many parts—phonology, morphology, syntax, pragmatics, vocabulary, word literacy, text literacy, and reading comprehension—must be analyzed and understood not only in terms of its mechanics (e.g., word attack and reading fluency) but also in terms of context (e.g., person-to-person interactions, relationships, activity settings). This necessitates an analysis of culture, which is inherent in language. While several studies have described the cultural context in which young Hispanics use and develop language, few have made the conceptual and methodological links necessary to understand how home and school contexts (including differences between contexts) influence early literacy and learning outcomes (Rueda, August, & Goldenberg, 2006). Representing a major gap in the literature, this issue is discussed at greater length in the final section of this paper. In addition to research on language and literacy development, we review the literature on school program effectiveness, including dual-language programs, research on assessment, English acquisition, cross-linguistic transfer, and directions for future research and practice.

It should be noted that a majority of the data presented in this paper focus on the school-age young Hispanic population—ages 5–8. While, conceptually, we discuss Hispanics ages 0–8 years, there is less research and empirical information available for infant, toddler, and preschool age Hispanics. We recognize, however, that this field is rapidly growing, in light of recent technological advances and a growing emphasis on publicly-funded preschool programs throughout the country. Where available, we present some work on Hispanics from infancy to age 4.

The study of young Hispanics in early education settings must better reflect current studies of how children acquire language. That is, as the study of early language has morphed from a consideration of habits (Skinner, 1957) and innate structures (Chomsky, 1959) to an interlocking study of linguistic, psychological, and social domains, educational researchers must continue to expand the integration of diverse theories and empirical research associated with language, cognition, and socialization to understand early development and educational appropriateness for young Hispanics (August & Hakuta, 1997; August & Shanahan, 2006; Cole & Cole, 2001; García, 2005).

This paper is organized thematically, and responds to the following questions:

- What is the range of linguistic proficiency of young Hispanic children in the US?
- How do linguistic properties between Spanish and English relate and develop for young Hispanic children?
- What relationship does social context have with the language and literacy development of young Hispanic children in the US?
- What schooling program options are available to young Hispanic children learning English and what does the evidence show in terms of programmatic features that promote literacy, academic achievement, and "academic" English proficiency?

We conclude with a summary of critical issues associated with the linguistic development and early education of young Hispanic children in the United States. In accordance with the literature reviewed, we offer a set of recommendations for future research endeavors.

LINGUISTIC PROFILE OF YOUNG HISPANIC CHILDREN

As mentioned, Hispanic children in the US are not a homogenous group. They come from diverse social, cultural, and linguistic backgrounds. Hispanic children represent, for example, long-term, native-born populations to the US, along with various countries-of-origin, each of which is associated with a unique combination of histories, cultural practices, perspectives, and traditions. At this age level, much like the Hispanic population in general, the growth in the population has been driven, to a high degree, by immigration patterns from Latin American and Caribbean countries to the US. In 2003, almost 25% of the total US birth cohort (some 4 million new-born) can be attributed to Hispanic mothers. Of this birth cohort, approximately 64% were born into a family in which at least one parent was born outside the US (Capps, Fix, Ost, Reardon-Anderson, & Passel, 2004; Hernandez, 2006; Hernandez, Denton, & Macartney, 2007). More than three in five Hispanic immigrant families were from Mexico, yet substantial groups also came from Central America, South America, and Spanish-speaking Caribbean nations.

Due to variation in nativity and national origin and related social factors, language development and language use vary within the young Hispanic population. Some young children acquire English as their first language and maintain monolingual proficiency throughout their life. These children are more likely to have native (US-born) parents. Others speak Spanish as their first language, and learn English as they enter public schooling—children often referred to as "sequential" bilinguals. The proportional size of this subpopulation has been growing rapidly over the past few decades (August & Shanahan, 2006). Indeed, the National Clearinghouse for English Language Acquisition (NCELA, 2006) reports that from the 1993–1994 to the 2003–2004 school year, K-12 enrollment of English language learners (ELL) grew over 65% while the total K-12 population grew less than 7%. Moreover, the increasing presence of native Spanish-speaking children is especially a function of immigration and high birth rates among the Hispanic population (García, Jensen, Miller, & Huerta, 2005). A final (and smaller) subset of Hispanic children develops English and Spanish fluency simultaneously and at comparable levels in the home and in school. Differences in language development are most commonly attributable to differing linguistic practices in the home.

In an analysis of data from the Early Childhood Longitudinal Study, Birth Cohort (ECLS-B), López , Barrueco, and Miles (2006) describe the home language environments of Hispanic 9-month-old infants in the country. Representing a national sample of children born between December 2001 and January 2002, López and colleagues found that Hispanic infants (constituting 26% of the total infant population) resided in various sorts of home language environments. The largest group (34%) of Hispanic infants lived in a home in which Spanish was the primary language, with some English. Twenty–two percent lived in a home in which English was primarily spoken, with some Spanish; 21% lived in English-only homes; and 19% lived in Spanish-only homes.

In another study, data from the US Census 2000 reveal that many parents of young Hispanic children have limited English proficiency (Hernandez, 2006). For example, three-fourths of young Hispanic children in immigrant families (71%) live with at least one parent who is Limited English Proficient (LEP), not speaking English exclusively or very well, and one-half (49%) live with two such parents (Hernandez, 2006).

Table 3.1 displays the prevalence of LEP Hispanic children compared to other racial/ethnic groups. While one–third of all young Hispanic children

TABLE 3.1 Limited English Proficiency of US Children Ages 0–8 by Race/Ethnicity

	Percent of Children							
	Bilingual	Limited English Proficiency						
	Child English fluent & speaks other language at home[a]	Child Limited English Proficient (LEP)[a]	Child LEP & father LEP[a]	Child LEP & mother LEP[a]	Father LEP	Mother LEP	Father or mother LEP	Both father & mother LEP
Total	10.0	8.7	3.0	2.9	12.2	11.7	14.0	9.3
Hispanic	32.8	32.7	11.7	11.2	45.0	41.8	49.5	35.2
White	2.8	1.4	0.3	0.3	1.7	1.9	2.5	1.0
Black	3.0	1.7	0.4	0.4	3.1	2.6	3.1	2.0
Asian	33.1	25.3	8.0	8.7	33.5	39.2	43.5	28.5
Native American	9.7	6.7	1.4	1.5	7.6	7.0	9.3	4.2
Hawaiian, Other Pacific Islander	6.2	2.8	0.4	0.5	3.3	3.4	4.7	1.5

[a] For children ages 5–8 years.
[b] Households in which no one over the age of 13 speaks English exclusively or very well.
Source: Calculated from Census 2000 5% microdata (IPUMS) by Donald J. Hernandez.

(ages 5–8) are bilingual—fluent in both English and Spanish—Hispanics are more likely than other racial/ethnic groups to be LEP, and to have one or two parents who are also LEP. That is, in 2000, over 50% of all Hispanic children ages 0–8 years old have either a mother or father whose primary language was Spanish. Moreover, Hispanic children, including those from native and immigrant families, are more likely than any other racial/ethnic group to live in linguistically isolated homes, households in which no one over the age of 13 speaks English exclusively or very well (Hernandez, 2006).

The quality and quantity of English and Spanish use in the home are associated with several demographic features. Associations have been found, for example, with national origin. Children of Mexican ancestry are less likely to be bilingual than those from other national origins (Hernandez, 2006). Furthermore, Hispanic children from Dominican, Mexican, and Central American backgrounds are more likely than Hispanics from others national origins to be LEP and to have one or two LEP parents. Bilingualism also varies by region. In 2000, the states with the highest relative proportion of bilingual Hispanic children were Florida and New Jersey, and the lowest relative proportion of bilingual Hispanic children was found in Colorado. Arizona, California, Illinois, and Texas had the highest relative proportions of young Hispanic children who were LEP (Hernandez, 2006).

The language proficiencies of young Hispanics are also associated with household income (Hernandez, 2006). While young Hispanic children are more likely than their general body of same-age peers to live in poverty, the likelihood is increased for Hispanic children who live in homes in which little or no English is spoken. For those Hispanic homes in which the father is fluent in English, 14% live below the official poverty line, compared to 29% of those Hispanic homes in which the father is not fluent in English.

Not surprising, Hispanic children from native families (i.e., 3rd generation or more) are more likely to demonstrate English proficiency than children of immigrant families (i.e., children who have at least one foreign-born parent). On the other hand, Hispanic children born to immigrant families (1st or 2nd generation immigrant) are more likely to show bilingual proficiency between 5–8 years old, compared to children in native-born families. Indeed, 40% of Hispanic children from immigrant families are proficient in English and Spanish, compared to 18% of children from native families—a trend present in every country-of-origin subgroup (Hernandez, 2006).

This general decrease in bilingual proficiency of Hispanic children from immigrant to native families exemplifies a phenomenon linguists and bilingual researchers call *language shift*. It also typifies Lambert's (1974) notion of *subtractive bilingualism*. With empirical evidence as early as the mid 1970s (Lieberson, Dalto, & Johnston, 1975), the language shift occurs when a language minority group gradually changes its language use and preference from the minority language to the locally dominant language. Census data indicate that Hispanic children of US-born parents are more likely to be monolingual English speakers, and that children of immigrant (1st and 2nd generation) are more likely to maintain bilingual proficiency (Hernandez, 2006), even when they demonstrate a preference for English in school settings (Oller & Eilers, 2002). Thus, the language shift—from Spanish to English, in this case—as Veltman (1983) suggested, tends to occur by the third generation after a family migrates from one country to another with a different majority language. In addition, some research suggests that a preference for English occurs in immigrant children attending US schools within the first generation, by grade 3.

Bilingualism, therefore, for many Hispanic children in the US tends to be of the *subtractive* sort. Lambert (1974) was the first to differentiate between *subtractive* and *additive* bilingualism. The basic distinction between the two depends on whether second language proficiency replaces native language proficiency (i.e., subtractive bilingualism) or adds to it (i.e., additive bilingualism). Data suggest that the linguistic development of many Hispanic children exemplifies the former type. In other words, competence in English has tended to come at the expense of Spanish proficiency (the heritage language) both within individuals and across generations.

Notwithstanding, some young Hispanic children from native as well as immigrant homes maintain proficiency in both languages. Indeed, 33% of all young Hispanic children ages 0–8 in 2000 had parents who reported their child spoke English and Spanish in the home—that they were bilingual (Hernandez, 2006). While impressive, this figure is to be interpreted cautiously, for at least two reasons. First, it is derived from Census data, which consists of surveyed information—we do not know the quality and type of bilingual language proficiency these children actually possess. That is, the level and type of proficiency of bilingual children are quite varied. They differ in terms of balanced competence and the extent to which the child is exposed to each language. Concerning balanced competence, McLaughlin (1995) notes that there tends to be an ebb and flow to children's bilingualism, and that it is rare for both languages to be perfectly balanced. However, a child is usually described as a balanced bilingual when he or she possesses age-appropriate competence in both languages. The amount of early exposure and opportunity to explore both languages also determines the type of bilingualism a child develops. A child exposed to English and Spanish at relatively comparable amounts in the home, and who is given adequate opportunity to use both, is likely to develop simultaneous bilingual proficiency. Whereas, another child exposed only to Spanish in the home and English in school will develop the two languages sequentially—either rapidly or successively, depending on the amount of opportunities to experiment with and use the second language.

The second reason the Census figure is to be interpreted with caution is that no indication is provided as to whether bilingual proficiency of Hispanic children is intermediary or permanent—whether bilingualism will diminish or be sustained over time. It is often the case that young bilinguals in the US do not develop their native language beyond early conversational skills learned in the home. Many Hispanic children, as previously indicated, lose native language proficiency at the expense of developing English skills. Several studies have been conducted with young Hispanics and their families to explore the various factors that influence Spanish maintenance, even as English skills are being developed (Hammer, Miccio, & Wagstaff, 2003; Lee & Samura, 2005; López, 2005; Pérez-Bazán, 2005). They found native language maintenance to be a result of interacting personal and family factors. While Hispanic children inevitably gain proficiency in English through interaction with the larger community, proficiency in Spanish was found to be associated with the quality and quantity of Spanish use in the home (Pérez-Bazán, 2005). Spanish maintenance also has been found to be related with parent education levels, where higher levels were associated with greater bilingual and Spanish proficiency (López , 2005), opportunities for native language use (Lee & Samura, 2005), as well as attitudinal and motivational features (López , 2005).

SOCIAL CONTEXT, DEVELOPMENT, AND LEARNING

Over recent decades, a growing interest has emerged among educational theorists and researchers concerning the social contexts of children as a critical variable related to their overall learning and development (Cole & Cole, 2001; García, 2002; Nasir & Hand, 2006; Portes, 2005; Rogoff, 2003). Though there is no one sociocultural theory to guide this work (Cole, 1996; Nasir & Hand, 2006; Portes, 2005), tenets among these theories find much overlap and relevance to language development and educational inquiry. Their roots are found in Vygotskyan thought (Vygotsky, 1978), and their aim is to find a unified way of understanding the development of psychological processes and cultural practices.

Sociocultural theorists posit that the psychology of the individual learner is deeply shaped by social interaction—in essence, that both children and those with whom they interact are engaged in the process of constructing knowledge primarily through social activity. Knowledge, therefore, is created between individuals primarily through social interaction. Higher-order mental processes, the tendency to look at things in certain ways, and values themselves are produced by shared activity and dialogue (Rogoff, 1990). In a broader sense, these social interactions are highly determined by culture and directly affect language, cognitive, and social development, as well as the acquisition of any new knowledge and behavior—that phenomenon we call *learning*.

Educators of culturally diverse students—including young Hispanic children learning English as a second language—often find this theoretical framework helpful, because it conceives of learning as an interaction between individual learners and an embedding context. This context may be as immediate as the social environment of the classroom or as indirect as the traditions and institutions that constitute the history of an educational system. Both contexts and many other factors come into play whenever teachers and students interact. Important contexts for teaching and learning range from (1) close detailed instruction of individual learners and (2) concern for the social organization of classrooms to (3) a consideration of the cultural and linguistic attributes of teachers, students, and peers. These contexts interweave, and we can follow their strands to gain a new understanding of the relationship between language, culture, and cognition.

It is useful, therefore, to conceive co-occurring linguistic, cognitive, and social character of a child's development as inherently interrelated (Hart & Risley, 1995, 1999; García, 2005). As children develop their ability to use language, they absorb more and more understanding of social situations and improve their thinking skills. This, in turn, allows them to learn how to control their own actions and thoughts. It is through a culturally bound and socially mediated process of language development that children construct mental frameworks (or *schema*) for perceiving the world around them. If language is a tool of thought, it follows that, as children develop more complex-thinking skills, the mental representations through which language and culture embody the child's world play a significant role. This perspective is especially important for young children negotiating two or more languages (Scheffner Hammer & Miccio, 2004).

Unfortunately, educational policy and practice discussions regarding the education of bilingual students are often overly simplistic and focus solely on linguistic deficiencies (i.e., limited English skills) (García, 2005; Jensen, 2008; Rolstad, Mahoney, & Glass, 2005; Tharp & Gallimore, 1989; Stritikus, 2001). They tend to neglect the complex interweaving of students' cultural, linguistic, and cognitive development. In their study of the possible effects of language on cognitive development, Hakuta, Ferdman, and Diaz (1987) recognize the importance of acknowledging these three important strands in children's development and addressing them in schools. They conclude that most of the variance in cognitive growth directly relates to the way in which society affects and manipulates cognitive capacities. Therefore, cultural and contextual sensitivity theories that examine the social and cultural aspects of cognitive development would best serve minority student populations.

Goldenberg, Rueda, and August (2006) present a research synthesis on the influences of social and cultural contexts on literacy development and attainment of language minority children and youth, including several studies that used young Hispanics as the target sample. They defined social and cultural influences broadly, as factors that contribute to the context in which children and youth go to school and live—including beliefs, attitudes, behaviors, routine practices, social and political relations, and physical resources connected with groups of people who share some characteristic (e.g., socioeconomic status, educational status, race/ethnicity, national origin, linguistic group). Moreover, they evaluated studies using six operational definitions and domains of social and cultural contexts: (1) immigration, (2) home/school discourse differences, (3) characteristics of students and teachers, (4) the influence of parents and families, (5) educational policy, and (6) language status or prestige. Here, we provide conclusions from each of these domains.

Again, research employing mixed and complex methodologies is greatly needed to better understand particular ways in which domains and levels of social and cultural contexts influence the literacy development of young Hispanics who often negotiate two languages and diverse cultural practices. These studies will need to account for differences across levels of parent education; SES; ethnicity; immigration status; beliefs and attitudes of parents, teachers, and students; discourse features at school, home, and in the community; instructional features in the classroom; parent involvement strategies; educational policy; language status/prestige; and so on. This work will require linking well-designed experiments with high-quality ethnographic research to cross-check findings, provide relative frequency of events or occurrences, examine competing explanations, and make generalizations based on available data. The combination of qualitative and quantitative methods will have a much greater probability of shedding light on complex topics than either one does individually (Green, Camilli, & Elmore, 2006; Smith, 2006; Weisner, 2005).

LANGUAGE, CULTURE, SCHOOLING, AND THE EVIDENCE

The knowledge base reviewed until this point is directly related to understanding instructional programs, teaching strategies, and educational policies that seek to provide optimal literacy and academic development for young Hispanic children. We showed that a majority of young Hispanic children come from homes in which Spanish is used, and that there are important associations between language development in Spanish and English and the development of certain cognitive features (especially those needed to do well in school). Moreover, we reviewed available theory and research on how various contexts (in and out-of school) influence early literacy learning. These issues should take top priority for those involved in educational delivery and research with young Hispanic children. It means instruction, curricular content, and schooling practices should be developed and evaluated to account for their linguistic and sociocultural circumstances, so as to leverage home resources and parental support, and to optimize student learning (Genesee, Geva, Dressler, & Kamil, 2006; Goldenberg, Gallimore, Reese, & Garnier, 2001; Goldenberg et al., 2006; Reese, Garnier, Gallimore, & Goldenberg, 2000; Scheffner Hammer & Miccio, 2004; Shannon, 1995; National Task Force on Early Childhood Education for Hispanics, 2007). In this section, we discuss what research presently suggests concerning the educational development of young Hispanics, including achievement trends and ways in which language-related practices in homes and schools influence this scenario.

Achievement Trends

Currently, Hispanics lag behind their White and Asian American peers at all proficiency levels of reading and mathematics (at least a half of a standard deviation) at the beginning and throughout K–12 schooling (Braswell, Daane, & Grigg, 2003; García, Jensen, Miller, & Huerta, 2005; NCES, 2003; Reardon & Galindo, 2006). Educational achievement patterns of virtually all racial/ethnic groups are established during the early years of school and change little thereafter. Although some of the difference between racial/ethnic groups is accounted for by socioeconomic status (SES) differences between groups (on average, Hispanics have lower SES than Whites and Asian Americans), much of it is not (Reardon & Galindo, 2006). In an analysis of national math and reading outcomes from kindergarten through fifth grade, Reardon and Galindo (2006) found racial/ethnic differences within SES groups. Hispanic children scored significantly lower than Whites in both subjects within each SES group, though, in some cases, the size of the gap decreased over time. In a separate analysis, Reardon (2003) found that racial/ethnic and SES achievement differences in early elementary education were attributable to processes within, between, and out-of school. That is, processes in the home and school accounted for the differences (García, Jensen, & Cuéllar, 2006).

Reardon and Galindo (2006) also found reading and mathematics achievement patterns from kindergarten through third grade to vary by home language environments. Hispanic children living in homes categorized as "primarily Spanish" or "Spanish only" lagged further behind White children than did Hispanics who lived in homes in which primarily English or English only was spoken (see Figure 3.1). The impact of language background on achievement outcomes should not necessarily be surprising given the relationship of SES with achievement, and the correlation between low SES and non-English home environments among Hispanics (Collier, 1987; Jensen, 2007; NCES, 1995).

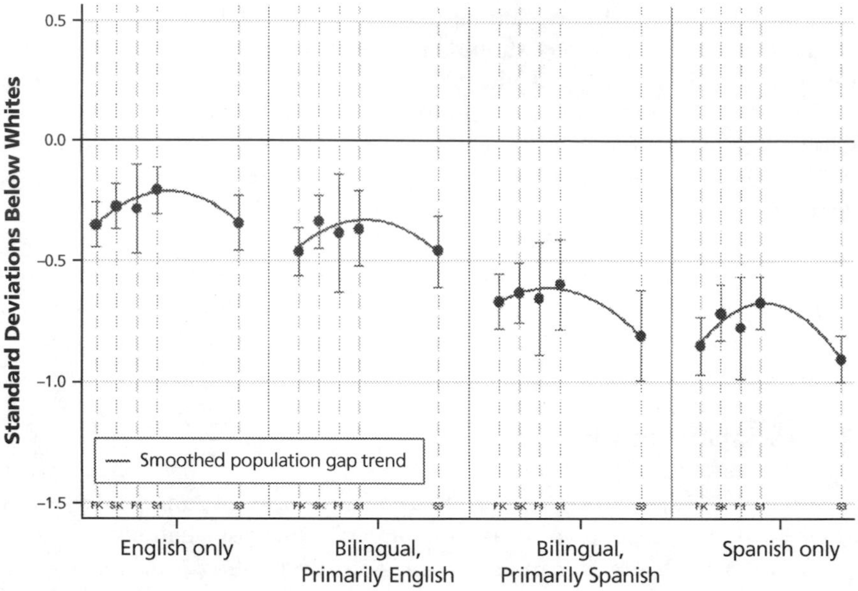

Figure 3.1 Estimated population Hispanic–White math gap, by home language-use (*Source:* Reardon & Galindo, 2006).

Thus, rather than pointing to one or two out-of-school factors that account for the low achievement of young Hispanic children, as a whole, it should be understood that early risk is due to a myriad of interrelated factors. Early risk factors include (but are not necessarily limited to) parent education levels, family income, parent English language proficiency, mother's marital status at the time of birth, and single- versus dual-parent homes (NCES, 1995). The more risk factors the child is subject to, the lower the probability the child will do well in school, in terms of achievement and attainment. Because Hispanic children, on average, exhibit more risk factors than Whites, they are generally at greater risk for academic underachievement and underattainment (Hernandez, Denton, & Macartney, 2007).

Moreover, it is important to clarify that risk is not due solely to non-English proficiency, but to a number of sociodemographic conditions that correlate with Spanish use in the home. In an analysis of national data, Jensen (2007) compared Spanish-speaking kindergarteners to their general education peers on a number of outcomes, including SES, parent education, and mathematics achievement (i.e., numeracy, shape/size recognition, and ordinality). He found that Spanish-speaking kindergartners, on average, scored four–fifths of a standard deviation lower than the general body of kindergartners in mathematics. They also fared an entire standard deviation below their peers in terms of SES and maternal educational attainment. Nearly half of the kindergarteners from Spanish-speaking homes had mothers who had not completed high school.

Schooling and Programs

The underlying concern in educational assessment of young Hispanic children is to provide an optimal classroom setting in which to learn and develop. Yet, ways in which schools approach curriculum and instruction for these children vary (sometimes greatly). For Hispanic children whose home language is Spanish, a critical concern is how and whether to integrate their native language. This has been a topic of empirical research and policy debate for several decades (García, 2005). Here, we present ways in which linguistics and policy analysts have approached the issue, and a summary of their findings. Moreover, we present two schooling programs—dual-language and prekindergarten programs—that appear promising for young Hispanics in terms of their ongoing educational performance.

Debates regarding program types that best develop the academic skills of children whose native language is not English continue to cause tumult among practitioners, academics, and policymakers. The fundamental issue underlying this argument has been whether bilingual or English-only approaches are more effective in boosting and sustaining the academic achievement of ELLs. Early research surrounding this issue was inconclusive. Some, such as Baker and de Kanter (1981) and Baker and Pelavin (1984), asserted that the research evidence did not support the effectiveness of bilingual instruction, and that bilingual education simply does not work. Others, such as Willig (1985) refuted this argument and provided evidence to support the efficacy of bilingual programs.

Rolstad, Mahoney, and Glass (2005) present another meta-analysis, including 17 studies conducted since 1985. Authors in this review decided to include as many studies as possible, instead of excluding on the basis of a priori criteria. Effect size of program effectiveness was computed by calculating mean outcome differences between new treatment and traditional treatment groups, and subsequently dividing by the standard deviation of the traditional treatment group (Glass, McGaw, & Smith, 1981). Using this method, authors found that bilingual approaches were consistently better than English-only approaches, yielding an average benefit of .23 of a standard deviation—a small, but important, finding.

Recent research, therefore, suggests academic benefits of bilingual over English-only programs—on average, an increase of .2 to .3 standard deviations in test performance. This is enough to close one-fifth to one-third of the overall Hispanic–White achievement gap in reading in the early elementary-school years.

One of the problems with broad comparisons of program types is that there is not one bilingual program or approach (García, 2005; García, Jensen, Miller, & Huerta, 2005), but several. As mentioned above, they differ in terms of required teacher qualifications, curriculum, the student population they are designed to serve, instructional approaches, and variations of Spanish/English use, among other aspects.

Relatively new in the United States, dual-language (DL) programs—also known as two-way immersion (TWI)—offer a unique approach to bilingual education. Designed to teach English to ELL students and Spanish to native English-speakers through dual-language content and instruction in a shared classroom (i.e., English-plus-Spanish [EPS] approaches), available research suggests positive effects for young Hispanics as well as for language majority populations (García & Jensen, 2006). It is important to note that the implementation of these programs vary, in terms of the amount of time they devote to each language (e.g., 50–50 vs., 90–10 models), the grade levels they intend to serve, language and curriculum division, and the populations they intend to serve (Center for Applied Linguistics [CAL], 2005). On the other hand, DL programs are unified by common notions of learning (based heavily on Vygotskyan [or sociocultural] notions of social interaction and naturalistic learning), second language acquisition, the importance of teaching language through content, and the goal of producing bilingual students (Genesee, 1999).

Extant research shows that DL programs are able to promote bilingual oral and academic skills for young ELL Hispanics, as well as for their language majority counterparts (Barnett, Yarosz, Thomas, & Blanco, 2006; Cazabon, Lambert, & Hall, 1999; Christian, 1994, 1997; Christian, Genesee, Lindholm-Leary & Howard, 2004; Cobb, Vega, & Kronauge, 2005; Figueroa, 2005; García & Jensen, 2006; Howard, Sugarman, & Christian, 2003; Lindholm, 1999; Sugarman & Howard, 2001). While the methodological rigor between studies varies from randomized trials controlling for student background, school environment quality, and the integrity of program implementation to measuring the academic progress of a small group of DL participants over time (Howard, Sugarman, & Christian, 2003), conclusions converge on comparisons between DL and other programs, and comparisons between Hispanic ELLs and native English speakers.

Comparisons between programs for Hispanic ELLs and native English-speakers show that DL participants score as well or better on standardized achievement tests in English and Spanish than same-age peers educated in other programs (Howard, Sugarman, & Christian, 2003). Indeed, studies document native Spanish speakers participating in DL programs to outperform other Spanish speakers enrolled in other programs in English reading and mathematics, as well as Spanish pre-reading, reading, writing, and mathematics (Barnett, Yarosz, Thomas, & Blanco, 2006; Christian, 1994;

Cobb, Vega, & Kronauge, 2005). Other studies have found no significant differences in outcomes for Hispanic ELL students (Cazabon, Lambert, & Hall, 1999; Howard, Sugarman, & Christian, 2003).

Studies measuring the academic benefits for native English speakers enrolled in DL programs also present a mixed picture. Some studies indicate benefits over and above other schooling programs, while others do not suggest significant differences (Cobb, Vega, & Kronauge, 2005; Howard, Sugarman, & Christian, 2003). Cobb, Vega and Kronauge (2005), for example, found the greatest academic benefits for native English-speakers enrolled in DL programs to be in reading skills, yet, in other areas, they found no differences.

A final topic regarding the schooling of young Hispanics concerns prekindergarten programs. In recent years, access to state-funded prekindergarten programs has expanded in several states where Head Start and other initiatives have come short (García & Jensen, 2007). The motivation—in most cases, to get children in school at age four (and, often, age three)—concerns the economic (Heckman & Masterov, 2004) and neurological (Ramey & Ramey, 1998; Shonkoff & Phillips, 2000) benefits of early education. Moreover, recent research shows young Hispanics are particularly positioned to benefit from involvement (Gormley, Gayer, & Dawson, 2004). Unfortunately, as García & Gonzáles (2006) indicate, they are less likely to be enrolled than their White, Asian, and African American peers, not because they prefer alternative care, but because early learning venues may be unavailable in the neighborhood, may be too costly, or knowledge of their existence may not be common among parents of this population.

The general academic benefits of participation in prekindergarten programs have been documented repeatedly, yet the sizes of the effects vary across programs and between racial/ethnic groups. Indeed, an evaluation of the public prekindergarten program in Tulsa, Oklahoma found that, while benefits for all racial/ethnic and SES groups were found, gains for Hispanic students in letter–word identification, spelling, and applied problem solving were each greater than for African American, Native American, and White children (Gormley, Gayer, & Dawson, 2004). Yet, no discussion was rendered concerning the curricular or instructional strategies that generated these results or their impact over time.

CONCLUSION

Current Knowledge Base

Though much is to be discovered through applied research to improve classroom practices and early learning opportunities for young Hispanic children (National Task Force on Early Childhood Education for Hispanics, 2007), the current body of knowledge reviewed in this paper allows for several conclusions. Most clearly, we know that a central feature concerning the education of young Hispanic children continues to be their language development. Diverse, in terms of their national origins, geographical location, and home circumstances, some Hispanic children grow up in homes in which Spanish is spoken regularly, and a large majority is exposed to Spanish through relatives and/or neighbors. The extent to which children speak Spanish in the home and maintain bilingual proficiency over time varies by national origin, generational status, and between states and regions. Moreover, Spanish maintenance is influenced by a combination of personal, familial, educational, and societal factors. Importantly, the amount of parent educational attainment is associated with the quality of native Spanish proficiency; more formal parent education is associated with the maintenance, proficiency, and literacy in Spanish.

Decades of linguistics research support the notion that children can competently acquire two or more languages (García, 2005). Associations of linguistic properties between languages are important, though quite complex. Among the available theories in second language acquisition, transfer theory is the most widely accepted. It asserts that language skills from the first language transfer to the second (Genesee, 1999). Literacy research also supports the general notion of transfer (August & Shanahan, 2006). The quality of literacy skill development in the second language is dependent on the quality of similar skills in the native language. Indeed, word- and text-level skills transfer between languages.

Schooling program options for young Hispanics differ, in terms of their goals, requirements for staff competency, and the student populations they are meant to serve. In terms of student achievement outcomes, meta-analyses and best evidence syntheses suggest that programs supporting bilingual approaches to curriculum and instruction are favorable to English-only or English immersion programs (García, 2005). DL (or TWI) programs, which integrate language minority and language majority students in the same classroom, teach both languages through course content. Studies suggest that students (from multiple language backgrounds) in DL programs perform at equal levels as their peers and, in many cases, outperform those enrolled in other programs (Howard, Sugarman, & Christian, 2003). Research also suggests that prekindergarten programs can increase early learning for young Hispanic children (Gormley, Gayer, & Dawson, 2004). Yet, further research evaluating the longitudinal benefits and curricular and instructional strategies of these programs is needed.

Further Research—In a Nutshell

Throughout this chapter, we have referred to needs for further research related to the language development and early education of young Hispanics. We see improving the scope and quality of research as vital to the improvement of early educational programs, practices, and policies for these children. Moreover, given the size and growth of the young Hispanic population in this country, and the inherent social consequences of low educational quality to society at large, we feel a comprehensive research agenda centered on raising early learning opportunities for young Hispanics to be critical. This research agenda will need to incorporate multiple research methods to systematically evaluate how school and non-school contexts influence language development, cognitive processing, and academic outcomes. In addition to exploring and understanding associations between contexts and student outcomes, there is a great need to evaluate the added value of educational policies and practices based on the research literature. This work will continue to require experts from several fields—such as reading, second language acquisition, and parenting—to explore improved assessment practices and the efficacy of rich language environments, DL programs, preschool programs (including curricular and instructional strategies), teacher quality, and educational policies.

REFERENCES

August, D., & Hakuta, K. (1997). *Improving schooling for language-minority children: A research agenda.* Washington: National Research Council, Institute of Medicine, National Academy Press.

August, D., & Shanahan, T. (Eds.) (2006). *Developing literacy in second language learners: Report of the national literacy panel on language minority youth and children.* Mahwah, NJ: Lawrence Erlbaum Associates.

Baker, K. A., & de Kanter, A. A. (1981) *Effectiveness of bilingual education: A review of the literature.* Washington, D.C.: US Department of Education.

Baker, K. A., & Pelavin, S. (1984). *Problems in bilingual education.* Paper presented at the annual meeting of the American Education Research Association, New Orleans, LA: American Institutes for Research, Washington, D.C.

Barnett, W. S., Yarosz, D. J., Thomas, J., & Blanco, D. (2006). *Two-way and monolingual English immersion in preschool education: An experimental comparison.* New Brunswick, NJ: National Institute for Early Education Research.

Braswell, J., Daane, M., & Grigg, W. (2003). *The Nation's Report Card: Mathematics Highlights 2003.* Washington, DC: US Department of Education, National Center for Education Statistics. (NCES 2004451.)

Capps, R., Fix, M., Ost, J., Reardon-Anderson, J., & Passel, J. (2004). *The health and well-being of young children of immigrants.* Washington, DC: The Urban Institute.

Cazabon, M., Lambert, W., & Hall, G. (1999). *Two-way bilingual education: A report on the Amigos Program.* Washington DC: Center for Applied Linguistics.

Chomsky, N. (1959) A Review of B. F. Skinner's Verbal Behavior. *Language, 35*(1), 26–58.

Christian, D. (1994). *Two-way bilingual education: students learning through two languages.* Washington DC: Center for applied linguistics.

Christian, D. (1997). *Directory of Two-way bilingual.* Washington DC: Center for Applied Linguistics.

Christian, D., Genesee, F., Lindholm-Leary, K., & Howard, L. (2004). *Project 1.2 two-way immersion: Final progress report.* Center for Research on Education, Diversity & Excellence, UC Berkeley.

Cobb, B., Vega, D., & Kronauge, C. (2005). *Effects of an elementary dual language immersion school program on junior high school achievement of native Spanish speaking and native English speaking students.* Paper presented at the American Education Research Association annual conference in Montreal, Canada.

Cole, M. (1996). *Cultural psychology: A once and future discipline.* Cambridge, MA: Harvard University Press.

Cole, M., & Cole, S. R. (2001). *The development of children.* New York: Worth.

Collier, V. P. (1987). Age and rate of acquisition of second language for academic purposes. *TESOL Quarterly, 21*(4), 617–641.

Collins, R., & Ribeiro, R. (2004). Toward an early care and education agenda for Hispanic children. *Early Childhood Research & Practice, 6*(2), 142–159.

Figueroa, L. (2005). *The development of pre-reading knowledge in English and Spanish: Latino English language learners in a dual-language education context.* Paper presented at the American Education Research Association annual conference in Montreal, Canada.

García, E. E. (2002). Bilingualism in schooling in the United States. *International Journal of the Sociology of Language, 155*(156), 1–92.

García, E. E. (2005). *Teaching and learning in two languages: Bilingualism and schooling in the United States.* New York: Teachers College Press.

García, E. E., & Gonzáles, D. (2006). *Pre-K and Latinos: The foundation for America's future.* Washington, D.C.: Pre-K Now.

García, E. E., & Jensen, B. T. (2006). Dual-language programs in the US: An alternative to monocultural, monolingual education. *Language Magazine, 5*(6), 30–37.

García, E. E., & Jensen, B. T. (2007). Advancing school readiness for young Hispanic children through universal prekindergarten. *Harvard Journal of Hispanic Policy, 19,* 25–37.

García, E. E., Jensen, B. T., & Cuéllar, D. (2006). Early academic achievement of Hispanics in the United States: Implications for teacher preparation. *The New Educator, 2,* 123–147.

García, E. E., Jensen, B. T., Miller, L. S., & Huerta, T. (2005). *Early childhood education of Hispanics in the United States.* Tempe, AZ: The National Task Force on Early Childhood Education for Hispanics. Available from http://www.ecehispanic.org/work/white_paper_Oct2005.pdf

Genesee, F. (Ed.) (1999). *Program alternatives for linguistically diverse students.* Center for Research on Education, Diversity & Excellence (CREDE): University of California, Berkeley.

Genesee, F., Geva, E., Dressler, C., & Kamil, M. (2006). Synthesis: Cross-linguistic relationships. In D. August & T. Shanahan (Eds.), *Report of the national literacy panel on language minority youth and children.* Mahwah, NJ: Lawrence Erlbaum Associates.

Glass, G. V., McGaw, B., & Smith, M. L. (1981). *Meta-analysis in social research.* Beverly Hills, CA: Sage.

Goldenberg, C., Gallimore, R., Reese, L., & Garnier, H. (2001). Cause or effect? A longitudinal study of immigrant Latino parents' aspirations and expectations and their children's school performance. *American Educational Research Journal, 38,* 547–582.

Goldenberg, C., Rueda, R., & August, D. (2006). Synthesis: Socioculutral contexts and literacy development. In D. August & T. Shanahan (Eds.), *Report of the national literacy panel on language minority youth and children.* Mahwah, NJ: Lawrence Erlbaum Associates.

Gormley, W., Gayer, T., & Dawson, B. (2004). *The effects of universal pre-k on cognitive development.* Washington, DC: Public Policy Institute, Georgetown University.

Green, J., Camilli, G., & Elmore, P. (Eds.). (2006). *Handbook of complementary methods for research in education.* Washington, DC: American Educational Research Association.

Hakuta, K., Ferdman, B. M. & Diaz, R. M. (1987). Bilingualism and cognitive development: Three perspectives. In S. Rosenberg (Ed.), *Advances in Applied Psycholinguistics Volume II: Reading, Writing and Language Learning.* (pp. 284–319). Cambridge, MA: Cambridge University Press.

Hammer, C. S., Miccio, A. W., & Wagstaff, D. A. (2003). Home literacy experiences and their relationship to bilingual preschoolers' developing English literacy abilities: An initial investigation. *Language, Speech, and Hearing Services in Schools, 34,* 20–30.

Hart, B., & Risley, T. (1995). *Meaningful differences in the everyday experience of young American children.* Baltimore, MD: Paul H. Brookes Publishing Co.

Hart, B., & Risley, T. (1999). *The social world of children learning to talk.* Baltimore, MD: Paul H. Brookes Publishing Co.

Heckman, J., & Masterov, D. (2004). *The productivity argument for investing in young children.* Chicago, Il: Committee for Economic Development.

Hernandez, D. (2006). *Young Hispanic children in the US: A demographic portrait based on Census 2000.* University at Albany, State University, NY: A report to the National Task Force on Early Childhood Education for Hispanics.

Hernandez, D. J., Denton, N. A., & Macartney, S. E. (2007). Young Hispanic children in the 21st century. *Journal of Latinos and Education, 6*(3), 209–228.

Howard, E. R., Sugarman, J., & Christian, D. (2003). *Trends in two-way immersion education: A review of the research.* Washington, DC: Center for Applied Linguistics.

Jensen, B. T. (2007). The relationship between Spanish use in the classroom and the mathematics achievement of Spanish-speaking kindergartners. *Journal of Latinos and Education, 6*(3), 267–280.

Jensen, B. T. (2008). Immigration and language policy. In J. González (Ed.), *Encyclopedia of Bilingual Education.* SAGE Publications.

Lambert, W. (1974). *Culture and language as factors in learning and education.* In F.E. Aboud and R.D. Meade (Eds.), The Fifth Western Symposium on Learning. Bellingham, Washington: Western Washington State College.

Lee, J. S., & Samura, M. (2005). *Understanding the personal, educational, and societal factors that lead to additive bilingualism.* Paper presented at the American Educational Research Association annual conference, Montreal, Quebec, Canada.

Lieberson, S., Dalto, G., & Johnston, M. (1975). The course of mother tongue diversity in nations. *American Journal of Sociology, 81*(1), 34–61.

Lindholm, K. J. (1999). *Two-way bilingual Education: Past and future.* Toronto: Presentation at the American Education Research Association.

López, L. (2005). *A look into the homes of Spanish-speaking preschool children.* Paper presented at the 5th International Symposium on Bilingualism, Barcelona, Spain.

López, M., & Barrueco, S., & Miles, J. (2006). *Latino infants and families: A national perspective of protective and risk factors for development.* A report to the National Task Force on Early Childhood Education for Hispanics. Arizona State University.

McLaughlin, B. (1995). *Fostering second language development in young children.* Washington, DC: Center for Applied Linguistics, NCRDSLL.

Nasir, N. S., & Hand, V. M. (2006). Exploring sociocultural perspectives on race, culture, and learning. *Review of Educational Research, 76*(4), 449–475.

National Center for Education Statistics (1995). *Approaching kindergarten: A look at preschoolers in the United States.* National household survey. Washington, DC: US Department of Education, Office of Educational Research and Improvement.

National Center for Education Statistics (2003). *Status and Trends in the Education of Hispanics.* (NCES 2003–007). Washington DC: US Government Printing Office.

National Clearinghouse for English Language Acquisition (2006). *The growing numbers of limited English proficient students: 1993–94–2003/04.* Office of English Language Acquisition (OELA): US Department of Education.

National Task Force on Early Childhood Education for Hispanics (2007). *Para nuestros niños: Expanding and improving early education for Hispanics—Main report.* Tempe, AZ: National Task Force on Early Childhood Education for Hispanics. Retrieved August 6, 2007 from http://www.ecehispanic.org/work/expand_MainReport.pdf

Oller, D. K., & Eilers, R. E. (2002). *Language and literacy in bilingual children.* Clevedon, UK: Multilingual Matters Limited.

Pérez-Bazán, M J. (2005). *Input rate: The pacemaker of early bilingual acquisition.* Paper presented at the 5th International Symposium on Bilingualism, Barcelona, Spain.

Portes, P. (2005). *Dismantling educational inequality: A cultural-historical approach to closing the achievement gap.* New York: Peter Lang Publishing.

Ramey, C. & Ramey, S. (1998). Early Intervention and Early Experience, *American Psychologist, 53*(2), 109–120.

Reardon, S. (2003). *Sources of educational inequality: The growth of racial/ethnic and socioeconomic test score gaps in kindergarten and first grade.* Population Research Institute. Pennsylvania State University.

Reardon, S., & Galindo, C. (2006). *K-3 academic achievement patterns and trajectories of Hispanics and other racial/ethnic groups.* Paper presented on April 11th at the Annual AERA Conference in San Francisco, CA.

Reese, L., Garnier, H., Gallimore, R., & Goldenberg, C. (2000). Longitudinal analysis of the antecedents of emergent Spanish literacy and middle-school English reading achievement of Spanish-speaking students. *American Educational Research Journal, 37*(3), 633–662.

Rogoff, B. (1990). *Apprenticeship in thinking: Cognitive development in social context.* Oxford, UK: Oxford University Press.

Rogoff, B. (2003). *The cultural nature of human development.* New York: Oxford University Press.

Rolstad, K., Mahoney, K., & Glass, G.V. (2005). The big picture: A meta-analysis of program effectiveness research on English language learners. *Educational Policy, 19*(4), 572–594.

Rueda, R., August, D., & Goldenberg, C. (2006). The sociocultural context in which children acquire literacy. In D. August & T. Shanahan (Eds.), *Report of the national literacy panel on language minority youth and children* (pp. 96–127). Mahwah, NJ: Lawrence Erlbaum Associates.

Scheffner Hammer, C., & Miccio, A. (2004). Home literacy experiences of Latino families. In B. H. Wasik (Ed.), *Handbook of family literacy* (pp. 216–241). Mahwah, NJ: Lawrence Erlbaum Associates.

Shannon, S. M. (1995). The hegemony of English: A case study of one bilingual classroom as a site of resistance. *Linguistics and Education, 7*(3), 175–200.

Shonkoff, J. P., & Phillips, D. A. (2000). *From neurons to neighborhoods: The science of early childhood development.* National Research Council and Institute of Medicine (2000). Washington, DC.: National Academy Press.

Skinner, B. (1957). *Verbal Behavior.* Englewood Cliffs, NJ: Prentice-Hall.

Smith, M. L. (2006). Multiple methodology in education research. In J. L. Green, G. Camili & P. B. Elmore (Eds.), *Handbook of complementary methods in education research* (pp. 314–346). Washington, DC: American Educational Research Association.

Stritikus, T. (2001). From personal to political: Proposition 227, literacy instruction, and the individual qualities of teachers. *International Journal of Bilingual Education and Bilingualism, 4*(5), 291–309.

Sugarman, J. and Howard, L. (September, 2001). Two-way immersion shows promising results: Findings from a new study. *Language links* (pp. 1–11). Washington, DC: Center for Applied Linguistics.

Tharp, R. G., & Gallimore, R. (1989). Rousing schools to life. *American Educator, 13*(2), 20–25, 46–52.

Veltman, C. (1983). *Language shift in the United States.* Amsterdam, the Netherlands: Mouton Publishers.

Vygotsky, L. S. (1978). *Mind in Society: The development of higher psychological processes.* Cambridge, MA: President and Fellows of Harvard College.

Weisner, T. S. (Ed.). (2005). *Discovering successful pathways in children's development: Mixed methods in the study of childhood and family life.* Chicago: University of Chicago Press. 57–70.

Willig (1985). A meta-analysis of selected studies on the effectiveness of bilingual education. *Review of Educational Research, 55*(3), 269–317.

CHAPTER 4

LANGUAGE AND LITERACY DEVELOPMENT IN LATINO DUAL LANGUAGE LEARNERS[1]

Promising Instructional Practices

Dina C. Castro, Ellen Peisner-Feinberg, Virginia Buysse, and Cristina Gillanders

ABSTRACT

In the last 15 years, the United States has experienced a demographic shift that has dramatically increased the racial, ethnic, cultural and linguistic diversity among young children and families who are enrolled in early childhood programs. For example, 30% of the children enrolled in Head Start programs in 2006–2007 spoke a language other than English at home, and almost 85% of these children were Spanish-speaking (Office of Head Start, 2007). A growing number of children under the age of 5 are from immigrant families. Many of these children and families do not speak English as their primary language and are much more likely to face economic hardships than native-born families, placing them at higher risk for limited school readiness and later school failure; the majority of these families are of Latino descent (National Center for Children in Poverty, 2006). Latinos, including immigrants and native-

Language and Cultural Diversity in Early Childhood Education, pages 65–93

born, are now the largest minority group in the country, estimated to be 15% of the population (U.S. Census Bureau, 2006). The percentage of Latinos is even larger among young children, with 23% of all babies born in the U.S. in 2004 born to Latino mothers (Hamilton, et al., 2005). Among children under 5 years of age, Latinos make up 21.4% of the total population (US Census Bureau, 2004).

The increasing number of Latino dual language learners (DLLs) constitutes a challenge and an opportunity for the provision of high quality early care and education. Furthermore, many of the widely used indicators of program quality would benefit from further addition of elements related to serving young diverse learners. The information presented in this chapter is intended to contribute to the current discussion about what is needed to effectively promote school readiness, specifically, language and literacy learning, in Latino DLLs. The purposes of this chapter are to review current research and to identify knowledge gaps and future research directions related to instructional practices to promote language and literacy development in Latino DLLs. We begin with a discussion of what we know about the early education experiences of Latino DLLs. Then, we present a brief summary of research about second language learning in young children, including the relationship between oral language and literacy development in children growing up in bilingual environments. Next, a review of instructional strategies to promote language and literacy in DLLs is presented, including a description of the Nuestros Niños Program, one example of a promising professional development intervention in this area. Finally, we conclude with a discussion of Recognition & Response, a Response to Intervention (RTI) approach for pre-K that could provide a framework for integrating a tiered intervention system to promote school readiness in DLLs.

EARLY EDUCATION EXPERIENCES FOR LATINO DLLs

In recent years, federal- and state-funded early childhood initiatives have helped increase access to early education, particularly for 4-year-olds; however, access to early education programs is still limited for Latino children. Data from the nationally representative Early Childhood Longitudinal Study, Birth Cohort (ECLS-B), showed that only 49% of Latino 4-year-olds were enrolled in a center-based program in 2005–06, compared to 60–62% of their Asian, American Indian/Alaska Native, Black, and White peers, and one–third of the Latino children did not participate in any type of non-parental care arrangement (Planty et al., 2008). Some research has described a cultural preference of Latina mothers for relative care versus center-based care as a potential explanation for the observed low participation rates among Latino children, compared with other racial/ethnic groups (Buriel & Hurtado-Ortiz, 2000; Fuller, Holloway, & Liang, 1996). However, other studies indicate that other factors, in addition to cultural preferences, might be involved. Becerra and Chi (1992), in a study of White, Mexican–American, and Chinese–American mothers, concluded that the low utilization rates of early care and education programs by Latino families may be explained by their limited knowledge about the availability of early childhood services, limited accessibility, and differences in child rearing perspectives.

In a recent study based on an analysis of Census 2000 data, Hernández (2006) found that among 3- and 4 year-olds in Mexican immigrant and U.S.-born Mexican–American families, which constitute 72% of all young Latino children, cultural influences (i.e., child's generation, number of years parents have been in the U.S., and mother's English fluency) accounted for no more than 15% of the early care and education enrollment gap, compared to White children, but socioeconomic and structural factors (i.e., poverty level, mother's education level, and parents' occupations) accounted for half or more of the enrollment gap.

However, the lower participation rate of Latino children in early education programs does not account entirely for the disparity that exists between Latino children and other groups, with respect to readiness for kindergarten. National studies have shown that, even among those who have attended an early childhood program, Latino children lag behind their peers when they enter kindergarten, and the gap in academic achievement appears to widen as children grow older. Among 3- to 5-year-olds not yet enrolled in kindergarten, White and African American children were more likely than Latinos to recognize most letters of the alphabet, participate in storybook activities, count up to at least 20, and write or draw rather than scribble (U.S. Department of Education, 2000). Among a national sample of kindergartners participating in the Early Childhood Longitudinal Study (ECLS-K), Latino children produced the lowest mean scores on reading proficiency and lagged behind their peers in letter recognition and phonemic awareness at kindergarten entry (Reardon & Galindo, 2006). These findings suggest that interventions focused on closing the school readiness gap should not only increase the access of Latino children to early education programs, but should also employ research-based instructional practices that take into account the specific developmental characteristics of DLLs (Ballantyne, Sanderman, D'Emilio, & McLaughlin, 2008; National Task Force on Early Childhood Education for Hispanics, 2007; The Future of Children, 2005).

Research on early childhood education programs shows that high quality classroom experiences can have positive effects on children's language development and early literacy skills (see Snow & Páez, 2004 for a review). Moreover, research also has shown that young children at risk for school failure, such as children from poor and minority backgrounds, are significantly more likely to succeed in school when they have attended high quality early childhood programs (Bowman, Donovan, & Burns, 2001; Peisner-Feinberg et al., 2001). However, much of the research on the long-term effects of early education has been conducted with African American children (e.g., Campbell et al., 2002—Abecedarian Study; Schweinhart et al., 2005—Perry Preschool Study). Although there is emerging evidence of the positive impact of high quality early education on Latino children's school readiness (Gormley & Gayer, 2005), the studies are few, assess a limited set of children's developmental outcomes, and most importantly, do not use longitudinal designs.

Regarding DLLs, some research has found that, even though there are practices that are beneficial to both monolingual and bilingual children, these may not be sufficient to support a comparable level of academic success among bilingual children (August & Shanahan, 2006). Also, this research suggests that instructional accommodations are needed, particularly in classrooms where instruction is provided only in English (Goldenberg, 2008). The research is more limited on effective instructional and intervention practices to promote language and literacy development in preschool DLLs, compared to the research that has been conducted with monolingual English-speaking preschool children.

SECOND LANGUAGE LEARNING IN PRESCHOOL DLLs

In order to develop curricular and instructional approaches that are effective for promoting school readiness in DLLs, it is necessary to have an understanding of how young children learn a second language and the factors that influence this process. Bilingual speakers may learn their two languages *simultaneously* or *sequentially*. A simultaneous process occurs when a child is exposed to two languages from birth or soon after, while the sequential process happens when the child is not exposed to the second language until after the basic components of the first language have been established, at about age 4 or later (McLaughlin, 1984). Children growing up in bilingual environments may achieve different degrees of proficiency in each language. The levels of bilingual proficiency are comprised within a continuum that goes from partial or minimal bilingualism, when the level of proficiency is higher in one language than the other, to balanced bilingualism, when the level of proficiency is high in both languages (Baker & Prys Jones, 1998). Depending on factors such as the amount and quality of the language input and opportunities for using the language, different children will acquire different levels of proficiency in each language and, thus, be at different points of the bilingual proficiency continuum.

The process of second language acquisition does not happen in isolation, and is influenced by many factors related to the child, family, early childhood setting, and community at large. For instance, individual characteristics, such as child motivation, personality, and learning style, can influence the speed and rate with which children learn a second language (August & Hakuta, 1997). Usually, a strong motivator for children to learn a second language is their desire to interact socially with peers and develop a sense of group belonging to the classroom and the broader community. However, individual personality traits influence the extent to which children initiate social interactions in order to make new friends or voluntarily participate in activities that involve speaking a new language. In addition, teaching strategies that take into account differences in learning styles are likely to be more effective in supporting second language learning than those based on the assumption that all children learn in the same way.

Regarding the role of the family, contrary to common belief, research suggests that the most important contribution of the family to their young children's second language learning is to help them develop and maintain their first language. This is particularly important for children attending an early childhood program in which the instruction is provided only in English. Research has shown that among children growing up bilingually, a strong basis in the first language promotes school achievement in the second language and is important for ensuring that children do not become alienated from their families and communities (August & Shanahan, 2006; Sánchez, 1999; Tabors, 1997; Wong Fillmore, 1991). Furthermore, most experts support the idea that learning two languages at the same time does not cause confusion or language delays in young children, but rather, that teaching both languages simultaneously actually facilitates English language learning (August & Hakuta, 1997; Bialystok, 2001). Previous knowledge of the different functions and rules of a language facilitates the process of learning a second language.

Studies conducted in the last four decades have shown positive effects of bilingualism on children's cognitive abilities, in particular, those related to metalinguistic abilities (or thinking about language). Bilingual children have been found to perform at a more advanced level than their monolingual peers in tasks such as comparing words by their meaning (semantic dimensions), identifying repetition and contradictions in a statement, judging the grammatical correctness of sentences in their two languages, and in a number of non-verbal capabilities (Bialystok, 1991; Hakuta, 1987; Galambos & Goldin-Meadow, 1990). Other areas of cognitive functioning that have also been found to be positively influenced by bilingualism are concept formation, reasoning by analogy, and problem-solving (Bialystok & Majumder, 1998; see Lee, 1996 for a review).

However, the positive cognitive consequences of being bilingual seem to be more evident among those who have an age-appropriate level of proficiency in both languages. High levels of bilingual proficiency are associated with cognitive advantages (Cummins, 2000). The associations among advanced bilingualism, cognitive ability, and academic performance have been demonstrated by studies showing that fluent bilinguals outperformed limited bilinguals and monolingual English-speaking children from the same national origin in standardized academic tests and grade point averages (GPAs) (Rumbaut, 1995). Furthermore, first- and second-generation fluent bilinguals had higher achievement scores than their native-born, English-speaking peers (Portes & Rumbaut, 1996).

According to Cummins (2000), the quality of the learning environments and experiences bilingual children are exposed to will determine their level of bilingual proficiency and, accordingly, the level of benefits from being bilingual. Based on this information, it seems reasonable to conclude that when early childhood professionals and parents provide experiences that support children in reaching advanced levels of proficiency in their two languages, the children will gain greater benefits from being bilingual (Castro, Ayankoya & Kasprzak, 2009).

LANGUAGE AND LITERACY DEVELOPMENT IN MONOLINGUAL AND BILINGUAL LEARNERS

The relationship between early language and literacy development and later reading achievement for monolingual children has been well documented in the research literature (e.g., Bryant, Bradley, Maclean, & Crossland, 1989; Whitehurst, 1999). Research examining the precursors to literacy has demonstrated that reading builds on (1) oral proficiency in the language of literacy (especially vocabulary development), (2) understanding of the concept of print, and (3) metalinguistic processes that allow children to become aware of the phonological forms of language. Numerous studies have shown the importance of oral language competence for the development of early literacy skills and later reading comprehension (e.g., Dickinson, McCabe, Anastasopoulos, Peisner-Feinberg, & Poe, 2003; Rapp, van den Broek, McMaster, Panayiota, & Espin, 2007). Specifically, research with monolingual children has shown that children with higher levels of oral proficiency and vocabulary development learn to read more easily (e.g., Adams, 1990; Dale, Crain-Thorenson, & Robinson, 1995; Dickinson & Tabors, 2001). Published reviews of the literature suggest that these three aspects each play a key role in helping pre-Kindergarten children learn to read (e.g., Bryant & Goswami, 1987; Scarborough, 2001; Wagner, Torgesen, & Rashotte, 1994). Furthermore, there is evidence to suggest that some specific interventions are effective in improving these abilities in this age group and in preventing reading difficulties later on (National Research Council, 1998; National Reading Panel, 2000).

For bilingual children, second language acquisition has been shown to influence development of these three aspects of literacy (Bialystok, 2007). In order to become literate in a second language, it is important to have an adequate level of oral proficiency in that language, and vocabulary development is a key component in that process. A study with preschool Latino DLLs examining the predictive relationship between language and literacy abilities found that Latino DLLs' growth in English and Spanish language abilities during their preschool year predicted their early reading abilities in both languages (Hammer, Lawrence & Miccio, 2007). Another study with this population found that English expressive vocabulary was strongly associated with English letter–word identification abilities, and Spanish expressive vocabulary predicted Spanish letter–word identification abilities (Lindsey, Manis, and Bailey, 2003). The development of knowledge about the concept of print also can be influenced by the process of second language acquisition; acquiring these concepts in either language facilitates the development of these abilities in the other language (Bialystok, 2007). Phonological awareness has been found to be one of the strongest predictors of the speed and efficiency of reading acquisition (Scarborough, 2001), and research with second language learners has shown that phonological awareness skills transfer from the first to the second language (Chiappe & Siegel, 1999; Cisero & Royer, 1995). Specifically for Spanish speaking children who are DLLs, it has been found that phonological awareness and word recognition in Spanish predicted word recognition in English (Durgunoglu, Nagy, & Hancin-Bhatt, 2003; Durgunglu, 1998).

The central processing framework needs to be considered and incorporated in the development of instructional strategies to support DLLs (Geva, 2006). The central processing framework describes the transferability of processing skills that are crucial for learning to read and write. Experts have observed that some aspects of learning to read, notably phonological processing, transfer easily across languages, whereas others, such as decoding, are more language-specific (Bialystok, 2007). Findings from several studies provide evidence to support the theory of cross-linguistic transferability in literacy learning between Spanish and English (e.g., Cisero & Royer, 1995; Durgunogly, Nagy, & Hancin-Bhatt, 1993; Quiroga et al, 2002). For example, a study examining the relationships between phonological awareness, expressive vocabulary, letter–word identification, memory for sentences, and concept of print in Spanish and English in a sample of preschool Latino DLLs found positive correlations between Spanish and English abilities in all areas except expressive vocabulary. In most areas, children's abilities in one language were related to their abilities in the other language (Tabors, Páez, & López, 2003). Another study with preschool Spanish DLL children concluded that, although the children were receiving instruction in English, they were applying their Spanish language skills to the English phonological awareness task (Páez, Tabors, & Lopez, 2007). One more study found that children in intervention classrooms where teachers received professional development related to teaching DLLs showed greater gains in acquiring phonological awareness skills in Spanish than in English, even though English was the language of instruction in those settings (Buysse, Castro, & Peisner-Feinberg, 2008). It may have been that Latino children in the study processed what they were learning about rhyming, alliteration, and letter sounds in their primary language before they could apply those skills in a new language. Additional research is needed to explicate these early reading processes, but these studies support the notion that preschool DLLs may acquire phonological skills in their stronger (primary) language before they emerge as observable skills in English.

Findings from these two lines of research on literacy development and second language learning suggest that interventions for DLLs should include activities that: (1) promote oral language proficiency in the language of literacy instruction and in the first language, (2) support the acquisition of concepts of print, and (3) emphasize the development of phonological and phonemic awareness that builds on children's first language skills. Each of these skills affect different aspects of literacy development—oral proficiency influences comprehension, concepts of print affect decoding, and phonological awareness impacts word recognition—all of which are necessary for children to become successful readers.

INSTRUCTIONAL PRACTICES FOR YOUNG DLLs

In recent years, some studies have been conducted to identify specific instructional practices that can improve academic outcomes for DLLs. A major research review conducted by the National Literacy Panel on Language-Minority Children and Youth provides general recommendations on instruction for DLLs (August and Shanahan, 2006). In addition, the Institute of Education Sciences' (IES) What Works Clearinghouse (available at http://ies.ed.gov/ncee/wwc/) has summarized recent studies in a document that provides recommendations for literacy and language instruction for DLLs in the elementary grades (Gersten, Baker, et al., 2007). These reports are a major contribution for the education of DLL children from kindergarten and beyond. However, there is still a gap in research to guide instruction for DLLs in pre-Kindergarten classrooms, although some of the strategies discussed for older children can be adapted to early childhood classrooms. The three main recommendations from these reports, as summarized by Goldenberg (2006; 2008), are presented below, along with adaptations we propose for early childhood classrooms:

1. *Supporting the primary language is important for promoting the school readiness of DLLs.* Findings from several research syntheses (August & Shanahan, 2006; Rolstad, Mahoney, & Glass, 2005; Slavin & Cheung, 2005) support the benefits of using the primary language for instruction in classrooms enrolling DLLs. For example, the National Literacy Panel on Language Minority Children and Youth (August and Shanahan, 2006) conducted a meta-analysis of 17 studies on reading instruction with DLLs, and found small to moderate positive effects on English reading outcomes among children who received instruction in their primary language as compared to those receiving instruction only in English. They concluded that the use of the primary language in the classroom, rather than confusing children, may support DLLs' reading achievement in their second language. The use of the first language (Spanish) in classrooms also has been found to be related to teachers' positive perceptions of children's behavior and social competence (Chang et al., 2007). At present, though, many early childhood programs lack the personnel and/or the resources to include a significant amount of primary language instruction during the day. In some parts of the country, bilingual teachers and teacher assistants may be available, but they may not know how to incorporate DLL children's primary language into classroom instruction.
2. *Effective instruction is the foundation of learning for all children, including DLLs.* The evidence found in recent studies conducted with school-age DLLs suggests that what constitutes effective instruction for non-DLLs is equally effective instruction for DLLs (Fitzgerald, 1995). DLL children seem to learn language and literacy skills much the same as non-DLL children. However, the question still remains, *What is considered effective instruction in early childhood education?* As stated by NAEYC in their position statement referring to curriculum, assessment, and program evaluation, effective early childhood instruction entails using a curriculum that is "thoughtfully planned, challenging, engaging, developmentally appropriate, culturally and linguistically responsive, comprehensive, and likely to promote positive outcomes for all young children"(NAEYC, 2003, p. 2). Furthermore, the indicators of effectiveness are: "children are active and engaged; the goals are clear and shared by all; the curriculum is evidence-based; the valued content is learned through investigation, play, and focused, intentional teaching; the curriculum builds on prior learning and experiences; and the curriculum is comprehensive." (NAEYC, 2003, p. 2).
3. *Instructional accommodations are needed for young DLLs.* While the previous recommendation focuses on the basic foundation for effective

instruction, instructional accommodations are critical for DLLs, especially when they are instructed only in English. Another important finding from the research reviewed by the National Literacy Panel on Language Minority Children and Youth (Shanahan & Beck, 2006) is that the impact of instructional practices or interventions tends to be weaker for DLLs than for monolingual English speakers (Goldenberg, 2006). An interpretation of this finding is that instructional accommodations may be needed for DLLs in order for them to benefit as much from effective instruction as their English-speaking counterparts. The following accommodations are recommended, based on findings from previous studies:

- *Conduct ongoing and frequent assessments that allow teachers to monitor children's English language acquisition and development in different domains.* Assessments are used to inform instruction and to improve the outcomes for young DLLs. Measures of phonological processing, letter and alphabetic knowledge, concepts of print, and the process of second language acquisition can help teachers plan specific instructional accommodations, such as the use of extra support in small group instruction (Lesaux & Siegel, 2003).
- *Provide focused small-group interventions for DLL children, especially with those who are at risk for reading and math difficulties.* The need for small-group interventions should be consonant with indications of school readiness difficulties, as determined by the assessment data. Previous randomized controlled trials of reading interventions for struggling DLLs in grades K–5 have indicated that small-group or peer-assisted interventions allow children multiple opportunities to respond to questions, to practice reading skills, and to receive explicit instruction on vocabulary instruction and phonological awareness (e.g., Vaughn et al., 2006; McMaster et al., 2008). Such interventions, however, would need to be adapted for children at the early childhood level.
- *Provide explicit vocabulary instruction during the day.* For most English-speaking children, vocabulary learning in English occurs incidentally. For DLLs, vocabulary development in English requires a combination of direct teaching of words and incidental learning through multiple exposures to words in a variety of meaningful social contexts (Carlo et al., 2004). Therefore, an important accommodation for DLLs in preschool settings is to address the meanings of everyday words, phrases, and expressions not yet learned in the context of play. Furthermore, teachers can promote vocabulary knowledge by using the children's primary language strategically, for example, through storybook reading activities (Gillanders & Castro, 2008). Even if teachers are not

fluent in the children's primary language, learning and using specific core words in the primary language can further support children's learning of the same concepts in English (Castro, Gillanders, Machado-Casas, & Buysse, 2006).

- *Ensure the development of formal or academic English.* To be successful in school, DLLs need to develop the specialized language of academic discourse that is different from conversational skills. Lack of proficiency in academic English can interfere with learning other academic content. As an example, although children might learn mathematical concepts and skills using manipulatives, they also need to learn the language of mathematics in order to be successful in school. Therefore, the curriculum should incorporate opportunities to provide explicit instruction of the academic language related to basic mathematics concepts and skills (Francis, Rivera, Lesaux, Kieffer, and Rivera, 2006).
- *Promote socioemotional development through effective teacher–child relationships and facilitate children's participation as members of the sociocultural group of the classroom.* Teachers can create positive teacher-child relationships when they are involved in learning with children, are consistent and firm, and support children's positive behaviors (Howes & Ritchie, 2002). In addition, classroom organization characteristics, such as predictable classroom routines, cooperative learning, and peer-assisted instruction, help foster positive relationships (Howes & Ritchie, 2002). Being purposeful in creating positive teacher–child relationships becomes especially important when monolingual English-speaking teachers are working with DLL children, because of the language barriers. In addition, effective teacher–child relationships can positively affect the social status of DLL children and their inclusion in the classroom community (Gillanders, 2007). An important aspect of teacher–child relationships is the interpretation of challenging behaviors. Some common behaviors of DLLs that are related to the process of second language acquisition are often misunderstood as challenging behaviors (e.g., not talking, difficulty expressing ideas and feelings, difficulty following directions). To the extent that teachers better understand the process of second language acquisition and learn effective strategies for dealing with challenging behaviors, they will better be able to establish positive relationships with DLL children (Santos & Ostrosky, 2004).
- *Promote family-school partnerships.* When teaching DLL children in an English-dominant environment, building family–school partnerships becomes especially critical, since the family can provide

> first language support that children may not receive at school. One way of achieving this support is by providing academic learning materials in the primary language that families can use with children at home. Several intervention studies have found that sending literacy materials to families' homes can increase the frequency of literacy events and, in turn, the literacy achievement of young DLLs (e.g., Goldenberg, Reese, & Gallimore, 1992; Hancock, 2002).

The limited research on this topic for pre-Kindergarten children suggests that there are multiple factors that can influence the effectiveness of a particular curriculum or instructional approach. Factors such as a child's exposure to his or her primary language and to English, opportunities to experience early literacy activities in multiple languages, and a variety of family characteristics (e.g., immigration status, family resources and structure, and access to print materials) likely moderate the effects of early education experiences designed to promote language and literacy learning (Castro et al, 2008).

Although there is ample empirical evidence on older DLL children to suggest that teaching reading in the primary language promotes higher levels of reading achievement in English, many questions remain about whether this approach is more beneficial for some students than others (e.g., those with higher or lower levels of English proficiency), and in what settings and under what conditions this approach should be used (Goldenberg, 2007). For children in pre-Kindergarten settings, similar research questions should be examined regarding the most effective ways of supporting children's development and learning in their primary language, with a particular focus on early education programs in which English is the language of instruction. In this regard, it will be especially important to determine how characteristics of the home and early education program coincide to support or inhibit early learning. Within the early childhood field, as a result of federal initiatives such as Early Reading First and the strong emphasis on school readiness skills, there are now a number of curricula and instructional approaches that can be used to support children's literacy skills related to phonological awareness (e.g., rhyming, alliteration, segmenting, blending, and letter-sound relationship; see, for example, the IES' What Works Clearinghouse). However, there is a pressing need in future research to focus on curricular and instructional approaches to support oral language development for DLLs, along with additional research on the benefits of early bilingualism on cognitive development and executive function (Yoshida, 2008). Previous studies have focused on methods to promote some aspects of language development, most notably, vocabulary development, using dialogic and interactive storybook reading activities. However, additional research should focus on the most effective ways to support other aspects of language development (e.g., syntax and oral language proficiency) in both the first and second language. A variety of approaches suggested in the literature, such as first language education, bilingual education, and two-way bilingual immersion programs (designed for both DLLs and native English speakers), should be evaluated through research to determine their effects on children's oral language development and academic learning, along with their feasibility and appropriateness in early education programs (Castro el al, 2009).

In the next section, we describe an intervention study aimed at improving the quality of teaching practices in early childhood programs enrolling Latino DLLs, as an example of a program that integrates many of the recommended instructional strategies discussed above.

THE NUESTROS NIÑOS EARLY LANGUAGE AND LITERACY PROGRAM

The Nuestros Niños Program consists of intensive, ongoing professional development for pre-Kindergarten teachers who serve Latino ELLs whose primary language is Spanish. The content of the Nuestros Niños program is based on the best available research evidence on effective instructional practices to promote language and literacy skills (e.g., oral language, phonological awareness, concepts of print, letter identification, and alphabetic principle) in pre-Kindergarten children in general, as well as the more limited literature on this topic, in order to address the specific learning characteristics of Latino DLLs (Espinosa, Castro, Crawford, & Gillanders, 2007). The instructional practices were designed to complement the core curriculum and to provide monolingual English-speaking teachers who use English as the primary language of instruction with specific accommodations for DLLs (e.g., the use of visual cues and props, implementing pre-reading activities in Spanish prior to group English storybook time, and systematically observing and documenting second language learning). The professional development components included: (1) professional development institutes to promote teachers' acquisition of core content knowledge and skills, (2) individualized consultation sessions to support teachers in implementing new instructional strategies in the classroom, and (3) community of practice meetings to provide participating teachers with opportunities for feedback, reflection, and collaborative problem-solving.

A preliminary investigation using a randomized, controlled study was conducted to assess the effects of the Nuestros Niños program on teachers' classroom practices and children's outcomes related to language proficiency and early literacy skills in both English and Spanish (see Buysse, Castro,

& Peisner-Feinberg, 2009 for a complete report of the study findings). The study was conducted with 55 teachers and 193 Latino DLLs enrolled in a state-funded pre-Kindergarten program targeting at-risk four-year-olds (particularly those not previously enrolled in early education), with a focus on promoting school readiness skills. Independent assessments of both classroom practices and children's skills were conducted at the beginning and end of the pre-K program year, to compare changes in intervention and control classrooms. The classroom observation scale, the literacy environment checklist, and the literacy activities rating scale from the Early Language and Literacy Classroom Observation (ELLCO) Toolkit (Education Development Center, 2002) were used to assess the quality of the classroom practices. The ELLCO Addendum (Castro, 2005) was developed as a companion measure to assess specific practices targeting ELLs for each of the three subscales of the ELLCO. Child knowledge and skills related to language proficiency, vocabulary, letter identification, and phonological awareness were assessed in both English and Spanish with the following measures: the Woodcock Language Proficiency Battery-Revised: English and Spanish Forms (WLPB-R; Woodcock, 1991; Woodcock & Muñoz-Sandoval, 1995); the Peabody Picture Vocabulary Test (PPVT-III; Dunn & Dunn, 1997) and corresponding Test de Vocabulario en Imágenes Peabody (TVIP; Dunn, Padilla, Lugo, & Dunn, 1986); the Phonological Awareness Tasks (PAT; Miccio & Hammer, 2002); Naming Letters (National Center for Early Development & Learning, 2003); and Where's My Teddy Story and Print Concepts (FACES: The Head Start Child and Family Experiences Survey, 2003).

As far as we know, this was one of the first experimental studies conducted to examine the efficacy of a professional development intervention targeting early language and literacy skills of Latino DLLs in pre-K. The study addressed two primary research questions. First, do teachers in pre-K classrooms receiving the Nuestros Niños intervention make greater improvements in their classroom practices related to facilitating language and literacy learning than teachers in control classrooms? Second, do Latino DLLs in pre-K classrooms receiving the Nuestros Niños intervention make greater gains in language and literacy skills than their peers in control classrooms?

With regard to classroom practices, the results showed greater improvements in three areas for intervention classrooms, compared to control classrooms, with effect sizes in the moderate to large range. Significant differences were found between intervention and control classrooms in the frequency of literacy activities, with increases in literacy activities over the school year for intervention classrooms, compared to decreases for control classrooms. In addition, intervention classroom teachers made greater improvements than control classroom teachers in setting up a supportive environment and in implementing activities that were specifically designed to address the language and literacy needs of Latino DLLs (e.g., incorporating Spanish books and other Spanish print materials into interest centers, as well as using Spanish in book reading and other classroom activities). With respect to child outcomes, children in intervention classrooms showed greater gains in overall phonological awareness skills in Spanish, particularly in the area of rhyming skills, and limited effects in English (only for the specific skill of segmenting and matching syllables), with effect sizes in the moderate to large range. However, there were no differences found in other areas of Spanish or English skills, including language proficiency, vocabulary, letter identification, and story concepts.

Taken together, these findings suggest that an initial attempt to design a professional development intervention focused on instructional strategies for Latino DLLs was more effective for improving teaching practices related to language and literacy than for enhancing children's outcomes in these areas. This finding is perhaps not too surprising, given that it is now widely acknowledged that research on the effectiveness of professional development relies on a chain of causal evidence with several critical links: evidence that teachers acquire new knowledge and skills; evidence that teachers apply knowledge and skills as these were intended to be implemented in practice; and evidence that teacher practices acquired through professional development produce positive outcomes for children's learning and development (Cochran-Smith & Zeichner, 2005). As the authors of previous studies that reported similar findings (e.g., Carlo et al., 2004; Landry et al., 2006), we hypothesize that teachers require extended opportunities of practice in order to effectively implement new instructional strategies learned through professional development. In addition, using measures that are insensitive to curricular influences might make it more difficult to find intervention effects. Within early childhood and the broader field of education, there is still much that is unknown about each of these causal linkages in professional development, as well as about the most effective assessment and instructional practices for DLLs. However, the finding related to the impact of the Nuestros Niños intervention on classroom practices is particularly important because it suggests that professional development aimed at improving instruction for DLL children can have broader effects for improving the quality of instruction for all children.

As research continues to advance knowledge on effective instructional strategies that promote school readiness for specific sub-groups, the need arises for a framework that can help organize and integrate knowledge and practices to ensure that interventions are based on sound research and are implemented systematically. We propose that the Response to Intervention (RTI) principles and practices can be used to integrate research-based intervention strategies for DLLs into a coherent and comprehensive system that can generate measurable outcomes. The content of the Nuestros Niños intervention—effective instructional strategies for promoting language and literacy in general, along with specific strategies to scaffold learning for DLLs—is consistent with models of RTI, suggesting that such models may hold particular promise in this regard.

RECOGNITION & RESPONSE AND THE EARLY EDUCATION OF DLLs

Within the field of early childhood education, RTI is considered an emergent practice. As meaningful access to the general curriculum for *all* children has become an important focus of pre-Kindergarten, there has been a corresponding need for models that accommodate diverse learners who need additional instructional supports. RTI is an instructional approach developed for school-age children which emphasizes a tiered model for prevention intervention or early intervening when children show signs of learning difficulties (e.g., Batsche et al., 2005; Jimmerson, Burns, & VanDerHeyden, 2007). The key idea behind RTI is to provide children with the supports needed to address learning difficulties as soon as they arise, rather than waiting until a child experiences school failure. While there are many variations on RTI models, they share at least three common elements undergirding sound instructional principles. These include: (1) the use of a research-based core curriculum and effective instruction for all students, (2) standardized prevention interventions which have been validated through research for targeted students who need additional instructional supports, and (3) an integrated assessment or data-collection system that includes universal screening and progress monitoring to inform instructional decision making.

A research synthesis conducted on 14 studies concluded that there is an emerging body of empirical evidence to support RTI as an effective method for identifying children with learning difficulties and for providing specific interventions that either ameliorate or prevent the occurrence of learning disabilities among school-age children (Coleman, Buysse, & Neitzel, 2006). The synthesis also revealed that the majority of studies focused specifically on literacy interventions, with a particular emphasis on improving students' reading skills (see, for example, Coyne, Kame'enui, Simmons, & Harn, 2004; McMaster, Fuchs, Fuchs, & Compton, 2005); however, two studies assessed the efficacy of RTI to improve math skills (Fuchs et al., 2004; Fuchs et al., 2005). All of the studies focused primarily on the effects of specific interventions at Tier 2. Consequently, although there is strong empirical evidence for many of the skill-based interventions used within RTI, including those addressing math, additional research is needed to evaluate the efficacy of a comprehensive RTI system in which multiple tiers are implemented by teachers (rather than researchers) in order of intensity. The synthesis also concluded that additional research was needed to assess the efficacy of such a system for younger, pre-Kindergarten children who experience learning difficulties in language development, phonological awareness, and early math skills. In a related study, a meta-analysis conducted on 24 studies involving school-age children found positive effects related to implementation of RTI for improvements in student outcomes (UEE = 1.02 for field-based efforts, 1.54 for university-based efforts), as well as for improvements in systemic outcomes (UEE = 1.80 for field-based efforts, 0.47 for university-based efforts; Burns, Appleton, & Stehouwer, 2005). The Institute of Education Sciences (IES) has released two practice guides related to research-based practices to support the implementation of RTI, one focused on early reading difficulties, the second focused on early math difficulties (Gersten et al., 2008; Gersten et al., 2009).

The instructional principles that serve as the foundation for RTI are consistent with the current emphasis in early childhood education on high quality curriculum and instruction and the importance of intervening early, using research-based approaches. Consistent with this perspective, connecting teaching and learning processes to child outcomes recently was identified as a key research priority for the early childhood field (Takanishi & Bogard, 2007).

While most models of RTI are designed for school-age children, the Recognition & Response (R&R) model has been specifically designed for pre-K (Buysse & Peisner-Feinberg, 2008a; Buysse & Peisner-Feinberg, 2008b; Recognition & Response Implementation Guide, 2008). R&R is a framework for creating an integrated system that links assessment to instruction designed for use across a number of content areas (e.g., language and literacy, math, and social–emotional development). As such, it can be used with a variety of curricular and assessment approaches that have been validated through research and found to be effective with young children. First described in a widely cited research synthesis (Coleman et al., 2006), and further defined in the Recognition & Response Implementation Guide (2008), the R&R model was developed by a research team at the FPG Child Development Institute at the University of North Carolina at Chapel Hill. The R&R model was endorsed by the National Center for Learning Disabilities (NCLD), the National Association for the Education of Young Children (NAEYC), and the Division of Early Childhood (DEC) of the Council for Exceptional Children (CEC). R&R is a tiered instructional model consisting of three key components that build on the principles of RTI, but adapted for younger children. These include: (1) recognition—the use of systematic assessment results to gauge children's progress in learning, including the incorporation of universal screening and progress monitoring; (2) response—the implementation of an effective core curriculum and instruction and the use of

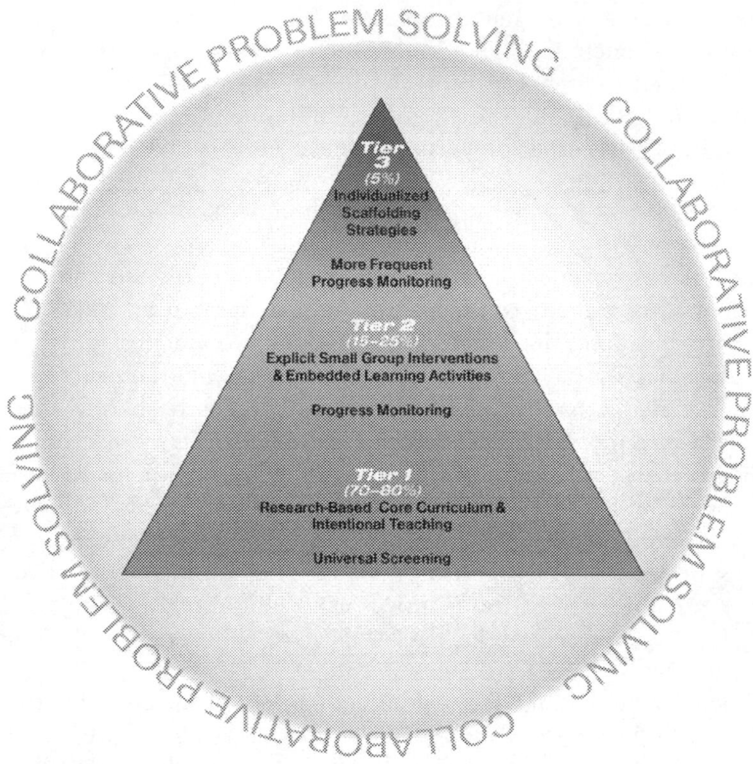

Figure 4.1 R&R conceptual framework.

focused interventions linked to assessment to support children's learning; and (3) collaborative problem-solving—a process for making informed decisions based on data to plan and evaluate instruction at all tiers.

The R&R model encompasses three layered tiers of increasing intensity, with different aspects of recognition and response at each tier, guided by the collaborative problem-solving process. The recognition component at Tier 1 includes universal screening of all children to gather data to inform decisions about who may need intervention support. The response component at Tier 1 consists of the use of a research-based core curriculum and intentional teaching for all children that provides the foundation for instruction. While Tier 1 focuses on all children, Tier 2 focuses on some children indicated as needing additional supports. Recognition at Tier 2 consists of progress monitoring for these children, and response consists of explicit small-group interventions and embedded learning activities. Tier 3 focuses on a few children who need more intensive support, in addition to the Tier 2 intervention. Recognition at Tier 3 includes more frequent progress monitoring for these children, while response includes the addition of individualized scaffolding strategies.

R&R appears to be a promising approach for instruction with young DLLs in particular, as it provides a means for discriminating between more generalized learning difficulties and difficulties due to knowledge of the language of instruction. The process of second language learning takes time, and thus, DLLs may appear to be delayed in their language development as compared with their monolingual peers. Geva (2006) cautioned that early educators should not mistake delays in developing language and literacy skills among DLLs as necessarily indicative of a specific learning difficulty, while, at the same time, recognizing the need to monitor each child's progress to identify persistent language and literacy problems that do not respond to high quality instruction and attempts to scaffold learning. Future research is needed to determine whether it may be possible to differentiate DLLs in pre-K who might benefit from additional instructional supports in language and literacy from those who may be at-risk for a specific reading disability that could require more intensive interventions. Models such as R&R hold particular promise in this regard (Coleman, Buysse, & Neitzel, 2006; Recognition & Response Implementation Guide, 2008; Vanderwood & Nam, 2007).

Many of the foundational principles of R&R are consistent with current beliefs about best practices for instruction for DLLs. These include insuring that a core curriculum and sound instruction that are effective for all children, including DLLs, are being utilized. Another area concerns the use of a variety of informational sources, including appropriate assessment tools, for making decisions about children's underlying knowledge and skills. A third area of similarity is the use of differentiated instruction for DLLs, as well as accommodations for children who require additional supports to learn. Moreover, the interventions selected to support children's learning need to offer research evidence of their efficacy. While there is acknowledgement about the need for such instructional approaches, scant research exists to help teachers determine precisely what interventions and which instructional accommodations and adaptations are most beneficial for Latino DLLs (Snow, 2006).

There is an urgent call in the field of early education for effective intervention approaches targeting DLLs, with the perspective that strong research-based practices can prevent inappropriate referral to special education and school failure (McMaster, Kung, Han, & Cao, 2008). RTI has the potential to positively impact DLL children's school readiness by providing a systematic approach that includes specific measures, instructional strategies, and decision-making processes. While most research using an approach consistent with RTI with DLLs has been conducted with school-age children, those studies provide evidence of the potential for such an approach to improve developmental and learning outcomes of DLLs in early childhood education (e.g.,Gerber et al., 2004; Vaughn, et al., 2006; Gunn et al., 2000). Specific recommendations related to the use of an RTI approach with DLL children presented by Brown & Doolittle (2008) suggest that such a framework should include: (1) a systematic process for examining the specific background variables of DLLs (i.e., first and second language proficiency, socio-economic status, immigration pattern, and culture); (2) examination of the appropriateness of classroom instruction and the classroom context, based on knowledge of individual children's factors; (3) information gathered through informal and formal assessments; and (4) nondiscriminatory interpretations of all assessment data. It is essential to build on DLL children's previous knowledge, considering their strengths as well as their needs.

While further research is needed to address the gaps in knowledge about effective instructional practices to promote language and literacy development in Latino DLLs, R&R offers a model for integrating current knowledge by organizing assessment and instruction in ways that can help teachers determine and effectively address the learning needs of all children in the classroom, attending to the particular needs of DLLs.

CONCLUSION

Given the dramatic increase in the Latino child population and the risk factors associated with their school readiness, there is an urgency to examine policies and practices that will increase access to early education programs and improve the quality of practices to promote development and learning of Latino DLLs. The research reviewed in this chapter indicates that implementing specific instructional accommodations is beneficial to meeting the educational needs of Latino DLL children. Moreover, although more research is required to expand our knowledge about specific instructional approaches that are effective in promoting language and literacy in young DLLs, there is a growing body of knowledge that provides a basis for the development of interventions with this population. For example, there is strong evidence that supports the use of the first language in the classroom. How the first language can be incorporated in early childhood instruction will be determined by the goals of the program, as well as the specific models and methods selected to reach these goals (i.e., bilingual transitional, two-way immersion, Spanish immersion, or English immersion). Further research is needed to determine how much first language use is needed for this to be effective in supporting learning among DLLs. However, even in classrooms where English is the only language of instruction, attempts to include DLLs' first language will be beneficial for promoting children's language and literacy development. There also is emerging research that supports the use of additional instructional accommodations. Some promising practices include the use of small-groups and one-on-one instruction, frequent and ongoing assessments to monitor children's progress and adjust practice implementation accordingly, explicit vocabulary instruction, and activities that promote social and emotional development, as well as those that help build partnerships with families. We presented the Nuestros Niños program as an example of an intervention that integrates many of the instructional accommodations described in this chapter for classrooms where English is the language of instruction. We proposed R&R, a broad framework based on the adaptation of RTI for pre-K, as an overarching model for instruction that can be helpful in promoting the language and literacy development of young DLLs. Although there are still many knowledge gaps in this area, there also are many promising practices that programs can begin implementing to promote Latino DLLs' school readiness and future school success.

REFERENCES

Adams, M. J. (1990). *Beginning to read: Thinking and learning about print.* Cambridge, MA: MIT Press.

August, D., & Hakuta, K. (1997) (Eds.). *Improving schooling for language-minority children. A research agenda.* Washington, DC: National Academy Press.

August,D., & Shanahan, T. (2006) (Eds.). *Developing literacy in second-language learners: Report of The National Literacy Panel on Language—Minority Children and Youth.* Mahwah, NJ: Erlbaum.

Baker, C. & Prys Jones, S. (1998). *Encyclopedia of Bilingualism and Bilingual Education.* Philadelphia, PA: Multilingual Matters Ltd.

Batsche, G., Elliott, J., Graden, J. L., Grimes, J., Kovaleski, J. F., Prasse, D., Reschly, D. J., Schrag, J., & Tilly, W. D. 2005. *Response to intervention: Policy considerations and implementation.* Alexandria, VA: NASDSE.

Becerra, R. M., & Chi, I. (1992). Child care preferences among low-income minority families. *International Social Work, 35,* 35–47.

Beech & A. M. Colley (Eds.), *Cognitive approaches to reading,* (pp. 213–243). New York: Wiley.

Bialystock, E. (1991). Metalinguistic dimensions of bilingual language proficiency. In E. Bialystok (Ed.) *Language processing in bilingual children* (pp. 113–40). Cambridge: Cambridge University Press.

Bialystok, E. (2001). *Bilingualism in development: Language, literacy, and cognition.* Cambridge, UK: Cambridge University Press.

Bialystok, E. (2007). Acquisition of literacy in bilingual children: A framework for research. *Language Learning, 57 (1),* 45–77.

Bialystok, E., & Majumder, S. (1998). The relationship between bilingualism and the development of cognitive processes in problem-solving. *Applied Psycholinguistics, 19,* 69–85.

Bowman, B. T., Donovan, M. S., & Burns, M. S. (Eds.). (2001). *Eager to learn: Educating out preschoolers.* Washington, D.C.: National Academy Press.

Bryant, P. E., & Goswami, U. (1987). Phonological awareness and learning to read. In J. R. Beech & A. M. Colley (Eds.), *Cognitive approaches to reading* (pp. 213–243). New York: Wiley.

Bryant, P. E., Bradley, L., Maclean, M., & Crossland, J. (1989). Nursery rhymes, phonological skills and reading. *Journal of Child Language, 16,* 407–428.

Buriel, R., & Hurtado-Ortiz, M. T. (2000). Child care practices and preferences of native- and foreign-born Latina mothers and Euro-American mothers. *Hispanic Journal of Behavioral Sciences, 22*(3), 314–331.

Burns, M. K., Appleton, J. J., & Stehouwer, J. D. (2005). Meta-analytic review of responsiveness-to-intervention research: Examining field-based and research-implemented models. *Journal of Psychoeducational Assessment, 23,* 381–394.

Buysse, V., Castro, D. C., & Peisner-Feinberg, E. (2009). Effects of a professional development program on classroom practices and outcomes for Latino English language learners. Manuscript submitted for publication.

Buysse, V. & Peisner-Feinberg, E. (2008a). *Recognition & Response.* Paper presented at the US Department of Education Global Summit 2008, Washington, DC.

Buysse, V. & Peisner-Feinberg, E. (2008b). *Recognition & Response: A Comprehensive Early Intervening System for Early Childhood.* Paper presented at the DEC 24th Annual International Conference on Young Children with Special Needs and Their Families, Minneapolis, MN.

Campbell, F. A., Ramey, C. T., Pungello, E. P., Sparling, J., & Miller-Johnson, S. (2002). Early Childhood Education: Young Adult Outcomes from the Abecedarian Project. *Applied Developmental Science, 6,* 42–57.

Carlo, M. S., August, D., McLaughlin, B., Snow, C. E., Dressler, C., Lippman, D., et.al. (2004). Closing the gap: Addressing the vocabulary needs for English language learners in bilingual and mainstream classrooms. *Reading Research Quarterly, 39,* 188–215.

Castro, D. C., (2005). *Early Language and Literacy Classroom Observation (ELLCO) Addendum for English Language Learners.* Chapel Hill, NC: University of North Carolina, FPG Child Development Institute.

Castro, D. C., Gillanders, C, Machado-Casas, M., & Buysse, V. (2006). *Nuestros Niños early language and literacy program.* Chapel Hill: The University of North Carolina, FPG Child Development Institute.

Castro, D. C., Páez, M., Dickinson, D. K., & Frede, E. (2009). Promoting language and literacy in young DLLs: Research, practice and policy. Manuscript submitted for publication.

Castro, D. C., Ayankoya, B., & Kasprzak, C. (in press). *New Voices ~ Nuevas Voces Guide for Cultural and Linguistic Diversity in Early Childhood.* Baltimore, MD: Paul Brookes Publishing Co.

Chang, F., Crawford, G., Early D., Bryant D., Howes, C., Burchinal, M., Barbarin, O., Clifford, R., & Pianta, R. (2007). Spanish-speaking children,s social and language development in pre-Kindergarten classrooms. *Early Education and Development, 18(2),* 243–269.

Chiappe, P., & Siegel, L. S. (1999). Phonological awareness and reading acquisition in English and Pujabi-speaking Canadian children. *Journal of Educational Psychology, 91,* 20–28.

Cisero, C. A., & Royer, J. M. (1995). The development and cross-language transfer of phonological awareness. *Contemporary Educational Psychology, 20,* 275–303.

Cochran-Smith, M., & Zeichner, K. M. (Eds.). (2005). *Studying teacher education: The report of the AERA panel on research and teacher education.* Mahwah, NJ: Lawrence Erlbaum.

Coleman, M. R., Buysse, V., & Neitzel, J. (2006). *Recognition & response: An early intervening system for young children at-risk for learning disabilities.* Full report. Chapel Hill: The University of North Carolina, FPG Child Development Institute.

Coyne, M. D., Kame'enui, E. J., Simmons, D. C., & Harn, B. A. (2004). Beginning reading instruction as inoculation or insulin: First-grade reading performance of strong responders to kindergarten intervention. *Journal of Learning Disabilities, 37,* 90–104.

Cummins, J. (2000). *Language, power and pedagogy: Bilingual children caught in the crossfire.* Clevedon, UK: Multilingual Matters.

Dale, P. S., Crain-Thoreson, C., & Robinson, N. (1995). Linguistic precosity and the development of reading: The role of extralinguistic factors. *Applied Psycholinguistics, 16,* 173–187.

Dickinson, D. K., & Tabors, P. O. (Eds.). (2001). *Beginning literacy with language: Young children learning at home and school.* Baltimore, MD: Paul, H. Brookes Publishing.

Dickinson, D. K., McCabe, A., Anastasopoulos, L., Peisner-Feinberg, E., & Poe, M. D. (2003). The comprehensive language approach to early literacy: The interrelationships among vocabulary, phonological sensitivity, and print knowledge among preschool-aged children. *Journal of Educational Psychology, 95*(3), 465–481.

Durgunoglu, A. Y. (1998). Acquiring literacy in English and Spanish in the United States/ In A. Y. Durgunoglu & L Verhoeven (Eds.), *Literacy development in a multilingual context: Cross-cultural perspectives,* (pp. 135–145), Mahwah, NJ: Erlbaum.

Durgunoglu, A. Y., Nagy, W. E., & Hancin-Bhatt, B. J. (1993). Cross-language transfer of phonological awareness. *Journal of Educational Psychology, 85,* 453–465.

Dunn, L. M., & Dunn, D. (1997). *Peabody Picture Vocabulary Test-Third Edition.* Circle Pines, MN: American Guidance Service.

Dunn, L. M., Padilla, E. R., Lugo, D. E., & Dunn, L. M. (1986). *Test de Vocabulario en Imágenes Peabody.* Diablo, CA: Dunn Educational Services.

Education Development Center (2002). *Early Language and Literacy Observation* (ELLCO) Toolkit. Baltimore: Paul H. Brookes.

Espinosa, L., Castro, D., Crawford, G., & Gillanders, C. (2007). Early school success for English language learners: A review of evidence-based instructional practices for pre-K to grade 3. In V. Buyssc & L. Aytch (Eds.), *Early school success: Equity and access for diverse learners.* Executive Summary. Chapel Hill: The University of North Carolina, FPG Child Development Institute.

FACES: The Head Start Family and Child Experiences Survey (2003). *Where's My Teddy Story and Print Concepts.* Washington, DC: Administration on Children, Youth, and Families.

Fitzgerald, J. (1995) English-as-a-second language learners' cognitive reading processes: A review of research in the United States. *Review of Educational Research, 65,* 145–190.

Francis, D. J., Rivera, M., Lesaux, N., Kiefer, M., & Rivera, H. (2006). *Practical guidelines for the education of English language learners: Research-based recommendations for instruction and academic intervention.* Retrieved from http://www.centeron-instruction.org/files/ELL1-Interventions.pdf

Fuchs, D., Fuchs, L. S., & Compton, D. L. (2004). Identifying reading disabilities by responsiveness-to-instruction: Specifying measures and criteria. *Learning Disabilities Quarterly, 27,* 216–227.

Fuchs, L. S., Compton, D. L., Fuchs, D., Paulsen, K., Bryant, J. D., & Hamlett, C. L. (2005). The prevention, identification, and cognitive determinants of math difficulty. *Journal of Educational Psychology, 97,* 493–513.

Fuller, B., Holloway, S. D., & Liang, X. (1996). Family selection of child-care centers: The influence of household support, ethnicity, and parental practices. *Child Development, 67(6),* 3320–3337.

Galambos, S. J., & Goldin-Meadow, S. (1990). The effects of learning two languages on levels of metalinguistic awareness. *Cognition, 34 (1),* 1–56.

Gerber, M., Jimenez, T., Leafsstedt, J., Villaruz, J., Richards, C., & English, J. (2004). English reading effects of small group effective intervention in Spanish for K–1 English learners. *Learning Disabilities Research & Practice, 19,* 239–251.

Gersten, R., Baker, S.K., Shanahan, T., Linan-Thompson, S., Collins, P., & Scarcella, R. (2007) Effective literacy and English language instruction for English learners in the Elementary grades: A Practice Guide (NCEE 2007–4011). Washington, DC: National Center for Education Evaluation and Regional Assistance, Institute of Education Sciences, U.S. Department of Education. Retrieved October 25, 2009 from http://ies.ed.gov/ncee

Gersten, R., Beckmann, S., Clarke, B., Foegen, A., Marsh, L., Star, J.R., & Witzel, B. (2009). *Assisting students struggling with mathematics: Response to Intervention (RtI) for elementary and middle schools* (NCEE200–4060). Washington, DC: National Center for Education Evaluation and Regional Assistance, Institute of Education Sciences, U.S. Department of Education. Retrieved October 25, 2009 from http://ies.ed.gov/ncee/wwc/publications/practiceguides/

Gersten, R., Compton, D., Connor, C.M., Dimino, J., Santoro, L., Linan-Thompson, S., and Tilly, W.D. (2008). Assisting students struggling with reading: Response to Intervention and multi-tier intervention for reading in the primary grades. A practice guide. (NCEE 2009–4045). Washington, DC: National Center for Education Evaluation and Regional Assistance, Institute of Education Sciences, U.S. Department of Education. Retrieved October 25, 2009 from http://ies.ed.gov/ncee/wwc/publications/practiceguides/.

Geva, E. (2006). Learning to read in a second language: Research, implications, and recommendations for services. *Encyclopedia on Early Childhood Development.* Retrieved on November 17, 2008 from http://www.enfant-encyclopedie.com/pages/PDF/second_language.pdf

Gillanders, C. (2007). An English-speaking prekindergarten teacher for young Latino children: Implications for the teacher-child relationship on second language learning. *Early Childhood Education Journal, 35(1)*, 47–54.

Gillanders, C., & Castro. D. (Fall, 2007). Reading Aloud to English Language Learners. *Children and Families: The Magazine of the National Head Start Association, Vol. XXI (3)*, 12–14.

Goldenberg, C. (2006). Improving achievement for English learners: What research tells us. *Education Week. 25(43)*, 34–36.

Goldenberg, C. (2008).Teaching English language learners. What the research does—and does not—say. *American Educator, Summer*, 8–44.

Goldenberg, C., Reese, L., & Gallimore, R. (1992). Effects of literacy materials from school on Latino children's home experiences and early reading achievement. *American Journal of Education, 100 (4)*, 497–536.

Gormley, W., & Gayer, T. (2005). Promoting school readiness in Oklahoma: An evaluation of Tulsa's Pre-K program. *Journal of Human Resources, (Summer)*, 533–558.

Gunn, B., Biglan, A., Smolkowski, K., & Ary, D. (2000). The efficacy of supplemental instruction in decoding skills for Hispanic and non-Hispanic students in early elementary school. *Journal of Special Education, 34*, 90–103.

Hakuta, K. (1987). Degree of bilingualism and cognitive ability in mainland Puerto Rican children. *Child Development, 58 (5)*, 1372–88.

Hamilton, B.E., Martin, J.S., Ventura, M.A., Sutton, P.D., & Menacker, F. (2005). "Births: Preliminary Data for 2004" *National Vital Statistics Reports, 54, 8*: 1–18.

Hammer, C.S., Lawrence, F.R., & Miccio, A. W. (2007). Bilingual children's language abilities and early reading outcomes in Head Start and kindergarten. *Language, Speech, and Hearing Services in Schools*, 38, 237–248.

Hancock, D. R. (2002). The effects of native language books on the pre-literacy skill development of language minority kindergartners. *Journal of research in Childhood Education, 17 (1)*, 62–68.

Hernández, D. (2006). Young Hispanic Children in the U.S.: A demographic portrait based on Census 2000. Report to the National Task Force on Early Childhood Education for Hispanics. Tempe, AZ: Arizona State University.

Howes, C., & Ritchie, S. (2002). A matter of trust. New York: Teachers College Press. Learners in U.S. Schools: An Overview of Research. *Journal of Education for Students Placed at Risk, 10(4)*, 363–385.

Jimmerson, S. R., Burns, M. K., & VanDerHeyden, A. M. (Eds). (2007). *Handbook of response to intervention: The science and practice of assessment and intervention.* New York: Springer.

Landry, S. H., Swank, P. R., Smith, K. E., Assel, M. A., and Gunnewig, S. B. (2006). Enhancing Early Literacy Skills for Preschool Children: Bringing a Professional Development Model to Scale. *Journal of Learning Disabilities, 4* (39), 306–324.

Lee, P. (1996). Cognitive development in bilingual children: A base for bilingual instruction in early childhood education. *The Bilingual Research Journal, 20 (3 & 4)*, 499–522.

Lesaux, N. K., & Siegel, L. S. (2003). The development of reading in children who speak English as a second language. *Developmental Psychology, 39(6),* 1005–1019.

Lindsey, K., Manis, F., & Bailey, C. (2003). Prediction of first –grade reading in Spanish-speaking English-language learnes. *Journal of Education Psychology, 95,* 482–494.

McLaughlin, B. (1984). Second-language acquisition in childhood: Volume 1, Preschool children. Hillsdale, NJ: Erlbaum.

McMaster, K. L., Fuchs, D., Fuchs, L. S., & Compton, D. L. (2005). Responding to nonresponders: An experimental field trial of identification and intervention methods. *Exceptional Children, 71,* 445–463.

McMaster, K. L., Shu-Hsuan Kung; I. H., & Cao, M. (2008) Peer-Assisted Learning Strategies: A "Tier 1 "Approach to Promoting English Learners' Response to Intervention. *Exceptional Children, 74 (2),* 194–214.

Miccio, A. W., & Hammer, C. S. (2002). *Phonological Awareness Tasks* (PAT). University Station, PA: Penn State.

National Association for the Education of Young Children (NAEYC) & National Association of Early Childhood Specialists in State Departments of Education (NAECS/SDE) (2003). Early childhood curriculum, assessment and program evaluation: Building an effective, accountable system in programs for children birth through age 8. Joint Position Statement. Washington, D C: NAEYC.

National Center for Children in Poverty (2006). Young children in immigrant families—the role of philanthropy: Sharing knowledge, creating services, and building supportive policies. Report of a Meeting, January 18–19, 2006. New York, NY.

National Center for Development & Learning (2003). *Naming letters.* Chapel Hill, NC: University of North Carolina, FPG Child Development Institute.

National Reading Panel. (2000). Teaching children to read: An evidence-based assessment of the scientific research literature on reading and its implications for reading instruction. Washington, DC: U.S. Department of Health and Human Services.

National Research Council (1998). Preventing reading difficulties in young children. Washington, DC: National Academy Press.

National Task Force on Early Education for Hispanics. (2007) Para nuestros niños: Expanding and improving early education for Hispanics. Main Report. Tempe, AZ: Arizona State University.

Office of Head Start (2007). Dual language learning: What does it take? Washington, D. C.: Administration for Children and Families, U. S. Department of Health and Human Services.

Páez, M., Tabors, P. O., & López, L. M. (2007). Dual language and literacy development of Spanish-speaking preschool children. *Journal of Applied Developmental Psychology, 28(2),* 85–102.

Peisner-Feinberg, E. S., Burchinal, M. R., Clifford, R. M., Culkin, M. L., Howes, C., Kagan, S. L., & Yazejian, N. (2001). The relation of preschool child care quality to children's cognitive and social developmental trajectories through second grade. *Child Development, 72(5),* 1534–1553.

Planty, M., Hussar, W., Snyder, T., Provasnick, S., Kena, G., Dinkes, R., KewalRamani, A., & Kemp, J. (2008). The Condition of Education 2008 (NCES 2008–031). National Center for Education Statistics, Institute of Education Science, U.S. Department of Education. Washington, DC.

Portes, A. & Rumbaut, R. G. (1996) (2nd. Ed.). *Immigrant America: A portrait.* Berkeley: University of California Press.

Quiroga, T., Lemos-Britton, Z., Mostafapour, E., Abbott, R.D., & Berninge, V.W. (2002). Phonological awareness and beginning reading in Spanish-speaking ESL first graders: research into practice. *Journal of School Psychology, 40,* 85–111.

Rapp, D.N., Van den Broek, P., McMaster, K.L., Kendeou, P., &Espin, C.A. (2007). Higher-order comprehension processes in struggling readers: A perspective for research and intervention. *Scientific Studies of Reading, 11,* 289–312.

Recognition & Response Implementation Guide (2008). Chapel Hill: The University of North Carolina, FPG Child Development Institute.

Rolstad, K., Mahoney, K. & Glass, G. V. (2005). The Big Picture: A Meta-Analysis of Program Effectiveness Research on English Language Learners. *Educational Policy, 19(4),* 1–23.

Rumbaut, R. G. (1995). The new Californians: Comparative research findings on the educational progress of immigrant children. In R. G. Rumbaut & W. A. Cornelius (Eds.). *California's immigrant children: Theory, research, and implications for educational policy.* La Jolla, CA: Center for U.S.–Mexican Studies, University of California-San Diego.

Sánchez, S. Y. (1999). Issues of language and culture impacting the early care of young Latino children. Vienna, VA: National Child Care Information Center Publications. Retrieved on April 19, 2000 from http://www.nccic.org/pubs/sanchez99.html

Santos, R.M., & Ostrosky, M.M., (2004). "Understanding the Impact of Language Differences on Classroom Behavior," What Works Issue Brief No.2. Champaign, Ill.: Center on the Social and Emotional Foundations for Early Learning, 2004.

Scarborough H.S. (1989). Prediction of reading disability from familial and individual differences. *Journal of Educational Psychology, 81,* 101–1008.

Scarborough, H.S., (2001). Connecting early language and literacy to later reading disabilities: Evidence, theory, and practice. In S.Newman & D. Dickinson (Eds.), *Handbook for research in early literacy* (pp.97–110). New York: Guilford Press.

Schweinhart, L. J., Montie, J., Xiang, Z., Barnett, W. S., Belfield, C. R., & Nores, M. (2005). *Lifetime effects: The High/Scope Perry Preschool study through age 40.* (Monographs of the High/Scope Educational Research Foundation, 14). Ypsilanti, MI: High/Scope Press.

Shanahan, T., & Beck, I.L. (2006). Effective literacy teaching for English –language learners. In D. August & T. Shanahan (Eds.), *Developing literacy in second-language learners: Report of the National Literacy Panel on Language-Minority Children and Youth* (pp. 415–488). Mahwah, NJ: Erlbaum.

Slavin, R. & Cheung, A. 2005. A synthesis of research of reading instruction for English language learners, *Review of Educational Research, 75(2)*: 247–284.

Snow, C. (2006). Cross-cutting themes and future directions. In D. August & T. Shanahan (Eds.), *Developing literacy in second-language learners: Report of the National Literacy Panel on Language-Minority Children and Youth* (pp. 631–651). Mahwah, NJ: Lawrence Erlbaum.

Snow, C. E., & Páez, M. M. (2004). The Head Start classroom as an oral language environment. What should the performance standards be? In E. Zigler & S. J. Styfco (Eds.), *The Head Start Debates.* Baltimore, MD: Brookes Publishing Co.

Tabors, P. O. (1997). *One child, two languages: A guide for early childhood educators of children learning English as a second language.* Baltimore, MD: Paul H. Brookes Publishing.

Tabors, P.O., Páez, M., & López, L. (2003). Dual language abilities of bilingual four-year olds: Initial findings from the early childhood study of language and literacy development of Spanish-speaking children. *NABE Journal of Research and Practice, 1,* 70–91.

Takanishi, R., & Bogard, K.L. (2007). Effective educational programs for young children: What we need to know. *Child Development Perspectives, 1,* 40–45.

The Future of Children. (2005). School readiness: Closing racial and ethnic gaps, Vol. 15(1). Retrieved February 16, 2005, from http://www.futureofchildren.org

U. S. Census Bureau (2004). Current Population Survey: Annual Social and Economic Supplement. Washington, DC.

U. S. Census Bureau (2006). Nation's Population One-Third Minority. May 10 Press Release.

U.S. Department of Education, National Center for Educational Statistics. (2000). Statistics in brief —March 2000: Home literacy activities and signs of children's emerging literacy, 1993–1999. Washington, DC: U.S. Government Printing Office.

Vanderwood, M. L., & Nam, J. E. (2007). Response to intervention for English language learners: Current development and future directions. In S. R. Jimerson, M. K. Burns, & A. M. VadDerHeyden (Eds.), *Handbook of response to intervention: The science and practice of assessment and intervention* (pp. 408–417). New York: Springer.

Vaughn, S., Matches, P. G., Linan-Thompson, S., Cirino, P. T., Carlson, C. D., Pollard-Durodola, S. D., et al. (2006). First-grade English language learners at-risk for reading problems: Effectiveness of an English intervention. *Elementary School Journal, 107,* 153–180.

Wagner, R. K., Torgesen, J. K., & Rashotte, C. A. (1994). Development of reading-related phonological processing ability: New evidence of bidirectional causality from a latent variable longitudinal study. *Developmental Psychology, 30,* 73–87.

Whitehurst, G. J. (1999, April). The role of inside-out skills in reading readiness of children from low-income families. In C.J. Lonigan (Chair), From prereaders to readers: The role of phonological processing skills in at risk and typically developing children. Symposium conducted at the meeting of the Society for Research in Child Development. Albuquerque, NM.

Woodcock, R. W. (1991). *Woodcock Language Proficiency Battery-Revised: English and Spanish Forms.* Itasca, IL: Riverside.

Woodcock, R. W., & Muñoz-Sandoval (1995). *Woodcock Language Proficiency Battery-Revised: Spanish Form.* Itasca, IL: Riverside.

Wong Fillmore, L. (1991). When learning a second language means losing the first. *Early Childhood Research Quarterly, 6*, 323–346.
Yoshida, H. (2008). The cognitive consequences of early bilingualism. *Zero to Three, 29*(2), 26–30.

NOTE

1. In this chapter, the authors use the terms *dual language learner* and *bilingual learner* or *bilingual child* interchangeably to refer to young children learning their first and second language simultaneously or sequentially, in different settings, and acquiring different levels of proficiency in each language.

CHAPTER 5

YOUNG ENGLISH LANGUAGE LEARNERS AS LISTENERS

Theoretical Perspectives, Research Strands, and Implications for Instruction

Mary Renck Jalongo and Nan Li

ABSTRACT

Dramatic growth in the immigrant population of the United States during recent decades has altered the educational landscape. The general population is increasing at the rate of two million people annually; approximately half of that growth is attributable to immigration (Gollnick & Chinn, 2008). Data from the National Clearinghouse for English Language Acquisition reveals that, since 1990, the enrollment of English Language Learners (ELLs) in U.S. public schools has grown by 105%, while growth in the general school population is only 12% (Kindler, 2002). Over four million school-aged children are ELLs; they now constitute nearly 10% of the U.S. school-age population and are an increasingly diverse group (Ovando, Collier, & Combs, 2005; Zelasko & Antunez, 2000). It is estimated that, by 2030, up to 40% of children will be recent immigrants to the United States and that most of them will speak a lan-

Language and Cultural Diversity in Early Childhood Education, pages 95–114

guage other than English at home (U.S. Census Bureau, 2003). At the same time that the student population becomes more diverse, the teaching force has become more homogeneous (Johnson, 2006). In 2003, nearly 40% of United States public school children were members of minority groups, while less than 10% of their teachers were members of minority groups (Snyder & Hoffman, 2003).

Although it is customary to assume that young ELLs are from families that have left desperate circumstances to pursue a better quality of life or that they reside only in urban areas, this describes only some of our immigrant population. True, nearly 80% of the ELLs in the United States are children living in poverty whose first language is Spanish; however, over 400 different languages are spoken by young ELLs (Kindler, 2002). The next most populous groups of ELLs in the U.S. are Vietnamese, Hmong, Cantonese, and Korean (Kindler, 2002). Thus, the 10 million children in the United States who speak a language other than English at home can be surprisingly diverse, not only in terms of their national origins and the amount of exposure to and practice with the English language they have amassed, but also with respect to their socioeconomic circumstances and the educational levels of other family members (Federal Interagency Forum, 2006). To illustrate just a few, frequently overlooked categories of young ELLs, they may be: children of international adoption who have varying levels of familiarity with their native language (Meacham, 2007); children whose first language (L1) actually consists of two languages (e.g., a tribal language and a national language); economically privileged children whose parents are employed in international trade, politics, science, or medicine; or young children who use one language for worship and a second for conversation. What unifies all of these ELLs is their dependence on listening to acquire proficiency in the language of instruction in most schools: English.

As contemporary definitions of listening would have it, listening is "the necessary, interactive process that enables the brain to construct meaning from the sounds that are heard" (McSporran, 1997, p. 15). Contrary to popular opinion, listening is an active process, rather than a passive one; it requires much more than keeping still, being quiet, or looking at the speaker (see Wolvin & Coakley, 2000, for an historical overview). Listening starts with *hearing*, or perceiving a message through sounds. If, for example, children are watching a nature program and the narrator states "no two zebras are exactly alike," we might expect listeners to be able to recall and repeat that information. Listening also involves *understanding*, which means listeners can interpret what they have heard and put it into their own words. In order to comprehend an aural message, listeners draw upon background knowledge and bring their accumulated linguistic knowledge (both in L1 and L2) to bear on the message. For example, when listeners hear that no two zebras are alike, they might infer, "Maybe this means that the pattern of stripes is different for each zebra." In addition to hearing and understanding, listening involves *evaluating*, which means that listeners reflect on the message and decide whether it is credible. Listeners may wonder, "How can the stripes be different for every zebra?

Oh, the fingerprints are different for every person. I think this makes sense" (Homework Center, 2010, paragraphs 2 and 3).

Listening has particular significance for young ELLs because listening is the first language skill to develop in children without hearing impairments. In addition, ELLs depend extensively on listening in the early stages of language acquisition, for first languages and any additional languages learned. In fact, most developmental charts of second language acquisition begin with a stage called *silent*, as ELLs often remain quiet for a period of time before attempting to produce utterances in L2 (Ellis, 2007). It is estimated that the young child's receptive vocabulary often is four times that of his or her expressive vocabulary, so listening is foundational to the expressive language tasks of speaking and writing (Fenson et al., 1993). Listening is also the language skill that young children use the most in formal learning situations. Across historical eras, observational studies estimate that between 50% and 75% of students' classroom time is spent listening to the teacher, other students, or audio media (International Listening Association, 2008; Smith, 2008). The demands placed on listening skills are magnified in second language contexts, where the receiver has incomplete control of the language (McKay, 2008; National Capital Language Resource Center, 2008). Due to the role that listening plays in children's early literacy development and academic success, effective listening skills and strategies merit far more attention in work with young ELLs (Jalongo, 2008).

This literature review on young children's listening uses Stephen Krashen's (1981; 1982; 2003) writings on second language acquisition as a theoretical base. The review is organized around three major strands of research on listening: the listening environment, the role that listening plays in vocabulary development, and the oracy/literacy connection. Implications of theory and research for practitioners, programs, policies, and practices conclude the chapter.

THEORETICAL PERSPECTIVES ON SECOND LANGUAGE ACQUISITION

Current theories of second language acquisition are based on years of research in a wide variety of fields, including linguistics, psychology, sociology, anthropology, and neurolinguistics (Freeman & Freeman, 2001; Mitchell & Miles, 2006: Lightbown & Spada, 2006). *Language acquisition* is the terminology used to describe the less formal, "natural" way of learning a second language through exposure to it (Mangubhai, 2006). The very word *acquisition* implies that language is "picked up" rather than directly taught. In their book, *Second Language Listening: Theory and Practice*, Flowerdew and Miller (2005) take issue with the prevailing assumption that learning to listen is automatic. Rather, they contend that listening is a skill that deserves equal treatment with other basic skills of speaking, reading, and writing.

Nunan (1997) refers to listening as the "Cinderella skill in second language learning" because it has been frequently overlooked by its elder sister, speaking. Nevertheless, throughout the first half of the 20th century, developing children's listening skills received scant attention in the literature. The tendency has been to treat listening as a means to an end, that end being literacy with print. The 1960s saw more emphasis on oral language skills, and then, in the 1980s, Stephen Krashen's (1982) theory of second language acquisition generated further interest in oral language skills. Of particular relevance to any discussion of listening were two hypotheses:

- *The input hypothesis*, which proposes that humans acquire language by understanding messages and receiving "comprehensible input." Language learning is supported when learners engage in meaningful interaction in the target language and strive to communicate. According to this hypothesis, the learner improves and progresses when second language input is one step beyond his/her current stage of linguistic competence.
- *The affective filter hypothesis*, which states that anxiety (e.g., being pressured, corrected, or ridiculed) creates "mental blocks" that interfere with language learning (Krashen, 1981; 1982). Low motivation, low self-esteem, and debilitating fear of making mistakes can combine to intensify the affective filter and slow the process of L2 acquisition. Positive affect is necessary, but not sufficient on its own, for acquisition to take place. (See Krashen, 2003 and Northwest Regional Educational Laboratory, 2003 for an overview).

Although Krashen's theory has been challenged by those who favor immediate immersion and direct instruction in English, it is a misconception that first providing support in L1 is at odds with acquiring L2. Support in the child's native language should be provided at some level (Thomas & Collier, 2002) and, even when that language is spoken by none of the educators, teachers need to reach out to identify community volunteers who can assist. Indeed, a focus on comprehensible input and a consideration of the affective filter is consistent with best practices in second language teaching (Coltrane, 2003; Linquanti, 1999), respect for language diversity (David et al., 2006) and culturally responsive teaching (Gay, 2000; Nieto, 2002).

We now turn to three major strands in the literature on listening and young ELLs: research on the listening environment, studies of ELLs' listening vocabulary development, and research on the linkages between oral language and written language.

STUDIES OF THE LISTENING ENVIRONMENT FOR YOUNG ELLs

From the perspective of a basic communication process, listening includes a sender who transmits a message, a message that is conveyed through a channel (and occurs in a particular environment), and a receiver who is expected to interpret what was heard. Therefore, when attempting to evaluate listening environments, three key variables are: (1) the listener's auditory development, (2) the quality and intensity of the acoustic signal relative to the presence of competing sounds, and (3) the listener's experience with the linguistic components contained in the signal (Nelson, Kohnert, Sabur, & Shaw, 2005). On all three counts, young ELLs are at high risk of failing to understand the messages that they hear.

In terms of auditory development, young children are less adept than adults at "filling in the blanks" when messages are incomplete or ambiguous (Soli & Sullivan, 1997; Stelmachowicz, Hoover, Lewis, Kortekaas, & Pittman, 2000). Nevertheless, preschoolers and children in the primary grades appear to be capable of identifying the behaviors associated with effective listening in their conversational partners and identify grandparents as the best listeners (Imhof, 2002). It also appears that young children tend to accept personal responsibility when communication breaks down. In a study that presented young children with deliberately confusing messages, McDevitt (1990) found that the children usually blamed themselves for being poor listeners when they failed to understand.

With respect to environmental variables that interfere with hearing a message, even an empty classroom is apt to be a poor listening environment due to noise from HVAC systems, the reverberation of sounds off hard surfaces, and noises from outdoors (Knecht, Nelson, Whitelaw, & Feth, 2002). Once the early childhood classroom is populated by groups of active young children and their teachers, the signal-to-noise ratios make listening difficult, even for children with normal hearing and English as their first language (Rogers, Lister, Febo, Besing, & Abrams, 2006). For young children listening to an unfamiliar L2, the listening demands are even greater, leaving them at "a distinct disadvantage in classrooms with typical noise and reverberation" (Nelson et al., 2005, p. 219). The magnitude of these challenges can best be appreciated when one considers that even adults who are native speakers of English must make an extra effort to listen when a fellow English speaker has an accent or dialectical differences.

The listener's experience with linguistic components is yet another consideration. A child who begins school without previous English language experience will be in the company of peers with a 4- to 5- year advantage (Hutchinson, Whiteley, Smith, & Connors, 2003). Thus, young ELLs "cannot rely on their cumulative oral language experience as a bridge to literacy to the same degree as their monolingual peers" (Nelson et al., 2005, p. 220). In an often quoted estimate from Cummins (1984), children learning English often take two to three years to acquire communicative language with peers, and another five to seven years to acquire proficiency with academic English (Hakuta, Butler, & Witt, 2000; Genesee, Lindholm-Leary, Saunders, & Christian, 2005). Children in classrooms are expected to engage in academic tasks that require more focused and persistent meaning-making efforts, and this places high demands on the young child's development as a listener (Field, 2001; Lund, 1991; McKay, 2008; Morley, 1991; Vandergrift, 2006). Take, for example, the common situation of listening to a picture book read aloud. As case study research describes, young children may come from a culture that emphasizes oral communication and have very little experience with books; they also may lack the prior knowledge to make sense out of what they hear and, therefore, show little interest in the stories that are shared (Gallas, 1994; Gallas, 1997). A picture story book read aloud requires sustained listening, filtering out distractions, drawing upon background knowledge, and using metacognitive strategies (Lundsteen, 1993). To support listening development, story sharing for ELLs evidently needs to be more engaging and interactive. In Cabrera and Martinez's (2001) study of the story comprehension of a group of students in their second year of a bilingual program, two simplified stories were presented, but the second one was accompanied by gestures, repetition, and comprehension checks. The second, more concrete and engaging way of presenting the story significantly improved comprehension in L2.

As we have seen, the communication process breaks down when the message cannot be heard above ambient noise and when the receiver encounters difficulties with interpreting the message. Both situations are apt to occur with young children, in general, and with ELLs, in particular.

THE ROLE OF LISTENING IN VOCABULARY DEVELOPMENT

In a British policy paper on language instruction for young children, an independent research team concluded that far more attention needs to be given to listening skills so that children build their vocabularies and learn to listen attentively (Rose, 2006). As a point of comparison, it is estimated that when monolingual English-speaking children begin formal reading instruction, they typically bring along a vocabulary of 5,000 to 7,000 words in English (Biemiller & Slonim, 2001). Thus, the vocabulary gap between an ELL who is completely new to English and monolingual peers can be enormous; it also can persist. Hutchinson et al.'s (2003) study of 43 ELLs found that they had weaker vocabulary and comprehension than monolingual peers, and this gap did not narrow significantly over a three-year period. The speed with which children recognize and understand words is also at issue. To illustrate, the typical adult processes speech sounds process at rates of 10 to 15 phonemes per second in order to follow a conversation, often identifying a word well before the utterance is complete (Cole & Jakimik, 1980). So, not only listening to and understanding vocabulary, but also the rate at which that is accomplished, affects ELLs' ability to engage in conversation and to accomplish academic tasks. Clearly, ELLs need more than word-by-word listening comprehension in order to succeed (August, Carlo, Dressler, & Snow, 2005; Gersten et al., 2007).

It is widely recognized that, both for adults and children, the concept of a word develops gradually and is constructed over time with additional experience (Nelson, 2007). Tasks used to assess listening comprehension in young children often are limited to items that can be represented pictorially. This approach falls short, not only of treating vocabulary learning as a process, but also of considering the cultural background and knowledge necessary to attribute meaning to the words that children hear (Brisk & Harrington, 2000). With respect to vocabulary development, it is clear that it needs to be studied formatively (i.e., while children are listening), as well as summatively (i.e., after the fact, with print materials). Advances in technology have made this possible. Equipment that records the focus of a child's gaze as words are spoken and an assortment of pictures is presented has been helpful in this regard. When the child looks at the correct picture after its name is spoken, it provides an assessment of listening comprehension in "real time"; it also makes it possible to study vocabulary development long before the child is able to provide verbal or written responses (Hurtado, Marchman, & Fernald, 2007). The speech processing ability of children becomes much more efficient and rapid at 24 months (Fernald, Perfors, & Marchman, 2006); however, the size of toddlers' vocabulary varies considerably, ranging from just a few words to hundreds (Jalongo, 2007). Studies that used technology to document language growth in preschoolers indicate that listening comprehension of vocabulary continues to advance as children mature (Snedeker & Trueswell, 2004; Song & Fisher, 2005).

Young children's vocabulary learning appears to follow the same basic sequence (but not at the same rate) for L1 and L2. When attempting to assess the listening comprehension and vocabulary of older children, researchers frequently use "rapid naming" approaches, in which children are presented with pictures to label verbally. One limitation in many studies of ELLs' vocabulary learning is that there is no effort to differentiate between ELLs with language disabilities or disorders and their ELL peers, a practice that tends to confound more generalized language problems with second language learning issues (Genesee et al., 2005). The level of language impairment, therefore, may be a better predictor of reading difficulties later on than the typical listening comprehension tasks (see

Lovett et al., 2008). Where listening and vocabulary are concerned, the field needs to move beyond quantitative methods that count the number of pictures young children can correctly identify in response to spoken words. In-depth, qualitative study of how ELLs build a concept of a word over time and how much the various L1s contribute to the process of learning the target language is needed.

In quantitative studies, the particulars of the ELLs' circumstances and the local situation often are overlooked, and the source of observed differences in vocabulary, not fully explored. Fernald, Perfors, and Marchman (2006), for example, ask not just whether some children have larger vocabularies, but why. If some children have more opportunities to use L2 both outside and inside school, for example, their greater vocabularies and efficiency in recognition of spoken words may be more of a practice effect than a difference in capacity for or willingness to become proficient in L2. Likewise, if quantitative researchers are claiming to study vocabulary growth, valid and reliable indicators of baseline vocabulary are needed. Approaches that would take those pre-existing differences into account (e.g., analysis of co-variance rather than correlational studies) are warranted.

THE LINKAGE BETWEEN ORACY AND LITERACY

Listening comprehension, defined as the young child's ability to understand what he or she hears, is highly predictive of overall academic achievement. Children with listening comprehension difficulties face serious learning challenges and are much more likely fall behind their peers as they progress through school (Field, 2001; Mendelsohn & Rubin, 1995). There is extensive documentation that oral language skills of listening and speaking—both in L1 and in L2—are linked to literacy with print; however, this should not be oversimplified (see Geva & Yaghoub-Zadeh, 2006 and Proctor, August, Carlow, & Snow, 2006 for a discussion). Oral language and written language are fundamentally different. This can best be demonstrated by two recurrent findings: first, that even though most young children without disabilities learn to speak or listen, not all become fluent readers and writers (Schultz, 2003), and second, that oral language deficits and reading problems frequently co-occur (Bishop & Snowling, 2004).

Although single grade level studies have mixed results, the longitudinal research suggests that oral language skills are highly effective predictors of later reading skill in English. In a longitudinal study of 249 Spanish-speaking ELLs, Lindsey, Manis, and Bailey (2003) found that oral language variables—even more than word identification—predicted reading comprehension in first grade. Nakamoto, Lindsey, and Manis (2008) studied 282 Spanish-speaking ELLs in 1st–3rd grade and concluded that facility with oral language (both in L1 and in L2) was a significant predictor of reading achievement in 6th grade. There is also support for cross-language transfer between L1 and L2, particularly in the area of phonological awareness (see Manis, Lindsey, & Bailey, 2004 for a review). The more similar L1 and L2 are, in terms of alphabet and phonetics, the greater the potential for transfer; some research suggests that cross-language transfer is greater for ELLs who have Italian or Spanish as L1 and are trying to learn English (D'Angiulli, Siegel, & Serra, 2000; Lindsey, Manis, & Bailey, 2003). The next section examines each of these three research strands for curriculum and instruction.

IMPLICATIONS FOR IMPROVING LISTENING INSTRUCTION

Furthering the academic achievement of ELLs is a national and international concern. In a report from 41 state education agencies in the U.S., only 18.7% of children classified as limited English proficient attained state norms for reading in their L2, English (Kindler, 2002). In order to increase comprehensible input, teachers need first to attend to characteristics of the listening environment. Flexer (1997) estimates that, on any given day, about 1/3 of first graders are not hearing normally, due to allergies, background noise, tinnitus (caused by medications), ear infections, and so forth. Such situations further compound the listening difficulties of young ELLs, so clinicians in the speech/hearing/language field endorse sound amplification systems to make the speaker's voice audible above classroom noise. Even simple changes, such as investing in chair glides to reduce background noise during classroom transitions, can make a difference.

Listening strategies are effective when they support listeners as they try to focus, recall, interpret, and evaluate a message (Field, 2001; Schwarts, 1998). Providing comprehensible input is an essential first step. A major way to increase comprehensible input is to combine what Bruner (2004) refers to as the enactive mode (physical activity and gesture) and the iconic mode (realia or pictures) with the symbolic mode (words and other symbols). The enactive mode engages the learners in actually doing something in order to connect it with language (e.g., a fingerplay or action song). The iconic mode uses concrete objects (e.g., fruit or plastic replicas of fruit) or pictorial representations of objects (e.g., photographs, clip art) to support vocabulary growth and make the language that is heard understandable. Total Physical Response (TPR), developed by James J. Asher in the 1960s, also emphasizes the relationship between language and the enactive mode (see Asher, 2000 for a review and sample lessons).

Audiovisual materials are another way to increase comprehensible input. They enable children to exercise greater control over an aural message as they pause, turn up the volume, repeat, slow down, or even stop. When teachers use such materials as picture books, cassettes or DVDs of bilingual books, captioned video, and multicultural folktales online, they increase opportunities for children to make sense of words that they hear (see Skouge, Rao, & Boisvert, 2007 for technology-supported learning activities). Deliberately linking the enactive, iconic, and symbolic modes in lessons also serves to differentiate instruction, because all children can participate at some level in the activity (Rothenberg & Fisher, 2007).

In addition to these general recommendations, two specific language arts activities that support ELLs and promote effective listening include:

- *The Talking Drawings Strategy.* In this activity, the teacher begins by sharing several different, accurately labeled diagrams, such as the parts of a plant (leaf, stem, roots, etc.), so that children can see how this is done. The teacher then asks the children to work with a partner and draw and label another such drawing, based on the lesson topic and goals (e.g., the Statue of Liberty). Next, the teacher shares a nonfiction passage that provides more details, such as a picture book, and the partners revise their drawings by discussing, redrawing, and labeling in greater detail (this can be done in both languages). Talking drawings encourage careful listening and enhance opportunities for peer interaction (Paquette, Fello, & Jalongo, 2007).
- *The Language Experience Approach.* This activity uses stories dictated by the child or children to create relevant reading material (Carasquillo & Rodriguez, 2002). When working with a group, the teacher can select a shared experience with cultural relevance (e.g., making an ethnic food for snack or learning a simple game from another culture). Each child suggests a sentence that results in a simple, sequential story, which the teacher writes on a wall chart. Sentences contributed to the chart story are labeled with the child's name to show her or his contribution. The concrete experience helps to make the words more understandable, because they are used in context and the focus on children's home cultures helps to engage the children and motivate them to participate.

Teachers will also find materials designed specifically for parents and families that offer information on early language development and advice on improving young children's listening skills to be a valuable resource (Lu, 2000; Smith, 2008). National organizations, such as the American Speech–Hearing–Language Association (www.asha.org), the International Reading Association (www.ira.org), and the National Association for the Education of Young Children (www.naeyc.org) offer free or inexpensive developmental charts, brochures about early literacy topics, and a variety of other resources, with some of them translated into Spanish. Creating an attractive display of these materials or sending them home so that parents and families with limited resources can access them easily helps to explain and reinforce the work that teachers are doing at school to promote English language learning.

Another major consideration in the education of young ELLs is Krashen's *affective filter*. Early childhood educators cannot hope to improve the situation for young ELLs without first genuinely welcoming them into classroom communities, treating them with respect and kindness, advocating for their needs, and valuing the funds of knowledge represented by their families, cultures, and communities (Fass, 1989; Houck, 2005; Parker & Pardini, 2006; Saracho, 2007). Unless and until we address deeply ingrained bias against young children for whom the language of instruction is not their first language, all of the recommendations, strategies, skills, and activities will be of little value (Bruns & Corso, 2001; Tabors, 2008). Educators need to recognize that the source of bias against young Spanish-speaking children in the U.S. often has more to do with the socioeconomic status of their families than with the fact that they are in the process of acquiring English. International comparisons are helpful in making this point. In Canada, for example, most ELLs are middle class (such as children learning French and English in the Province of Québec) and attitudes about bilingual education generally have a more positive, *enrichment* approach (Lovett et al., 2008). In Britain, children from Pakistan and Bangladesh who are learning English generally come from low-income families; historically, these children tend to struggle academically, particularly with respect to literacy in English (Hutchinson et al., 2003). Such international trends suggest that it is not the task of learning the mainstream language alone that creates a challenge; rather, the issues of English language learning are clouded by larger social issues and factors that put children at risk, such as poor nutrition, inadequate housing, and other health and safety considerations. Therefore, educators need to implement the essential principles of programs that have been successful in supporting not only second language learning, but also children living in poverty: (1) focusing on children in the lowest quintiles for services, (2) timing interventions in ways that match learners' developmental levels, (3) increasing the intensity of support programs, (4) providing ongoing professional training, (5) coordinating services with other agencies, (6) creating more time for and investing more time in opportunities for children to learn, and (7) carefully monitoring and evaluating attainment of programmatic goals (Neuman, 2009).

Teachers cannot hope to be effective unless they can see promise and potential in every child; they need, first and foremost, to practice "an ethic of caring" (Messiou, 2006; Noddings, 2005). Informal classroom observations of Madhu, the three-year-old son of recent immigrants from India, illustrate what happens when teachers absolve themselves of responsibility for young ELLs, simply because they do not speak the child's native language. Madhu speaks almost no English and, sadly, his preschool teacher has concluded that it is hopeless to try to communicate with him beyond some pantomimed gestures. When she first learned that Madhu would be joining her class, she approached it as a problem and treated the boy as if he were an imposition. A second-generation immigrant to the U.S. herself, she lacked compassion for Madhu's situation and openly stated that "He will just have to learn to speak English on his own and fend for himself. That's how *my* family managed to become successful." This teacher's negative attitudes have affected Madhu's classmates as well. When a visitor walks out to the playground, she finds Madhu sitting off by himself and softly crying. As she attempts to comfort him, two children come over and reveal their misconceptions about the boy's capabilities. The first says, "He can't hear you," while the second one adds, "Yeah, he don't know how to talk yet." By failing to care, Madhu's teacher has branded him as an incompetent and unworthy as a language partner to all of his peers; her inexcusable behavior also has robbed Madhu of opportunities for comprehensible input and has raised his affective filter to the point where he is demoralized about trying to communicate in English.

On the other hand, educators who approach young ELLs with warmth, acceptance, and a genuine desire to communicate—irrespective of their knowledge level in the child's L1—exert a positive effect on language outcomes for young children (Tabors, 2008). Effective instruction for ELLs draws upon the sum of their experiences in listening, speaking, reading, and writing, as a whole, for their literacy growth (Mendelsohn & Rubin, 1995; Vandergrift, 2006). To illustrate, in a multisite study of 141 kindergarten teachers that observed each early childhood educator instructing ELLs during several reading classes, teacher quality variables were related positively to student engagement and negatively to time spent in noninstructional activities (Cirino, Pollard-Durdola, Foorman, Carlson, & Francis, 2007). Ongoing professional training in second language acquisition is necessary to improve the ability of mainstream teachers to serve the culturally and linguistically diverse students in their classrooms (Ellis, 2007; Fillmore & Snow, 2000; Purdy, 2008). It is encouraging to note that in Lovett et al.'s (2008) study of 166 struggling readers with different L1 statuses, the children who had the greatest impairment also demonstrated the greatest growth following 105 hours of participation in a Response to Intervention Program. A commitment to children and families, despite the adversity they face, is the surest way to make progress.

Krashen's (2003) theory posits that a low-anxiety context promotes L2 learning. From a program and policy perspective, this means that young

ELLs need the support of teachers, volunteers, and peers with proficiency in both languages if they are expected to make connections between languages and master content across the curriculum (Parker & Pardini, 2006). However, this is not always the case, particularly if the child's L1 is shared by few or no other teachers, volunteers, and peers. The reality is pure supply and demand; schools with large groups of students who speak the same L1 tend to provide services, while others do not. Young ELLs under these circumstances are expected to figure it out for themselves; if their teachers seek assistance, the responses invariably include a short list of things that will not cost the district any money, such as "use collaborative learning." Producing positive outcomes from pairing ELLs with monolingual peers, however, depends upon such variables as the ELLs' language proficiency (both in L1 and in L2), the nature of the task, and the skills and attitudes of the non-ELLs (Genesee et al., 2005). If these peers treat the ELL as immature, odd, or incompetent, this will raise the young ELLs' affective filter, lower self-esteem, and may engender negative attitudes toward learning English. As Lightbown (2000) notes, there is no acceptable substitute for programs that consider the particular needs of individual ELLs:

> No matter how sound the research on which new ideas, materials and techniques are based, pedagogical innovations must be implemented and adapted according to local conditions, the strengths of individual teachers and students, the available resources, the age of the learner, and the time available for teaching. (p. 454)

To summarize, young ELLs need:

- A school environment that is positive and reflects high-quality, respectful and meaningful exchanges between and among children and families, teachers and administrators.
- Teachers who understand second language development and treat L1 as an asset (rather than a liability) and L2 as enrichment (rather than remediation of deficiencies); teachers with education, continuing professional development, and established competence in implementing best practices of instruction (Gibbons, 2002; Goh & Taib, 2006; Hawkins, 2004).
- Curriculum that is supported by research, developmentally suited for diverse learners, incorporates higher-order thinking skills, and is aligned with standards and assessment (Crosse, 2007).
- Educators who fully appreciate that no single approach or method is likely to be effective for all ELLs, given the tremendous diversity in their cultural and language backgrounds, levels of proficiency in both L1 and L2, and their beliefs, values, and attitudes about the acquisition of L2 (Genesee et al., 2005; Montecel & Cortez, 2002).

CONCLUSION

Listening ability lies at the very heart of all human growth, beginning even prior to birth and continuing across the lifespan (Brown, 1987). Language is a social tool, as well as an academic one; thus, listening comprehension has major implications for interpersonal relationships, as well (McKay, 2008). When a young child arrives at school with a limited understanding of the language of instruction, it has important consequences for everyone involved—for the learner, the family, peers, educators, professionals in related fields, and for communities, both small and large. Whether a classroom in the United States contains one child with very limited English proficiency, several ELLs who speak the same first language, or a veritable United Nations of different first languages, such as some schools in major cities, there is no doubt that supporting the listening development of young ELLs should be a major consideration in an inclusive and appropriate education for the very young.

REFERENCES

Asher, J. J. (2000). *Year 2000 update for the Total Physical Response, known world-wide as TPR.* Los Gatos, CA: Sky Oaks Productions. Retrieved April 22, 2003, from www.tpr-world.com/tpr-y2k.html

August, D., Carlo, M. Dressler, C., & Snow, C.E. (2005). The critical role of vocabulary development for English language learners. *Learning Disabilities Research and Practice, 20,* 50–57.

Biemiller, A., & Slonim, N. (2001). Estimating root word vocabulary growth in normative and advantaged populations: Evidence for a common sequence of vocabulary acquisition. *Journal of Educational Psychology, 93,* 498–520.

Bishop, D. V., & Snowling, M. J. (2004). Developmental dyslexia and specific language impairment: Same or different? *Psychological Bulletin, 130*(6), 858–886.

Brisk, M. E., & Harrington, M. M. (2000). *Literacy and bilingualism: A handbook for all teachers.* London: Lawrence Erlbaum.

Brown, H. D. (1987). *Principles of language learning and teaching.* Englewood Cliffs, NJ: Prentice Hall.

Bruner, J. S. (2004). *The process of education* (revised ed.). Boston: Harvard University Press.

Bruns, D.A., & Corso, R. M. (2001). *Working with culturally and linguistically diverse families.* Washington, DC: ERIC Clearinghouse on Languages and Linguistics (ERIC Digest No. ED 455 972).

Cabrera, M., & Martinez, P. (2001). The effects of repetition, comprehension checks, and gestures on primary school children in an EFL situation. *English Language Teachers Journal, 55*(3), 281–288.

Carasquillo, A.L., & Rodriguez, V. (2002). *Language minority students in the mainstream classroom* (2nd ed.). Philadelphia, PA: Multilingual Matters.

Cirino, P. T., Pollard-Durodola, S. D., Foorman, B. R., Carlson, C. D., & Francis, D. J. (2007). Teacher characteristics, classroom instruction, and student literacy and language outcomes for bilingual kindergartners. *Elementary School Journal, 107*(4), 341–364.

Cole, R., & Jakimik, J. (1980). A model of speech perception. In R. Cole (Ed.), *Perception and production of fluent speech* (pp. 133–163). Hillsdale, NJ: Lawrence Erlbaum.

Coltrane, B. (2003). *Working with young English Language Learners: Some considerations.* Washington, DC: ERIC Clearinghouse on Language and Linguistics (ERIC Digest No. 481 690).

Crosse, K. (2007). Introducing English as an additional language to young children. London: Paul Chapman.

Cummins, J. (1984). *Bilingualism and special education: Issues in assessment and pedagogy.* Clevendon, U.K.: Multilingual Matters, Ltd.

D' Angiulli, A., Siegel, L. S., & Serra, E. (2000). The development of reading in English and Italian in bilingual children. *Applied Psycholinguistics, 22,* 479–507.

David, J., Onchonga, O., Drew, R., Grass, R. Stuchuk, R., & Burns, M.S. (2006). Head Start embraces language diversity. *Young Children, 60*(6), 40–43.

Ellis, R. (2007). Educational settings and second language learning. *Asian EFL Journal, 9*(4), Article 1. Available from http://www.asian-efl-journal.com/Dec_2007_re.php

Fass, P. (1989). *Outside in: Minorities and the transformation of American education.* New York: Oxford University Press.

Federal Interagency Forum on Child and Family Statistics (2006). America's children: Key indicators of child well-being, 2006. Available from http://childstats.gov/

Fenson, L., Dale, P. S., Reznick, J. S., Thal, D., Bates, E., & Hartung, J. et al. (1993). *User's guide and technical manual for the MacArthur Communicative Development Inventories.* Cambridge, MA: MIT Press.

Fernald, A., Perfors, A., & Marchman, V.A. (2006). Picking up speed in understanding: Speech processing efficiency and vocabulary growth across the 2nd year. *Developmental Psychology,* 42(1), 98–116Feyten, C. M. (1991). The power of listening ability: An overlooked dimension in language acquisition. *The Modern Language Journal, 75*(2), 173–180.

Field, J. (2001). Finding one's way in the fog: Listening strategies and second-language learners. *Modern English Teacher, 9,* 29–34.

Fillmore, L.W., & Snow, C.E. (2000). *What teachers need to know about language.* Washington, DC: Office of Educational Research and Development. Retrieved January 13, 2010 from http://faculty.tamu-commerce.edu/jthompson/Resources/FillmoreSnow2000.pdf

Flexer, C. (1997). Individual sound-field systems: Rationale, description, and use. *The Volta Review, 99*(3), 133–157.

Flowerdew, J., & Miller, L. (2005). *Second language listening: Theory and practice.* London: Cambridge University Press.

Freeman, D.E., & Freeman, Y.S. (2001). *Between worlds: Access to second language acquisition* (2nd ed.). Portsmouth, NH: Heinemann.

Gallas, K. (1994). *The languages of learning: How children talk, write, dance, and sing their understanding of the world.* New York: Teachers College Press.

Gallas, K. (1997). Story time as a magical act open only to the initiated: What some children don't know about power and may not find out. *Language Arts, 74*(4), 248–254.

Gay, G. (2000). *Culturally responsive teaching: Theory, research, and practice.* New York: Teachers College Press.

Genesee, F., Lindholm-Leary, K., Saunders, W., & Christian, D. (2005). English Language Learners in U.S. Schools: An overview of research findings. *Journal of Education for Students Placed at Risk, 10* (4), 363–385.

Gersten, R., Baker, S. K., Shanahan, T., Linan-Thompson, S., Collins, P., & Scarcella, R. (2007). *Effective literacy and English language instruction for English Learners in the elementary grades.* Washington, DC: Institute of Education Sciences.

Geva, E., & Yaghoub-Zadeh, Z. (2006). Reading efficiency in native English-speaking and English-as-a-Second Language children: The role of oral proficiency and underlying cognitive-linguistic processes. *Scientific Studies of Reading, 10*(1), 31–57.

Gibbons, P. (2002). *Scaffolding language, scaffolding learning: Teaching second language learners in the mainstream classroom.* Portsmouth, NH: Heinemann.

Goh, C., & Taib, Y. (2006). Metacognitive instruction in listening for young learners. *ELT Journal: English Language Teachers Journal, 60*(3), 222–232.

Gollnick, D. M., & Chinn, P. C. (2008). *Multicultural education in a pluralistic society* (8th ed.). Upper Saddle River, NJ: Merrill Prentice Hall.

Hakuta, K., Butler, Y.G., & Witt, D. (2000). *How long does it take English learners to attain proficiency?* Santa Barbara, CA: University of California, Linguistic Minority Research Inst.

Hawkins, M. R. (2004). Researching English language and literacy development in schools, *Educational Researcher, 33*(3), 14–25.

Homework Center (2010). Speaking & listening skills: Listening skills. Retrieved January 13, 2010 from www.infoplease.com/homework/speaklisten.html

Houck, F. A. (2005). *Supporting English language learners: A guide for teachers and administrators.* Portsmouth, NH: Heinemann.

Hurtado, N., Marchman, V., & Fernald, A. (2007). Spoken word recognition in Latino children learning Spanish as their first language. *Journal of Child Language, 34*(2), 227–249.

Hutchinson, J. M., Whiteley, H.E., Smith, C. D., & Connors, L. (2003). The developmental progression of comprehension-related skills in children learning EAL. *Journal of Research in Reading, 26*(1), 19–32.

Imhof, M. (2002). In the eye of the beholder: Children's perception of good and poor listening behavior. *International Journal of Listening, 16,* 40–56.

International Listening Association (ILA). (2008). Facts on listening. Retrieved January 13, 2010 from http://www.listen.org/

Jalongo, M. R. (2007). *Early childhood language arts* (4th ed.). Needham Heights, MA: Allyn and Bacon.

Jalongo, M. R. (2008). *Learning to listen, listen to learn: Building essential skills in young children.* Washington, DC: National Association for the Education of Young Children.

Johnson, S. M. (2006). *Finders and keepers: Helping new teachers survive and thrive in our schools.* San Francisco: Jossey-Bass.

Kindler, A. (2002). Survey of the states' limited English proficient students and available educational programs and services 2000–2001 summary report. National Clearinghouse for English Language Acquisition & Language Institution Educational Programs, Washington, D.C.

Knecht, H., Nelson, P., Whitelaw, G., & Feth, L. (2002). Structural variables and their relationship to background noise levels and reverberation times in unoccupied classrooms. *American Journal of Audiology, 11,* 65–71.

Krashen, S. D. (1982). *Principles and practice in second language acquisition.* Oxford: Pergamon.

Krashen, S. D. (2003). *Explorations in language acquisition and use.* Portsmouth, NH: Heinemann.

Krashen, S.D. (1981). *Second language acquisition and second language learning.* New York: Pergamon Press.

Lightbown, P. (2000). Classroom SLA research and second language teaching. *Applied Linguistics, 21*(4), 431–462.

Lightbown, P., & Spada, N. (2006). *How languages are learned* (2nd ed.). Oxford: Oxford University Press.

Lindsey, K. A., Manis, F. R., and Bailey, C. E. (2003). Prediction of first-grade reading in Spanish-speaking English-Language Learners. *Journal of Educational Psychology, 95*(3), 484–494.

Linquanti, R. (1999). Fostering academic success for English Language Learners: What do we know? (Section 5: English language acquisition and academic Success: What do we know?). http://www.wested.org/policy/pubs/fostering/know.htm

Lovett, M. W., DePalma, M., Frijters, J., Steinbach, K., Temple, M., Benson, N., & Lacerenza, L. (2008). Interventions for reading difficulties: A comparison of Response to Intervention by ELL and EFL struggling readers. *Journal of Learning Disabilities, 41*(4), 333–352.

Lu, M. Y. (2000). Language development in the early years. (ERIC Document Reproduction Service No. ED 446 336). Available from http://www.vtaide.com/png/ERIC/Language-Early.htm

Lund, J. R. (1991). A comprehension of second language listening and reading comprehension. *Modern Language Journal, 75,* 196–204.

Lundsteen, S. W. (1993). Metacognitive listening. In A. D. Wolvin & C.G. (Eds.). *Perspectives on listening* (pp. 106–123). Westport, CT: Greenwood.

Mangubhai, F. (2006). What do we know about learning and teaching second languages? *Asian EFL Journal, 98*(3), unpaged. Retrieved January 1, 2009, from http://www.asian-efl-journal.com/Sept_06_fm.php

Manis, F. R., Lindsey, K. A., & Bailey, C. E. (2004). Development of reading in grades K–2 in Spanish-Speaking English-Language Learners. *Learning Disabilities Research and Practice, 19*(4), 214–224.

McDevitt, T.M. (1990). Encouraging young children's listening. *Academic Therapy, 25*(5), 569–577.

McKay, D. R. (2008). Career planning: Here is why you need good listening skills. Retrieved January 13, 2010 from http://careerplanning.about.com/cs/miscskills/a/listening_skill.htm

McSporran, E. (1997). Towards better listening and learning in the classroom. *Educational Review, 49*(1), 13–21.

Meacham, A. N. (2007). Language learning and the internationally adopted child. *Early Childhood Education Journal, 34*(1), 73–79.

Mendelsohn, D. J., & Rubin, J. (1995). A *guide for the teaching of second language listening.* San Diego, CA: Dominie Press.

Messiou, K. (2006). Conversations with children: Making sense of marginalization. *European Journal of Special Needs Education, 21*(1), 39–54.

Mitchell, R., & Myles, F. (2006). *Second language learning theories* (2nd ed.). London: Hodder Arnold.

Montecel, M. R., & Cortez, J. D. (2002). Successful bilingual education programs: Development and the dissemination of criteria to identify promising and exemplary practices in bilingual education at the national level. *Bilingual Research Journal, 26,* 1–22.

Morley, J. (1991). Listening comprehension in second/foreign language instruction. In M. Celce-Murcia (Ed.), *Teaching English as a second or foreign language* (pp. 81–106). Boston: Heinle & Heinle.

Nakamoto, J., Lindsey, K. A., & Manis, F. R. (2008). A cross-linguistic investigation of English Language Learners' reading comprehension in English and Spanish, *Scientific Studies of Reading, 12* (4), 352–371.

National Capital Language Resource Center (NCLRC). (2008). *The essentials of language teaching: Teaching listening.* Retrieved January 13, 2010 from www.nclrc.org/essentials/listening/liindex.htm

Nelson, K. (2007). *Young minds in social worlds: Experience, meaning and memory.* Cambridge, MA: Harvard University Press.

Nelson, P., Kohnert, K., Sabur, S., & Shaw, D. (2005). Classroom noise and children learning through a second language: Double jeopardy? *Language, Speech, and Hearing Services in Schools, 36,* 219–229.

Neuman, S. B. (2009). *Changing the odds for children at risk: Seven essential principles of educational programs that break the cycle of poverty.* Westport, CT: Praeger.

Nieto, S. (2002). *Language, culture, and teaching: Critical perspectives for a new century.* Mahwah, NJ: Lawrence Erlbaum.

Noddings, N. (2005). *The challenge to care in schools* (2nd ed.). New York: Teachers College Press.

Northwest Regional Educational Laboratory (2003). Overview of second language acquisition theory. Retrieved January 2, 2009, from http://www.nwrel.org/request/2003may/overview.html

Nunan, D. (1997). Listening in language learning. *The Language Teacher* http://www.jalt-publications.org/tlt/files/97/sep/nunan.html

Ovando, C. J., Collier, V. P., & Combs, M. C. (2005). *Bilingual and ESL classrooms: Teaching in multicultural contexts (4th ed.).* New York: McGraw Hill.

Paquette, K. R., Fello, S. & Jalongo, M. R. (2007). The Talking Drawings Strategy: Using primary children's illustrations and oral language to improve comprehension of expository text. *Early Childhood Education Journal, 35*(1), 65–73.

Parker, E. L, & Pardini, T. H. (2006). *The words came down: English language learners read, write, and talk across the curriculum, K–2.* Portland, ME: Stenhouse.

Proctor, C. P., August, D., Carlo, M.S., & Snow, C. (2006). The intriguing role of Spanish language vocabulary knowledge in predicting English reading comprehension. *Journal of Educational Psychology, 98*(1), 159–169.

Purdy, J. (2008). Inviting conversation: Meaningful talk about texts for English Language Learners. *Literacy, 42*(1), 44–51.

Rogers, C. L., Lister, J. J., Febo, D. M., Besing, J. M., & Abrams, H. B. (2006). Effects of bilingualism, noise, and reverberation on speech perception by listeners with normal hearing. *Applied Psycholinguistics, 27*(3), 465–485.

Rose, J. (2006). Independent review of the teaching of early reading: Final report. London, UK; The Rose Review Support Team. Retrieved January 13, 2010 from www.standards.dfes.gov.uk/phonics/report.pdf

Rothenberg, C. & Fisher, D. (2007). *Teaching English language learners: A differentiated approach.* Upper Saddle River, NJ: Pearson/Merrill Prentice Hall.

Saracho, O. N. (2007). A literacy program for fathers: A case study. *Early Childhood Educational Journal, 35*(4), 351–356.

Schultz, K. (2003). *Listening: A framework for teaching across differences.* New York: Teachers College Press.

Skouge, J. R., Rao, K., & Boisvert, C. (2007). Promoting early literacy for diverse learners using audio and video technology. *Early Childhood Education Journal, 35*(1), 5–11.

Smith, C. (2008). How can parents model good listening skills? Retrieved January 13, 2010 from www.eric.ed.gov/ERICWebPortal/recordDetail?accno=ED376481.

Snedeker, J., & Trueswell, J. C. (2004). The developing constraints on parsing decisions: T he role of lexical-bases and referential scenes in child and adult sentence processing. *Cognitive Psychology, 49,* 238–299.

Snyder, T., & Hoffman, C. (2003). *Digest of educational statistics 2002* (NCES 2003–060). Washington, DC: National Center for Educational Statistics, U.S. Department of Education.

Soli, S.D., & Sullivan, J.A. (1997). Factors affecting children's speech communication in classrooms. *Journal of the Acoustical Society of America, 101,* S3070.

Song, H., & Fisher, C. (2005). Who's "she"? Discourse prominence influences preschoolers' comprehension of pronouns. *Journal of Memory and Language, 52,* 29–57.

Stelmachowicz, P.G., Hoover, B. M., Lewis, D. E., Kortekaas, R.W., & Pittman, A.L. (2000). The relation between stimulus context, speech audibility, and perception for normal-hearing and hearing-impaired children. *Journal of Speech, Language, and Hearing Research, 43,* 902–914.

Tabors, P. O. (2008). *One child, two languages: A guide for early childhood educators of children learning English as a second language.* Baltimore: Paul H. Brooks.

Thomas, W.P., & Collier, V.P. (2002). *A national study of school effectiveness for language minority students' long-term academic achievement.* Santa Cruz, CA: Center for Research on Education, Diversity & Excellence. Retrieved January 12, 2009, from http://crede.berkeley.edu/research/llaa/1.1pdfs/1.1_10northwest.pdf

U.S. Census Bureau. (2003). Language use and English-speaking ability: 2000. Census 2000 Brief. Issued October 2003. Washington, DC: Author. Available from www.census.gov/prod/cen2000/doc/sf3.pdf

Vandergrift, L. (2006). Second language listening: Listening ability or language proficiency? *The Modern Language Journal, 90*(1), 6–18.

Wolvin, A.D., & Coakley, C.G. (2000). Listening education in the 21st century. *International Journal of Listening, 12,* 143–152.

Zelasko, N., & Antunez, B. (2000). *If your child learns in two languages: A parent's guide for improving educational opportunities for children acquiring English as a second language.* Washington, DC: National Clearinghouse for Bilingual Education.

PART II

LINGUISTICALLY AND CULTURALLY DIVERSE FAMILIES AND COMMUNITIES

CHAPTER 6

THE INTERFACE OF THE AMERICAN FAMILY AND CULTURE

Olivia N. Saracho

Teachers cannot hope to begin to understand who sits before them unless they can connect with the families and communities from which their children come. To do that it is vital that teachers and teacher educators explore their own beliefs and attitudes about non-white and non-middle-class people.

—Lisa Delpit (1996/2006)

ABSTRACT

Young children and their families represent an increasing diversity of language and culture. The National Association for the Education of Young Children (NAEYC, 2005) emphasizes that children need an environment that respects diversity and encourages their relationship with their families and community, as well as preserves children's home languages and cultural identities. Supporting young children's development requires that educators recognize, understand, respect, and accept cultural differences (Saracho & Martínez-Hancock, 2005). Since children and families represent different cultures, it is important to provide a brief overview of culture and how it affects young children.

Language and Cultural Diversity in Early Childhood Education, pages 117–146

CULTURE AND CHILDREN

Culture is characterized by a group of people's values, beliefs, behaviors, language, customs, and traditions (Saracho & Martínez-Hancock, 2005). There are many definitions of culture. Franz Boas began to use the term *culture* at the end of the nineteenth century to refer to the distinct body of customs, beliefs, and social institutions that seemed to characterize each separate society (Goodenough, 1971; Verdon, 2007). Boas (1908, 1910) believed that most of the individuals' customs have *unconscious* origins. According to Boas,

> Men act largely according to habit. The earlier in life the habit is inculcated the more difficult it is to alter, the more automatic is its action, and the stronger are the emotions associated with it. Habit is fundamentally activity, not thought; and thought about habitual activity is usually rationalization. (Boas, 1908, p. 280)

Boas felt that most customs are based on automatic and emotional responses to repetitive activities in which people act first and later justify their actions. Such customs develop unconsciously or consciously, and then vanish, while the people's explanations that they use to justify their customs may not have anything to do with their true origin, or *cause*, which makes them secondary in nature. In the Freudian view of the term, they are *rationalizations* (Verdon, 2007). Earlier, Goodenough (1957) thought that a society's culture was the knowledge that groups of people needed to know or believe in order to appropriately function and perform in an acceptable way in their community. Culture is the individuals' way of thinking, perceiving, associating, and interpreting.

Goodenough (2001) considers culture to be an "information pool." Real culture is in the culture messengers' frame of mind. Consequently, culture is the information that individuals must know about their heritage to function successfully within their society. Culture is composed of an assemblage of values, assumptions, customs, physical objects, clothing, houses, food, tools, and art that a cluster of individuals have endorsed to provide structure to their daily life (Stassen-Berger & Thompson, 2000). Additional cultural elements include geography, history, architecture, religion, folk medicine, music, dance, and socialization practices. Gender, class, race, and culture are major elements that influence the individual's identity development (Robinson, 1993). Stassen-Berger and Thompson (2000) assume that culture and ethnicity are comparable and interconnect. An ethnic group consists of a group of individuals with similar antecedent characteristics (such as national origin, religion, upbringing, and language), beliefs, values, and cultural experiences.

CULTURAL DIFFERENCES

Children's development also requires that their cultural differences be recognized, understood, respected, and accepted (Saracho & Martínez-Hancock, 2005). For example, Laosa (1980) studied Mexican American mothers and their child-rearing interactions, and found that differences were related to social class within ethnic and immigrant populations. Bowman (1994) discusses the difficulty of making generalizations concerning minority groups. She asserts that poverty complicates the understanding of culture. She questions the impact that the social class environment, as opposed to an ethnic group's cultural norms, has on its members' cultural differences, and believes that it is important to make this distinction between social class environment and cultural norms. In her book, *Poverty: A Framework for Understanding and Working with Students and Adults from Poverty*, Payne (1995) presents a framework that helps understand the way poverty influences the concept of time (i.e., living for the present versus living for the future to meet survival needs). She describes in detail the importance of learning the middle-class rules. Payne (1995) does not hold the students responsible for their own problems; rather, she proposes how educators can develop relationships with students as a means to give them the support they need to succeed. She explains that poverty students have limited options.

There are differences between schools' and families' beliefs, which lead to differences in their goals for children. The National Association for the Education of Young Children (NAEYC) encourages concern and respect for the family, and they identify and support the concept of "culturally appropriate practices" in early childhood education (Copple & Bredekamp, 2009; NAEYC, 1996, 2005). Although teachers attempt to know the children and their families, they find it difficult to identify the children's strengths. Still, teachers must assess their own attitudes, biases, and stereotypes, and develop family relationships, attentively observe, communicate, and make a commitment to move toward more family-centered practices. Such progression requires that teachers acquire an ethical commitment to provide child-centered and family-centered practices. First, they need to assess their own attitudes, biases, prejudices, and stereotypes to be able to develop an integrated multicultural and anti-bias curriculum for all children (York, 1998). Family-centered practice recognizes the importance of the family organization for child development, respects families as decision-makers, and supports families in their role as parents (McBride, 1999).

Children are born and socialized in a family environment to become productive citizens in their society. Family members belong to various cultures (Culturally and Linguistically Appropriate Services, 2002). The children's hereditary environment makes them unique individuals within their family of origin and cultural heritage.

FAMILY SUPPORT

Children's emotional and academic success depends on the support of their significant others. Supportive relationships, such as the family's positive encouragement, contributes to their school success (Prelow & Loukas, 2003). Steidel and Contreras (2003) credit this support to *familism*, which is based on the family members' commitment to the family and to family relationships. Familism has three dimensions: *structural*, *behavioral*, and *attitudinal*. The *structural* dimension refers to the spatial and social boundaries that establish the presence or absence of nuclear and extended family members (for instance, the number of adult relatives who live within driving distance of the family's home). The *behavioral* dimension of familism refers to the behavioral feelings and attitudes about the family (for instance, those family members who contact the family through telephone calls or visits) (Valenzuela & Dornbusch, 1994). The *attitudinal* dimension of familism refers to the cultural value that establishes the children's identity that is attached to their nuclear and extended families. It also includes their strong feelings of loyalty, reciprocity, and solidarity for their family members (Cauce & Domenech-Rodriguez, 2002). Burgess, Locke, and Thomes (1963) define *attitudinal familism* to be

> 1) the feeling on the part of all members that they belong pre-eminently to the family group and that all other persons are outsiders; 2) complete integration of individual activities for the achievement of family objectives; 3) the assumption that land, money, and other material goods are family property, involving the obligation to support individual members and give them assistance when they are in need; 4) willingness of all members to rally to the support of a member if attacked by outsiders; and 5) concern for the perpetuation of the family as evidenced by helping adult offspring in beginning and continuing an economic activity in line with family expectations and in setting up a new household (pp. 35–36)

Familial support is the practice of offering any necessary assistance to nuclear or extended family members in their everyday life. Such a component of attitudinal familism is based on the idea that family members support each other during difficult times. Familism is the basic meaning for the family's culture and has attracted the researchers' interests, because of its anticipated outcomes. Most researchers, except George (1986), define attitudinal familism in a similar way as Burgess et al. (1963). George (1986) added to the definition that family members need to maintain closeness.

Recently, Steidel and Contreras (2003) wanted to create a clear and comprehensive definition of attitudinal familism, and, thus, identified and combined several components from several theoretical definitions. Steidel and Contreras (2003) showed that attitudinal familism is composed of the following structural elements:

1. *Familial Interconnectedness* provides family members with both physical and emotional support, including spending and cherishing time with relatives. This element of attitudinal familism demonstrates the belief that the family should have a strong emotional and physical loyalty. Although the family members continue to have an independent personal life, families live near each other to participate in their everyday lives.
2. *Familial Honor* is the practice of protecting and defending the family's name and integrity. This element of attitudinal familism demonstrates the belief that family members have the responsibility to maintain, protect, and defend the family's name and honor.
3. *Subjugation of Self for Family* requires family members to respect and obey the family's rules. This element of attitudinal familism demonstrates the belief that family is more important than each individual member. Therefore, the family's needs are met, even at the expense of the other family members' personal needs and wishes (cited in Saracho, 2007b, p. 405).

Research on families needs to merge these factors with other variables in the studies, because such factors identify vital information related to the individuals' psychological performance (Steidel & Contreras, 2003).

The sociological literature views familism as the traditional allegiance of family members to the family and to family relationships. The family's support determines their children's emotional, personal, and intellectual success (Prelow & Loukas, 2003). The family's support and involvement in school and non-school learning is a critical element in the children's educational success (Bernal et al., 2000). Families contribute to their children's successful development and their daily lives. Family and school learning differ in life characteristics, including child rearing practices, values, and education. For instance, schools may believe that children need to learn to be both obedient and independent, that is, "to submit to rules which protect the rights of others, and to develop a progressive independence" (Johnson 1985, p. 123); while families and communities may be more nurturing. Families and schools may have similar values and educational goals; but they differ in their beliefs, expectations, and goals for young children. Children are challenged when they have to substitute the school's values for their family values. The schools need to accept and respect the culture and context of the different family groups. The school needs to consider (1) family and community elements outside the school and (2) shared values, trust, expectations, and obligations (Redding, 2001), including those of children from immigrant groups.

IMMIGRANT FAMILIES

A large number of immigrants has migrated and continues to migrate into the United States (Bhavnagri & Krolikowski, 2000). Between 1900 and 1910, a total of 8.9 million immigrants entered the United States, while between 1980 and 1990, the number increased to 9.5 million immigrants (Fix & Zimmermann, 1993). "The United States Immigration Commission reported that in 1909, 57.8 percent of the children in the schools of the nation's thirty–seven largest cities were of foreign-born parentage. In New York City the percentage was 71.5, in Chicago 67.3, and in San Francisco it was 57.8" (Weiss, 1982, p. xiii). At least 54 nationalities have been enrolled in the New York City public schools (Hunt, 1976). New York teachers declared that the arrival of every ship amplified their class enrollment. For example, if the immigrants "landed on Saturday, they settled on Sunday, and reported to school on Monday" (Berrol, 1976/1991, p. 28).

Before this massive immigration, the public schools were already ineffective, corrupt, completely politicized, and totally inadequate (Berrol, 1976/1991). In New York, immigration progressed and changed the schools, causing them to expand their services, adding kindergartens, high schools, vacation schools, social service programs, and curriculum modifications. The schools' purpose was to provide normal American experiences to the immigrant children from different cultures. Dewey (1915, 1916) promoted progressive education as the foundation for learning how to participate in a democratic society. During the Reform Era, reformers and public school educators focused on standardizing the various ethnic immigrants to acculturate through "universalism" and "democratization and Americanization of citizenry through compulsory schooling," and ignored reinforcing individual ethnic identity through "celebrating diversity" and "cultural pluralism" (Bhavnagri & Krolikowski, 2000).

Recently, the African American and Hispanic populations have been quickly expanding, indicating that by the year 2020 these school-age children will be the predominant group in the public schools (Berliner & Biddle, 1995). The United States Bureau of Census (1997) showed that the number of immigrant children continues to increase in the American schools. However, the immigrants are from different geographic regions than those in the past. Now, immigrants are from all topographical territories. Society and the schools have had a reaction similar to that of the

New York public schools to this ceaseless increase of immigrants, developing programs and strategies such as bilingual education, English as a second language, and California's Proposition 227. Moreover, the public schools continue to make critical modifications in an effort to offer these immigrants an education that will help them succeed in society (Saracho & Spodek, 2005).

Currently, immigrants in the United States are mostly from Latin America and the Caribbean, as well as Asia (Adler & Gielen, 2003). Foner (2001) refers to Caribbean immigrants to New York as *Islands in the City*. Documented and undocumented new immigrants persist in coming, and cluster in several states, especially New York and California, with large concentrations of immigrants that attend sub-standard schools in underprivileged urban neighborhoods in major metropolitan areas, such as Los Angeles, Miami, and Houston. Suarez-Orozco (2001) estimates that one out of five children in the United States is from an immigrant family. The young children of immigrants need to be provided with culturally-appropriate early childhood educational experiences.

Immigrants have different patterns of adjustment to a new society (Adler & Gielen, 2003). When they arrive in the United States, they differ in the level of training, education, language skills, and economic resources. Most societies around the world know about life in the United States. Many immigrants from Asia, the Caribbean, Mexico, and other Latin American countries learn about "American cultural values" through the media and communication with relatives who mail allowances and merchandise to them, and take a trip to the United States as guest workers or visitors. Current immigrants are more knowledgeable about life in the United States than their ancestors who migrated to the United States decades ago. As a result, the acculturation or adjustment of immigrant families and children in the United States differs. Their cultural pride, focus on ethnic identity, socialization, and values vary in their acculturation process (Roopnarine & Metindogan, 2005).

Numerous typologies on the ways that immigrants adapt to their new culture have been identified. Roopnarine, Bynoe, and Singh (2004) identified the following typologies:

- *Synchronous pattern of adjustment*: Immigrant families take the socialization and education values from their birth culture and combine them with those in their new society when they increasingly come into contact with those predominate members in their new society. They replace their beliefs and practices with those that help them function in their new society. Families provide their children with a good deal of support for their educational efforts. Their parent–

teacher communications and educational goals focus on the children's best possible school success.

- *Staggered patterns of adjustment*: Immigrant families retain their well-established birth, childrearing, and education beliefs throughout the preliminary adjustment stage, but renounce and/or alter them steadily as they become more firmly embedded in the United States. Families may encounter some dissonance when children adopt the school's socialization values and principles, and families are compelled to accordingly modify several childrearing practices and belief systems about schooling, health, and childrearing (Berry, 1998). Families tend to focus on the values they were raised with, which causes them to develop their expectations about schooling, and parent–teacher partnerships evolve over time.
- *Asynchronous* and *disorganized/disoriented patterns of adjustment*: Families and their children have many difficulties compressing and conforming to their life in a new country. In the *asynchronous adjustment patterns of adjustment*, families have rigid childrearing values and beliefs (e.g., strict discipline, traditional husband/wife roles, etc.) that were appropriate in their old country, and strongly advocate that they are transferred and implemented in the United States. They believe that the childrearing values are a drawback of life in America, because parents are very lenient with their children and it seems to them that children have more rights than their parents, including the right to ignore their parental authority. Parents may use improvised strategies in their childrearing practice, while their children challenge the inherent problems of their birth culture value systems (e.g., harsh discipline, unilateral respect for older members of the family, total obedience). Disagreements between the family and school systems cause parents to increasingly become separated from their children and the schooling practice. The *disorganized/disoriented* parents' and children's relationship increasingly declines in quality. Families encounter severe adjustment and acculturation problems. They may become isolated from their community and may permanently join the urban *underclass* (Portes & Zhou, 1993). Parent–child relationships become tense and parents become detached from the schools that refer them to social or psychological services. As a result, school effects become unpredictable (Roopnarine & Metindogan, 2005).

Research studies have not examined these categorizations; therefore, they remain tentative. They offer an initial attempt to avoid far-reaching descriptions to explain immigrant adjustment to American society. Some families are successful when they arrive in the United States, and are able to progress from "inner city to suburb" and from "the mailroom to the boardroom." Other researchers need to consider economic needs and cultural/linguistic differences with methods of childrearing and schooling practices that focus on democratic principles, as well as simple and non-punishable ways to discipline children. Many immigrants are able to function in more than one culture, and children are able to make a back-and-forth transition for schooling and cultural identity reasons (e.g., parachute children in Los Angeles, Asian Indians, and African Caribbeans). A few surrender to their own failure to meet the daily needs of their families and children and may become defenseless, abandoning the dominant society completely (Zhou, 1997).

Childrearing Beliefs and Practices

The diverse immigrant groups' childrearing practices and styles have been examined for parenting style typologies and their meaning for childhood social and intellectual abilities. In addition, many researchers have examined the differences in parent–child interactions and childrearing beliefs and their meaning for childhood development across immigrant groups in the United States and other cultures (Brown, Larson, & Sarsawathi, 2002; Roopnarine & Gielen, 2004; Suarez-Orozco, 2001). Cultural and cross-cultural studies on childrearing beliefs and practices in the original cultures of immigrant groups in the United States show that

- Cultures (e.g., Taiwanese, Korean, Thai, East Indian) with Confucian and Buddhist religious traditions focus on calmness, self-restraint, behavioral self-consciousness, obedience to adults, and parental control of childhood activities, which parents consider to be appropriate for social development (Tulananda & Roopnarine, 2001).
- Cultures (e.g., Caribbean) with severe discipline and embarrassment child rearing practices attempt to control childhood behaviors. Physical punishment to discipline children is still customary in several cultural groups (Roopnarine & Metindogan, 2005).

Cultural Play Beliefs

Parents of young children differ in their cultural beliefs about (1) the value and meaning of play, (2) the importance of academic learning, and (3) the assignment of large amounts of homework. Families from developing countries (e.g., Caribbean, Latin American) minimize the importance of play for the development of early social and cognitive skills. Both immigrant and non-immigrant parents in the United States emphasize the value of academic activities such as reading, learning the alphabet, and basic mathematics, and place less emphasis on play. Many immigrant parents, including those from the English-speaking Caribbean, think that it is important to assign daily homework assignments to help preschool children improve academic skills that are taught in school. Many teachers use a combination of academic strategies in play-based programs for European American children (Roopnarine, Shin, Jung, & Hossain, 2003).

HISPANIC AMERICAN FAMILIES

One out of seven children in the United States is from a different culture. Since the size and characteristics of the different cultural groups have been growing, this development is reflected in the population of young children (Saracho & Martínez-Hancock, 2005). Since 1976, culturally different children between the ages of birth and four years have increased; therefore, Oxford (1984) estimated an increase of 5.1 million in the year 2000. Currently, there are more than two million young children who are culturally different (Macias, 2000) in the public schools. The *Survey of the states' limited English proficient students and available educational programs and services: 1999–2000 Summary Report* showed that there were more than 400 languages spoken by Limited English Proficiency (LEP) students nationwide, and the great majority (77%) of LEP students had Spanish as their native language (Kindler, 2002). In addition, it is estimated that by the year 2020, the culturally different population will grow to more than five million, and for the group of those who have Spanish as their birth language, its number will triple by the year 2050 (National Coalition of Advocates for Students, 1988; Natriello, McDill, & Pallas, 1990). Thus, the majority of LEP students will be Hispanic children. Hispanic children are often labeled *at-risk* because of their lack of language proficiency. Schools have used conventional instructional strategies that have caused them to fail and continue to be at-risk throughout their school years (Saracho & Spodek, 2002).

Most Hispanic children rely on the support of significant others to succeed personally and academically. Research shows that supportive relationships (such as their families' positive encouragement) influences their school achievement (Prelow & Loukas, 2003). Such support is vital for Hispanic immigrant children who encounter challenges, such as a new country, a new language, and a new culture (Chavkin & Feyl-Gonzalez, 2000; Sands & Plunkett, 2005). Hispanic immigrant children need experiences in which they develop and practice their new language, both in the classroom and in other contexts, such as the home environment. Hispanic families can offer unique types of support that will promote their children's education. They can contribute to their children's language and literacy development in their real life and the real world (Quezada, Díaz, & Sánchez, 2003).

Researchers have found that the family's involvement in school and non-school learning is the most crucial component in Hispanic children's educational success (Bernal et al., 2000). The family's support is the basis upon which children can build personal and academic success (Prelow & Loukas, 2003), particularly those Hispanic children who are confronted with a different language and culture (Chavkin & Feyl-Gonzalez, 2000; Sands & Plunkett, 2005) in the school. Hispanic families' involvement can improve the children's academic and language learning (Quezada, Díaz, & Sánchez, 2003).

Since the Hispanic population has grown in both size and diversity, researchers have identified family characteristics that encourage their children's positive development (Rodriquez & Morrobel, 2004; Sands & Plunkett, 2005). Steidel and Contreras (2003) found that relatively unacculturated and primarily Hispanic families had the following schemes:

- *Familial Support*: Family members support immediate or extended family members in times of need and in everyday life.
- *Familial Interconnectedness*: Family members are both physically and emotionally close to each other, including those relatives who spend and value their time together.
- *Familial Honor*: Family members assume responsibility to protect the family name and defend any attacks against the family's integrity.
- *Subjugation of Self for Family*: Family members are submissive to and respect the family's rules. (cited in Saracho, 2007a, p. 105)

MEXICAN AMERICAN FAMILIES

Among Spanish speakers and other cultural groups, one of the largest cultural groups in the United States is the Mexican American group. They view themselves as America's forgotten minority. The Mexican American family's purpose is based on its essential needs, perceptions, and roles. According to Bigner (1994), the roles in the family systems justify acceptable behaviors and control their working system.

Family Roles

Mexican American families rely on their family's basic human needs, their perceptions, and their functions. Although society has identified them as passive, their constitutive role continues to increase in the industrial, agricultural, artistic, intellectual, and political life of the country. Mexican

American families' most important values are their relationships with the family, leisure time activities, and the Catholic church. They perform rituals on religious or national holidays and retain their folkways and customs such as (1) accepting authority in the home, church, and state, (2) being personally loyal to friends, (3) being responsive to praise and criticism, and (4) exercising folk medicine. Their economic condition and social status varies with each family (Saracho & Martínez-Hancock, 2005).

Mexican American families usually respond to others' feelings and follow their rules of conduct, such as respect for the status of others. Age and sex determine the roles and status in their culture. Older family members have a higher status and are given higher respect than others in the community. They appreciate their life experiences and knowledge of the history of the community, culture, and ethnic group (Ramírez & Castañeda, 1974). At a very young age, children learn to respect all elders, but give parents a special respect.

Family roles are based on age. The eldest children have more responsibilities, but their status is based on the quality with which the children complete their responsibilities. Larger families give older children the responsibility to socialize, teach, or tutor their younger siblings. Such socialization practices facilitate the classroom teachers' instructional organization of learning experiences. Culturally knowledgeable Mexican American children and young adults who inherently performed these social roles and behaviors are usually considered to be "well educated." Mexican American families believe that being socially well educated is more important than being academically well educated. Children who satisfactorily perform their responsibilities and who carry out appropriate behaviors bestow honor on their family in the eyes of the community (Saracho & Martínez-Hancock, 2005).

Family Values

Most of the values in the traditional Mexican American culture are similar to those of other ethnic groups, but they are very different from the typical American school's values. These traditional values are related to those values that are distinctive of communities that are (1) rural, (2) located near the Mexican border, and (3) inhabited by primarily Mexican American families. Assimilation and outside factors may affect the maintenance of the core traditional values that influence Mexican American families' behavior without considering any transformations that have developed within the Mexican American females (Ramírez & Castañeda,1974; Saracho & Martínez-Hancock, 2005). According to Valdés (1996), Mexican American children have functioning roles in the family. They have to respect and obey their parents, take care of their siblings, and to meet family goals. Valdés (1996) believes that these socialization practices conflict with the values of the school culture. Since this is a social class dilemma, the individuals in these situations know what they need to do to survive. One of the Ten Commandments for Mexican American Catholic families is to honor their parents. Since faith in the Mexican American family's religion is important, this becomes an important commandment.

Educators need to implement the wealth of the Mexican American home-based knowledge in their school-based practices to create a strong groundwork that can guide Mexican American children's learning and school success (Ortiz & Ordoñez-Jasis, 2005), including establishing collaborative programs. School and community collaborative programs must use the Mexican American families' cultural values to (1) concentrate on personal contacts, (2) encourage communication, (3) offer a warm and positive environment, and (4) adjust to the families' needs to reinforce their involvement (Quezada, Díaz, & Sánchez, 2003). Goldenberg and Gallimore (1991) encourage teachers to merge the children's school learning with their home and community values to promote Mexican American children's learning. Families can actively engage in their children's learning if teachers integrate the wealth of home-based knowledge with school-based practices to develop a framework for the children's school success (Saracho, 2007a).

AMERICAN-INDIAN FAMILIES

Since the first contact between the Europeans and indigenous citizens, issues on American-Indian[1] children's education and socialization have been challenged. The term *first contact* usually conjures a vision of European soldiers landing on a beach in the New World, their ship anchored just offshore, while a large cluster of Natives moves toward the soldiers. Both groups are careful, but they are also curious. Beyond the physical confrontation of two groups, there is also a metaphysical clash between different cultural styles for understanding reality and establishing truth, and viewing their relationship within physical and spiritual contexts. In brief, several, possibly incompatible, understandings of cosmology, jurisprudence, and religion are communicated (Russell, 2009).

When early childhood education is considered today, history is inescapable. The prevailing American culture continuously banned American-Indian cultures, educational traditions, and child rearing practices (Hubbs-Tait, Tait, Hare, & Huey, 2005). The imposition of the Euro-American educational system intruded in their lives. Hubbs-Tait, Tait, Hare, and Huey (2005) believe that the dislocation of American-Indian citizens and sending their children to boarding schools developed a legacy of dissonance and mistrust. Such a legacy and ongoing cultural discrepancies between American-Indian families and educational traditions limited educational parental involvement. Fixico (1998) states, "Historians, in particular, wrote Indians out of their textbooks for whatever insecure reasons of justifying the past actions of America's heroes, racial bigotry, or White guilt. By ignoring the dark episodes of the destruction of Indians and their cultures, historians in effect denied that these ever happened" (p. 86). Hawthorne (1967) states:

> It is difficult to imagine how an Indian child attending an ordinary public school could develop anything but a negative self-image. First, there is nothing from his culture represented in the school or valued by it. Second, the Indian child often gains the impression that nothing he or other Indians do is right when compared to what non-Indian children are doing. Third, in both segregated and integrated schools, one of the main aims of teachers expressed with reference to Indians is to "to help them improve their standards of living, or their general lot, or themselves," which is another way of saying that what they are and have now is not good enough, they must do and be other things. (p. 142)

In March of 1824, President James Monroe founded The Office of Indian Affairs in the Department of War to focus on the country's issues concerning Indian affairs. According to Kevin Gover[2] (2000), in the past, the Office of Indian Affairs intensely hurt American-Indian communities. Their initial goal was to remove the southeastern tribal nations. The Office of Indian Affairs used threat, deceit, and force to make the tribal nations march 1,000 miles to the west and leave thousands of their old, young, and ill in graves along the "Trail of Tears." They attempted to conveniently extinguish the American Indian cultures. After annihilating tribal economies and deliberately making the tribes dependent on the agency's services, the Office of Indian Affairs attempted to destroy the American Indians' language and culture. It prohibited them from speaking their Indian languages and engaging in traditional religious activities, banned the traditional government, and humiliated the American Indians' identity. The Office of Indian Affairs was supposed to serve the American-Indian population, but instead it executed these actions against the American-Indian children and provided emotional maltreatment to the American-Indian children who were in its boarding schools.

Presently, the Bureau of Indian Affairs (BIA) is an advocate for American Indians in an environment that communicates mutual respect. However, the legacy of the historical transgressions continues to be disturbing. The trauma of shame, fear, and anger persists through generations. Apparently, most of the American Indians' current problems (e.g., poverty, ignorance, disease) are the results of the historical offenses of the BIA (Gover, 2000). The BIA is attempting to commit to the people and communities that it serves, renew the hope and prosperity of American tribal communities, and protect them from the following:

- Hate and violent crimes committed against them
- Policies that humiliate them due to the assumption that they have less human genius than other races
- Those who attempt to steal their property
- Appointments of false leaders who serve purposes that conflict with those of the tribes
- Critical and stereotypical images that deface government halls or guide the American people to develop superficial and misinformed beliefs about American Indians
- Any attacks on their religion, language, rituals, or any of their tribal customs
- Having their children seized
- Those who teach their children to be ashamed of their identify

Non-Indian scholars began to write about these injustices. For example, Lucien Lévy-Bruhl, a professor of philosophy at the Sorbonne[3] from 1899 to 1927, was a French philosopher who wrote on the psychology of primitive people. His work provided anthropology with a new technique for understanding irrational factors in social thought and primitive religion and mythology. Since he believed that the theoretical moralities could succeed, he devoted his work to the mentality of people in so-called primitive societies, which he first investigated and described at length (Lévy-Bruhl, 2009) in his (1910/1985) book, *How Natives Think (Les Fonctions Mentales dans les Sociétés Inférieures)*. He theorized that American Indians were undeveloped and uncivilized individuals; were inferior races; had primitive, savage, and unintelligible mentalities; and had simple and naïve reasoning procedures.

Non-Indian researchers also reported that American-Indian children were deficient in their natural intelligence and their capacity to succeed in formal school programs (Guthrie, 2004). Fixico (1998) declare that it is ethically wrong to use research to destabilize the fair historical representation of other peoples, leaders, and non-mainstream situations. Mihesuah (1993) argues that researchers need to carefully examine their purpose for conducting research and to avoid considering American-Indian populations as curiosities. Smith (1999) believes that the word *research* is inevitably associated with European imperialism and colonialism:

> The word itself, "research" is probably one of the dirtiest words in the Indigenous world's vocabulary. When mentioned in many indigenous contexts, it stirs up silence, it conjures up bad memories, and it raises a smile that is knowing and distrustful. It is so powerful that indigenous people even write poetry about research. The ways in which scientific research is implicated in the worst excesses of colonialism remains a powerful remembered history for many of the world's colonized people. It is a history that still offends the deepest sense of our humanity. (p. 1)

In addition, Spindler and Spindler (1994) support this problematic research concept. These anthropologists have encountered similar problems when they conducted cultural studies. According to Spindler and Spindler (1994), "Psychological anthropologists are not left in a chartless swamp of cultural particulars for they have encountered the human psyche, as well as culture, and the interactions and combinations of both become their subject matter" (p. 4).

At the beginning of a new millennium, Gover (2000) believes that life for the American tribal communities will improve. However, Russell (2009) believes that the ghosts of the past cultural conflicts will continue to haunt them. Just like their ancestors, they will continue to wonder how to deal with their culture (e.g., cosmology, jurisprudence, religion) and the demands of modern American culture in a way that allows both cultures to merge without the more destructive components.

Cultural Values

Researchers show that American-Indian students have unique cultural values, such as conforming to authority and respect for elders, taciturnity, intense tribal social hierarchy, patrimonial/matrilineal tribes, and a focus on learning, which are strongly based on the teachings of their elders. Such cultural attributes are observed in the family socialization configurations that are characteristic of their particular ethnic groups (Yellow Bird, 2001; Yellow Bird & Snipp, 2002). Guthrie (2004) believes that information can assist educators to understand the current problems concerning American-Indian education.

Most tribal nations used their own very diverse educational systems, which were culturally responsive to the American Indians' needs. Their educational system consisted of informally observing the children and having the children informally interact with parents, relatives, elders, and religious and social groups. The American Indians' traditional educational practices helped their children to acquire the necessary skills to appropriately function within their natural environment in any tribal society (Pewewardy, 2002).

Before the arrival of the Europeans, American-Indian parents, relatives, and elders informally educated young American Indians. They had a wide range of Indian educational systems, studying tribal history and the natural world, undergoing religious training, and learning respect for elders. American Indians usually favored their own methods rather than the European ones. In 1744, the colonial Virginia legislature proposed to educate six youths at the College of William and Mary, but an Iroquois spokesperson graciously and firmly refused the proposal. Previously, a number of Iroquois had been at northern colleges. When they returned home, they were not capable of performing expected responsibilities in their society, or even appropriately speaking the language (DeJong, 1999). However, several other Eastern tribes appreciated the European education, and some members received a European general education equal to that of their non-Indian peer classmates (Hale, 2002).

American-Indian cultural values are essential in American Indians' learning. These cultural values should be integrated into instructional methods for American Indian students. Essentially, these methods are based on the belief that American-Indian students are strongly influenced by their language, culture, and heritage. Even though their way of learning is different, it is effective (Pewewardy, 2002).

Home Learning Environment

Studies on home learning show a difference between American-Indian children and middle-class European American children. Hubbs-Tait, Tait, Hare, and Huey (2005) identified several of these differences, which focus on (1) nonverbal, rather than verbal, communication, (2) oral storytelling, rather than reading, (3) non-English home language, (4) warmer and supportive parenting, and (5) promotion of American-Indian autonomy.

- *Nonverbal rather than verbal communication* (Long & Christensen, 1998; Seideman et al., 1994). The meaning of certain kinds of nonverbal activities differs among American Indians. The Lakota focus on traditional dance (Zimiga, 1982); the Navajo, Yaqui, Kwakuitl, and Pueblo children depend on a visual method to learn; the Navajo, Lakota, and Yaqui children learn through an observation–practice–demonstration approach (Swisher & Deyhle, 1989); and the parents of Papago (Tohono O'odham) children use a nonverbal modeling and gesturing technique (Macias, 1987). These cultural differentiations are academic strengths that can be integrated into their learning (Swisher & Deyhle, 1989). Although there are few studies on the use of nonverbal instructional techniques with American-Indian children, research supports visual learning, demonstration–observation–practice (Plank, 1994; Swisher & Deyhle, 1989), and activity-based instruction. Activity-based instruction shows considerable increases in science achievement scores for American-Indian children (Zwick & Miller, 1986).
- *Oral storytelling rather than reading* (Levin, Moss, Swartz, Khan, & Tarr, 1997). For instance, Yaqui parents prefer to tell stories and share information about Yaqui culture and tradition, rather than reading books. Of those Yaqui parents who participated in the Even Start

program, the staff estimated that 40% read books and approximately 80% told stories to children (Levin et al., 1997). Akaran and Fields (1997) describe how the parents' oral storytelling with Yup'ik kindergarten children has been successfully implemented to promote the children's early literacy development.

- *Non-English home language.* Before the end of the 20th century, several tribes and countries lacked a written symbol system that would record their language (Boseker, 1994; Watahomigie & McCarty, 1994), which made it difficult to read books to American-Indian children in their native language. Public schools and Bureau of Indian Affairs schools used programs with language and culture of instruction that replaced the children's native language and culture, which may have decreased the language scores in young children. The differences between family and school language may have caused problems with parent–children communication and the children's language proficiency (NAEYC, 1996). At the beginning of the new millennium, the political surroundings may be negative, but the preservative language programs for American-Indian children seem to relate to their school success (e.g., Watahomigie & McCarty, 1994).
- *Warmer and more supportive parenting.* American Indians provide a home learning environment that is warmer and more commendable than the one of European American parents (Seideman et al., 1994). MacPhee, Fritz, and Miller-Heyl (1996) explored the social networks and parenting among 500 American-Indian (Ute, Navajo, Laguna Pueblo), Hispanic, and European American parents or guardians of children, ages two to five years of age. They found that American-Indian parents used the least physical punishment. Their warm and supportive parenting has been found to influence American-Indian children's school success. Whitbeck, Hoyt, Stubben, and LaFromboise (2001) examined the school success and positive school attitudes of 212 American-Indian children from three reservations in the upper Midwest. The children's reports were used to examine how often their mother encouraged them (They answered such questions as, "How often does your mother talk with you about things that bother you?"). The results showed that maternal support predicted the children's school success. The maternal supportiveness influenced their children's cognitive scores (Hubbs-Tait, Culp, Culp, & Miller, 2002), which emphasized the importance of emotional support in the American-Indian children's home learning environment.
- *Promotion of American-Indian autonomy.* American-Indian children receive a lower promotion of autonomy than European American

> children (Abraham, Christopherson, & Kuehl, 1984; MacPhee et al., 1996). It seems that autonomy promotion is absent in the American-Indian culture. The major concern may be the cultural differences in the meaning of autonomy. For example, autonomy promotion for Papago (Tohono O'odham) parents means avoiding pressuring children to comply with adult demands and respecting the children as individuals (Macias, 1987). Autonomy promotion encourages children to experiment with innovative ideas (Abraham et al., 1984).

The aforementioned differences in home learning environments (e.g., supportive parenting) between American-Indian and European American children relate to the school success within groups of American-Indian children. Information on American-Indian parents and community participation acknowledges that inter-nation, inter-tribe, and inter-band discrepancies in beliefs and practices may be as quantitatively great and as qualitatively meaningful as those dissimilarities between the majority culture and American-Indian parents (Littlebear, 1992).

Parental goals and encouragement are attributes that can lead to American-Indian children's school success. Most of the studies in the areas of American-Indian parent and community involvement were conducted with older children. Presently, the importance of the characteristics of both home and classroom learning environments with preschool children has been examined (e.g., Hubbs-Tait, Culp, Huey, et al., 2002), however, there is a need to examine approaches that are used with American-Indian children in a variety of contexts, with families who differ in educational backgrounds, parental involvement, and educational goals. American-Indian families have pleaded that their culture and values be integrated into the curriculum. Selecting American-Indian classroom teachers and administrators may facilitate this process (Hubbs-Tait, Tait, Hare, & Huey, 2005).

ECONOMICALLY CHALLENGED FAMILIES

Originally, the policy debates before the enactment of the 1996 Personal Responsibility and Work Opportunity Reconciliation Act (PRWORA) related to the well-being of low-income children. Several of the policy debates addressed whether children would benefit from reforms of welfare and employment policy. Some people argued that families may become motivated to work when their wages are increased and are able to become self-sufficient; this would provide role models for children and increase family resources to invest in their children. Others claimed that children may pay the price of welfare reform. Attempting to balance employment with family responsibilities adds to the parents' stress and has a negative impact on their parenting abilities, especially if children are left unsupervised or are provided with poor quality environments or unsafe care arrangements (Gennetian & Miller, 2002).

Bradley, Corwyn, McAdoo, and Coll (2001) found that the affects of being poor were predominant in all six environmental domains that they studied: from parental responsiveness to parental teaching, from the quality of the physical environment to the level of stimulation for learning that is accessible, and from the likelihood of being spanked to the likelihood of having major contact with the children's father. Furthermore, the poverty status made a significant difference.

Home Learning Environment

For more than half a century, researchers have investigated the impact of children's home environments. Present developmental theories suggest that children living in different environments encounter definite actions, objects, events, and conditions in various quantities and patterns (Bronfenbrenner, 1979, 1995). These results were similar in relation to ethnicity and poverty status (Bradley, Corwyn, McAdoo, & Coll, 2001). The theories also hypothesize that children give a different meaning to each environment they experience. For instance, ethnic groups differ in their perception of appropriate childrearing practices and developmental goals for their children (Greenfield, 1995). Deater-Deckard, Dodge, Bates, and Pettit (1996) show that harsh discipline may indicate an out-of-control, parent-centered environment for European Americans, whereas lack of physical discipline among African Americans may indicate a relinquishment of the parenting role. Bradley, Corwyn, McAdoo, and Coll (2001) examined the frequency with which children were exposed to various parental actions, materials, events, and conditions as part of their home environments, and how those exposures related to their well-being in relation to age, ethnicity, and poverty status. In a follow up study, Bradley, Corwyn, Burchinal, McAdoo, and Coll (2001) examined the relationship between major characteristics of the home environment (e.g., maternal responsiveness, learning stimulation, spanking) and developmental results for children whose ages ranged from birth to age 13, in both poor and non-poor European American, African American, and Hispanic American families. They found a relationship between (1) learning stimulation and children's developmental status; (2) parental responsiveness; and (3) spanking based on age, ethnicity, and poverty status. The relationship was slightly stronger for younger, as compared with older, children.

War on Poverty

The "War on Poverty" attracted educational psychology, developmental psychology, and sociology researchers to study low income families' needs. These researchers attempted to identify the home factors that contributed to the young children's success and failure in school. Coleman and his associates (1966) explained the status of Black families in America and their children's problems in becoming admitted to the educational system. Moynihan (1965) described the hurdles Black families encountered in national programs. Billingsley (1968) examined the sociology of Black families, while Blassingame (1972) developed an historical perspective on Black families.

The families' environmental situations were modified in an effort to diminish their poverty level. Such attempts were particularly important for those children who were at risk of educational and social failure. During the Reform Era, the "War on Poverty" assumed that the environment caused poverty, instead of the individuals' weak character, body, or intelligence (Handlin, 1982; Holbrook, 1983; Bremner, 1956). They assumed that if they changed the environment (e.g., offering satisfactory health care, housing, support services, public welfare), poverty could be reduced. This concept was implemented from 1890 to 1920 (Mattson, 1998) and from 1904 to 1920 (Shapiro, 1983), which was considered the Progressive Era. Currently, child advocates share the same belief that the United States can and should improve the situation of its children through radically altering their present environmental conditions and through reasonable reforms (Bhavnagri & Krolikowski, 2000; Children's Defense Fund, 1997).

The attributes of poor families and their children during the reform and today are comparable. Children of poverty have hazardous housing, have treacherous health, endure school failure, have an elevated school dropout rate, and have a higher risk of delinquency than children from wealthy families. Poor families lack the required education, knowledge, and resources to cultivate positive health and developmental learning (Bhavnagri & Krolikowski, 2000; National Center for Children in Poverty, 1990).

In the past and present periods, "welfare reform" has been different, but its usual authorized rationalization is the same—that is, to improve services for the poor. According to Trattner (1992), "conditions in today's inner cities are similar to those in our nineteenth-century ghettos and slums and . . . current attacks on the poor and the programs established to help them echo many of the sentiments expressed in the earlier dialogue" (p. xii). Poverty and welfare remain a cause of intense debate and argument concerning the function of the communities, government, law, philanthropy, economy, individual responsibility, and personal morality (Bhavnagri & Krolikowski, 2000).

CONCLUSION

The family and school domains have been viewed as isolated cultural territories, even thought they have always had an impact on one another. A culture of idiosyncrasy continues to be a fundamental premise in American society, the family, and the school. It is essential that researchers investigate the effect that the family and school have on each other and the challenges that they encounter, especially with linguistically and culturally diverse families. This information can be used to better prepare educators and to guide researchers in these areas to address the challenges. For more than two centuries, sociologists' philosophies have made an effort to cure many of the social afflictions to increase the perception of the power of family ties (Redding, 2001).

Family and school relationships continue to be a disjointed problem. Currently, it is essential that families (especially those families of different cultures) and schools join forces to improve and insure their success in the future (North Central Regional Educational Laboratory, 1996). When families and schools work together, children will be able to benefit throughout their education, from before the time they enter early childhood programs until they graduate from the public schools. Families and schools need to cooperate with each other to advance the present and future social challenges that affect the schools, children, and families (Saracho & Spodek, 2005).

REFERENCES

Abraham, K. G., Christopherson, V. A., & Kuehl, R. O. (1984). *Journal of Comparative Family Studies, 15,* 372–388.

Adler, L. & Gielen, U. (2003). (Eds.). *Immigration, emigration, and migration in international perspective.* Westport, CT: Praeger.

Akaran, S. E., & Fields, M. V. (1997). Family and cultural context: A writing breakthrough. *Young Children, 52*(4), 37–40.

Berliner, D. C. & Biddle, B. J. (1995) *The manufactured crisis: Myths, fraud, and the attack on America's public schools.* Reading, MA: Addison-Wesley.

Bernal, V., Gilmore, L. A., Mellgren, L., Melandez, J., Seleme-McDermott, C., & Vázquez, V. (2000). Hispanic fathers and family literacy: strengthening achievement in Hispanic communities. A report on a dialogue with community providers of services for Hispanic fathers, national Hispanic organizations, literacy programs, and advocates for fatherhood held on January 13, 2000. Washington, DC: U. S. Department of Health and Human Services, Hispanic Association of Colleges and Universities, and National Practitioners Network for Fathers and Families. Retrieved on August 11, 2009, from http://purl.access.gpo.gov/GPO/LPS20410 and http://fatherhood.hhs.gov/hispanic01/

Berrol, S. C. (1991/1976). School days on the old east side: The Italian and Jewish experience. In G. E. Pozzetta (Ed.), *American immigration & Ethnicity:*

A 20–volume series of distinguished essays :Vol. 10. Education and the immigrant (pp. 27–39). New York: Garland. Reprinted from *New York History,* (1976), *57*(2), 201–213.

Berry, J. W. (1998). Acculturation and health: Theory and research. In S. S. Kazarain & D. R. Evans (Eds.), *Cultural clinical psychology: Theory, research, and practice.* (pp. 39–57). New York: Oxford University Press.

Bhavnagri, N. P., & Krolikowski, S. (2000). Home-Community Visits During an Era of Reform (1870–1920). *Early Childhood Research & Practice (ECRP), 2*(1). http://ecrp.uiuc.edu/v2n1/bhavnagri.html

Bigner, J. J. (1994). Individual and family development: A lifespan interdisciplinary approach. Englewood Cliffs, NJ: Prentice Hall.

Bilingsley, A. (1968). *Black families in white America.* Englewood Cliffs, NJ: Prentice-Hall.

Blassingame, J. (1972). *The slave community.* New York: Oxford University Press.

Boas, F. (1908). Anthropology: A lecture delivered at Columbia University in the series on science, philosophy, and art in December 18, 1907. New York: The Columbia University Press. Reprinted in 1974 in G. Stocking, Jr, (Ed.) *The shaping of American anthropology, 1883–1911: a Franz Boas reader* (pp. 267–281). Chicago: University Press.

Boas, F. (1910). Psychological problems in anthropology. *The American Journal of Psychology, 21*(3), 371–384. Reprinted in 1974 in G. Stocking, Jr, (Ed.) *The shaping of American anthropology, 1883–1911: a Franz Boas reader* (pp. 243–253). Chicago: University Press.

Boseker, B. J., (1994). The disappearance of American Indian languages. *Journal of Multilingual and Multicultural Development, 15*(2–3), 147–160.

Bowman, B. T. (1994). *Cultural Diversity and Academic Achievement.* Retrieved on July 18, 2009, from http://www.ncrel.org/sdrs/areas/issues/educatrs/leadrshp/le0bow.htm

Bradley, R. H., Corwyn, R. F., Burchinal, M., McAdoo, H. P., & Coll, C. G. (2001). The home environments of children in the United States Part II: Relations with behavioral development through age thirteen. *Child Development, 72*(6), 1868–1886.

Bradley, R. H., Corwyn, R. F., McAdoo, H. P., & Coll, C. G. (2001). The home environments of children in the United States Part I: Variations by age, ethnicity, and poverty status. *Child Development, 72*(6), 1844–1867.

Bremner, R. H.(1956). *From the depths: The discovery of poverty in the United States.* New York: New York University.

Bronfenbrenner, U. (1979). *The ecology of human development.* Cambridge, MA: Harvard University Press.

Bronfenbrenner, U. (1995). The bioecological model from a life course perspective: Reflections of a participant observer. In P. Moen, G. H. Elder, & K. Luscher (Eds.), *Examining lives in context* (pp. 599–618). Washington, DC: American Psychological Association.

Bronfenbrenner, U. & Morris, P.A. (1998). The ecology of developmental processes. In R.M. Lerner (Ed.), Theory, Volume 1, *Handbook of child sychology (5th edition),* (pp. 993–1028). New York: Wiley.

Brown, B. B., Larson, R. & Sarsawathi, T. S. (Eds.). (2002). *The world's youth: Adolescence in eight regions of the globe.* New York: Cambridge University Press.

Burgess, E. W., Locke, H. J.,&Thomes, M. M. (1963). *The family: From institution to companionship* (3rd ed.). New York: American Book Company.

Cauce, A. M., & Domenech-Rodriguez, M. (2002). Latino families: Myths and realities. In J. M. Contreras, K. A. Kerns,&A. Neal-Barnett (Eds.), *Latino children and families in the United States: Current research and future directions* (pp. 3–25). New York: Praeger.

Chavkin, N., & Feyl-Gonzalez, J. (2000). *Mexican immigrant youth and resiliency: Research and promising programs.* Charleston, WV: ERIC Clearinghouse on Rural Education and Small Schools. (ERIC Document Reproduction Service No. ED447990)

Children's Defense Fund. (1997). *The state of America's children: Leave no child behind.* Washington, DC : Author.

Coleman, J. S., Campbell, E. Q., Hobson, C. J., McPartland, J., Mood, A. M., Weinfeld, F. D., & York, R. L. (1966). *Equality of educational opportunity.* Washington, D. C.: Government Printing Office, pp. 7–23.

Copple, C., & Bredekamp, S. (2009). *Developmentally appropriate practice in early childhood programs Seraing children from birth through age 8* (3rd ed.). Washington, D. C.: National Association for the Education of Young Children.

Culturally and Linguistically Appropriate Services. (CLAS, 2002). *Early Childhood Research Institute on Culturally and Linguistically Appropriate Services.* Retrieved on July 18, 2009, from http://clas.uiuc.edu/aboutclas.html

Deater-Decker, K., Dodge, K. A., Bates, J. E., & Pettit, G. S. (1996). Physical discipline among African American and European American mothers: Links to children's externalizing behaviors. *Developmental Psychology, 32,* 1065–1072.

DeJong, D. H. (1993). *Promises of the past: A history of Indian education.* Golden, CO: North American Press.

Delpit, L. (1996/2006). *Other people's children: Cultural conflict in the classroom* . New York: The New Press.

Dewey, J. (1915). *Schools of tomorrow.* New York: E. P. Dutton.

Dewey, J. (1916). *Democracy and education.* New York: Macmillan.

Deyhle, D., & Margonis, F. (1995). Navajo mothers and daughters: Schools, jobs, and the family. *Anthropology and Education Quarterly, 26,* 135–167.

Fix, M., & Zimmermann, W. (1993). *Educating immigrant children: in the changing city.* (Urban Institute Report 93–3) Washington DC: The Urban Institute.

Fixico, D. L. (1998). Ethics and responsibilities in writing American Indian history. In D. A. Mihesuah (Ed.), *Natives and academics: Researching and writing about American Indians* (pp. 84–99). Lincoln, NE: University of Nebraska Press.

Foner, N. (2001). *Islands in the City: West Indian migration to New York.* Berkeley, CA: University of California Press.

Gennetian, L, A., & Miller, C. (2002). Children and welfare reform: A view from an experimental welfare program in Minnesota. *Child Development, 73*(2), 601–620.

George, L. K. (1986). Caregiver burden: Conflict between norms of reciprocity and solidarity. In K. A. Pillemer & R. S. Wolf (Eds.),*Elder abuse: Conflict in the family* (pp. 67–92). Greenwood, CT: Auburn House.

Goldenberg, C.N., & Gallimore, R. (1991). Local knowledge, research knowledge, and educational change: A case study of early Spanish reading improvement. *Educational Researcher, 20*, 2–14.

Goodenough, W. (1957). *Cultural Anthropology and Linguistics.* In Report of the Seventh Annual Round Table Meeting on Linguistics and Language Study. Monograph Series on Languages and Linguistics, no. 9. Washington, DC: Georgetown University.

Goodenough, W. (1971). *Culture, language and society.* Module in Anthropology, no. 7. Reading, MA: Addison-Wesley.

Goodenough, W. (2001). *Theory and methodology. Lecture 17: Cognitive anthropology.* Retrieved June 30, 2009, from http://www.neurognosis.com/54.310/Lecture%2017%20-%20Cognitive20Anthropology.rft

Gover, K. (2000). Remarks of Kevin Gover, Assistant Secretary—Indian Affairs: Address to tribal leaders, *Journal of American Indian Education, 39*(2), 4–6.

Greenfield, P. M. (1995, Winter). Culture, ethnicity, race, and development: Implications for teaching theory and research. *SRCD Newsletter* (pp. 3, 4, 12). Chicago, IL: Society for Research in Child Development.

Guthrie, R. V. (2004). *Even the rat was white: A historical view of psychology.* Boston: Allyn and Bacon.

Hale, L. (2002). *Native American education: A reference handbook.* Santa Barbara: ABC-CLIO.

Handlin, O. (1982). Education and the European immigrant, 1820–1920. In B. J. Weiss (Ed.) *American education and the European immigrant: 1840–1940.* (pp. 3–16). Urbana: University of Illinois.

Hawthorne, H.B. (1967). *A survey of the contemporary Indians of Canada: Economic, political, educational needs and policies, Volume II.* Ottawa: Indian Affairs Branch.

Holbrook, T. (1983). Going among them: The evolution of the home visit. *Sociology and Social Welfare. 10*, 112–135.

Hubbs-Tait, L., Culp, A. M., Culp, R. E., & Miller, C. E. (2002). Relation of maternal cognitive stimulation, emotional support, and intrusive behavior during Head Start to children's kindergarten cognitive abilities. *Child Development, 73*, 110–131.

Hubbs-Tait, L., Tait, D., Hare, C., & Huey, E. (2005). Involvement of American Indian families in early childhood education. In O. N. Saracho & B. Spodek (Eds.) *Contemporary perspectives on families, communities and schools for young children.* (pp. 225–246). Greenwich, Connecticut: Information Age Publishing.

Hunt, T. (1976). The schooling of immigrants and Black Americans: Some similarities and differences. *Harvard Educational Review, 45*, 423–431.

Johnson, F. (1985). The Western concept of self. In A. J. Marsala, G. Demos, & F. L. K. HS (Eds.) *Culture and self: Asian and western perspectives* (pp. 91–140). London: Tavistock.

Kindler, A. L. (2002). *Survey of the states' limited English proficient students and available educational programs and services: 1999–2000 Summary Report.* Washington, DC.: National Clearinghouse for English Language Acquisition and Language Instruction Educational Programs, Office of English Language Acquisition, Language Enhancement and Academic Achievement for Limited English

Proficient Students. Retrieved on August 26, 2009, from http://www.ncela.gwu.edu/files/rcd/BE021854/Survey_of_the_States.pdf

Laosa, L. M. (1980). Maternal teaching strategies in Chicano and Anglo-American families: The influence of culture and education on maternal behavior. *Child Development, 51,* 759–765.

Levin, M., Moss, M., Swartz, J., Khan, S., & Tarr, H. (1997). *National evaluation of the Even Start family literacy program: Report on Even Start projects for Indian tribes and tribal organizations.* Bethesda, MD: Abt Associates, Inc.; Fu Associates, Ltd. (Eric Document Reproduction Service No. ED415084). Retrieved on August 15, 2009, from http://www.eric.ed.gov/ERICDocs/data/ericdocs2sql/content_storage_01/0000019b/80/15/1e/3b.pdf

Lévy-Bruhl, L. (1910/1985). *How Natives think (Les fonctions mentales dans les sociétés inférieures.* London, England: George Allen and Unwin, Ltd. (Republished in 1985 by Princeton, N.J.: Princeton University Press).

Lévy-Bruhl, L. (2009). In *Encyclopædia Britannica.* Retrieved on August 26, 2009, from Encyclopædia Britannica Online: http://www.britannica.com/EBchecked/topic/338063/Lucien-Levy-Bruhl

Littlebear, D. (1992). Getting teachers and parents to work together. In J. A. Reyhner (Ed.), *Teaching American Indian students* (pp. 104–111). Norman: University of Oklahoma Press.

Long, E. E., & Christensen, J. M. (1998). Indirect language assessment tool for English-speaking Cherokee Indian children. *Journal of American Indian Education, 37*(3), 1–14.

Macias, J. (1987). The hidden curriculum of Papago teachers: American Indian strategies for mitigating cultural discontinuity in early schooling. In G. Spindler & L. Spindler (Eds.), *An interpretive ethnography of education: At home and abroad* (pp. 363–380). Hillsdale, NJ: Erlbaum.

Macias, R. (September 2000). *Summary report of the survey of the states' limited English proficient students and available educational programs and services.* Washington, D. C.: National Clearinghouse for Bilingual Education.

MacPhee, D., Fritz, J., & Miller-Heyl, J. (1996). Ethnic variations in personal social networks and parenting. *Child Development, 67,* 3278–3295.

Mattson, K. (1998). *Creating a democratic public: The struggle for urban participatory democracy during the Progressive Era.* University Park PA: The Pennsylvania State University.

McBride, S. L. (1999). Family-centered practices. *Young Children, 54*(3), 62–68.

Mihesuah, D. A. (1998). American Indian identities: Issues of individual choices and development. *American Indian Culture and Research Journal, 22*(2), 193–226.

Moynihan, D. P. (1965). *The Negro family: The case for national action.* Washington, DC: United States Department of Labor, Office of Policy, Planning, and Research. (pp. 8–28).

National Association for the Education of Young Children. (1996). NAEYC Position Paper: Responding to linguistic and cultural diversity—Recommendations for effective early childhood education. *Young Children, 52*(2), 4–12.

National Association for the Education of Young Children. (2005). NAEYC Position Paper: where we STAND summary: Many languages, many cultures:

Respecting and responding to diversity. Retrieved on July 8, 2009, from http://208.118.177.216/about/positions/pdf/diversity.pdf

National Center for Children in Poverty. (1990). *Five million children: A statistical profile of our poorest young citizens: Summary report.* New York.

National Coalition of Advocates for Students (1988). *New voices: Immigrant students in U.S. public schools.* Boston, MA. Author.

Natriello, G., McDill, E., & Pallas, (1990). *Schooling disadvantaged children: Racing against catastrophe.* New York: Teacher's College Press.

North Central Regional Educational Laboratory (NCREL). (1996, January). School-community collaboration. *New Leaders for Tomorrow's Schools, 2*(1). Retrieved on August 18, 2009, from http://www.ncrel.org/cscd/pubs/lead21/2-1a.htm

Ordoñez-Jasis, R., & Ortiz, R. W. (2006). Reading their worlds: Working with diverse families to enhance children's early literacy development, *Young Children, 61*(1), 42–48.

Ortiz, R. W., & Ordoñez-Jasis, R. (2005). Leyendo juntos (reading together): New directions for Latino parents' early literacy involvement. *Reading Teacher, 59,* 110–121.

Oxford, C. (1984). *Demographic projections of non-English background and limited English proficient persons in the Unites States in the year 2000.* Rossyln, VA: InterAmerica Research Associates.

Payne, R. (1995). *Poverty: A framework for understanding and working with students and adults from poverty.* Baytown, TX: RFT Publishing.

Pewewardy, C. (2002). Learning styles of American Indian/Alaska native students: a review of the literature and implications for practice, *Journal of American Indian Education, 41*(3), 22–56.

Plank, G. A. (1994). What silence means for educators of American Indian children. *Journal of American Indian Education, 34*(1), 3–19.

Prelow, H., & Loukas, A. (2003). The role of resource, protective, and risk factors on academic achievement-related outcomes of economically disadvantaged Latino youth. *Journal of Community Psychology, 31,* 513–521.

Portes, A. & Zhou, M. (1993). The new second generation: Segmented assimilation and its variants. *Annals of the American Academy of Political and Social Science, 530,* 74–96.

Quezada, R. L., Díaz, D. M., & Sánchez, M. (2003). Involving Latino parents. *Leadership, 33*(1), 32–38.

Ramírez, M., III, and Castañeda, A. (1974). *Cultural democracy, bicognitive development, and education.* New York: Academic Press.

Redding, S. (2001). The community of the school. In S. Redding & L. G. Thomas (Eds.), *The Community of the School.* (pp. 1–24). Lincoln, IL: Academic Development Institute.

Robinson, T. L. (1993). The intersections of gender, class, race, and culture. *Journal of Multicultural Counseling and Development, 21,* 50–58.

Rodriquez, M.,& Morrobel, D. (2004). A review of Latino youth development research and a call for an asset orientation. *Hispanic Journal of Behavioral Sciences, 26,* 107–127.

Roopnarine, J. L., Bynoe, P. B., & Singh, R. (2004). Factors tied to the schooling of English-speaking immigrants in the United States. In U. Gielen, & J. L. Roopnarine (Eds.), *Childhood and adolescence across cultures.* (2 Vols.). (pp. 319–349). Westport, CT: Praeger.

Roopnarine, J. L. & Gielen, U. (2004). *Families in global perspectives.* Boston, MA: Allyn & Bacon.

Roopnarine, J. L., & Metindogan, A. (2005). Cultural beliefs about childrearing and schooling in immigrant families and "developmentally appropriate practices": Yawning gaps! In O. N. Saracho & B. Spodek (Eds.) *Contemporary perspectives on families, communities and schools for young children.* (pp. 181–202). Greenwich, Connecticut: Information Age Publishing.

Roopnarine, J. L., Shin, M., Jung, K., & Hossain, Z. (2003). Play and early education and development: The instantiation of parental belief systems. In O. N. Saracho & B. Spodek (Eds.), *Contemporary issues in early childhood education.* Westport, CT: New Age Publishers.

Russell, C. (2009). Cultures in collision: Cosmology, jurisprudence, and religion in Tlingit territory. *The American Indian Quarterly, 33*(2), 230–252

Sands, T., & Plunkett, S. W. (2005). A new scale to measure adolescent reports of academic support by mothers, fathers, teachers, and friends in Latino immigrant families. *Hispanic Journal of Behavioral Sciences, 27,* 244–253.

Saracho, O. N. (2007a). Hispanic families as facilitators of their children's literacy development. *Journal of Hispanic Higher Education, 6*(2), 103–117.

Saracho, O. N. (2007b). Fathers and young children's literacy experiences in a family environment. *Early Child Development and Care, 177*(4), 403–415.

Saracho, O. N., & Martínez-Hancock, F. (2005). Mexican American families: Cultural and linguistic influences. In O. N. Saracho & B. Spodek (Eds.) *Contemporary perspectives on families, communities and schools for young children.* (pp. 203–224). Greenwich, Connecticut: Information Age Publishing.

Saracho, O. N., & Spodek, B. (2002). Introduction: Contemporary theories of literacy. In O. N. Saracho, O. N. & B. Spodek (Eds). *Contemporary perspectives in literacy in early childhood curriculum,* Volume 2 (pp. ix–xv). Greenwich, CT: Information Age Publishing.

Saracho, O. N., & Spodek, B. (2005). Challenges and realities: Family-community-school partnership. In O. N. Saracho & B. Spodek (Eds.) *Contemporary perspectives on families, communities and schools for young children.* (pp.1–20). Greenwich, Connecticut: Information Age Publishing.

Seideman, R. Y., Williams, R., Burns, P., Jacobson, S., Weatherby, F., & Primeaux, M. (1994). Culture sensitivity in assessing urban Native American parenting. *Public Health Nursing, 11*(2), 98–103.

Shapiro, M. S. (1983). *Child's garden: The kindergarten movement from Froebel to Dewey.* University Park, PA: The Pennsylvania State University Press.

Spindler, G. & Spindler L. (1994). General introduction. In Suarez-Orozco, M.M., Spindler, G. & Spindler, L. (Eds). *The making of psychological anthropology II* (pp. 1–7). Orlando: Harcourt Brace.

Smith, L. T. (1999). *Decolonizing methodologies: Research and Indigenous peoples.* New York: Zed Books Ltd.

Stassen-Berger, K., & Thompson, R. A. (2000). *Developing Person Through the Life Span.* (5th Ed.). New York: Worth Publishers.

Steidel, A. G. L., & Contreras, J. M. (2003). A new familism scale for use with Latino populations. *Hispanic Journal of Behavioral Sciences, 25*(3), 312–330.

Suarez-Orozco, M. (2001). Globalization, immigration, and education: The research agenda. *Harvard Educational Review, 71*, 345–365.

Swisher, K., & Deyhle, D. (1989). The styles of learning are different, but the teaching is just the same: Suggestions for teachers of American Indian youth. *Journal of American Indian Education, 28*(Special Issue), 1–14.

Trattner, W. I. (1992). Introduction to the transaction edition. In R. H. Bremner (Ed.) *The discovery of poverty in the United States.* (pp. xi–xxvii). New Brunswick: Transaction.

Tulananda, O., & Roopnarine, J. L. (2001). Mothers' and fathers' interactions with preschoolers in the home in Northern Thailand: Relationships to teachers' assessments of children's social skills. *Journal of Family Psychology, 15*, 676–687.

United States Bureau of the Census. (1997). *Statistical abstract of the United States, 1997.* (117th Edition). Washington, DC: Author.

Valdés, G. (1996). *Con respeto: Bridging the distances between culturally diverse families and schools, an ethnographic portrait.* New York: Teachers College Press.

Valenzuela, A., & Dornbusch, S. M. (1994). Familism and social capital in the academic achievement of Mexican origin and Anglo adolescents. *Social Science Quarterly, 75*, 18–36.

Verdon, M. (2007). Franz Boas: cultural history for the present, or obsolete natural history? *Journal of the Royal Anthropological Institute, 13*(2), 433–451.

Watahomigie, L., J., & McCarty, T. L. (1994). Bilingual/bicultural education at Peach Springs: A Hualapai way of schooling. *Peabody Journal of Education, 69*(2), 26–42.

Weiss, B. J. (Ed.). (1982). *American education and the European immigrant: 1840–1940.* (pp. 3–16). Urbana: University of Illinois.

Whitbeck, L. B., Hoyt, D. R., Stubben, J. D., & LaFromboise, T. (2001). Traditional culture and academic success among American Indian children in the upper Midwest. *Journal of American Indian Education, 40*(2), 48–60.

Yellow Bird, M. (2001). Critical values and First Nations peoples. In R. Fong & S. Furuto (Eds), *Cultural competent social work: Interventions* (pp. 61–74). Boston: Allyn and Bacon.

Yellow Bird, M., & Snipp, C. M. (2002). American Indian families. In R. L. Taylor (Ed.), *Minority families in the United States: A multicultural perspective* (pp. 227–249). Upper Saddle River, NJ: Prentice-Hall.

York, S. (1998). *Big as life, the everyday inclusive curriculum.* St. Paul, MN: Red Leaf Press.

Zhou, M. (1997). Segmented assimilation: Issues, controversies, and recent research on the new second generation. *International Migration Review, 31*, 975–1008.

Zimiga, A. W. (1982). The influence of traditional Lakota thought on Indian parent group involvement on the Pine Ridge Indian Reservation: A case study. *Dissertation Abstracts International, 42*(8), 3488A. (UMI No. 8125501)

Zwick, T. T., & Miller, K. W. (1996). A comparison of integrated outdoor education activities and traditional science learning with American Indian students. *Journal of American Indian Education, 35*(2), 1–9.

NOTES

1. The term "American Indians" is suggested by the *Journal of American Indian Education.* This term refers to the indigenous population of the continental United States.
2. Kevin Gover was Assistant Secretary of Indian Affairs (1997 to 2000), is a member of the Pawnee Tribe, is a native of Lawton, Oklahoma, and is presently director of the Smithsonian Institution's National Museum of the American Indian.
3. One of Europe's most respected and important institutions of higher learning. The Sorbonne refers both to the University of Paris and to the first college that was established before it became the university.

CHAPTER 7

CULTURE AS FRAMEWORK VERSUS INGREDIENT IN EARLY CHILDHOOD EDUCATION

A Native Hawaiian Perspective

C. Kanoelani Nāone and Kathryn Au

ABSTRACT

The concept of developmentally appropriate practice has long served as the touchstone for discussions of early childhood education, bringing with it universalistic assumptions about the proper teaching of young children and the normative course of learning, regardless of children's cultural and linguistic backgrounds. Perhaps as a result, research in early childhood education based on assumptions of difference, rather than deficit, is much less common than in elementary and secondary education, as recent reviews attest (Castagno & Brayboy, 2008; Osborne, 1996). Yet, the urgency of promoting research in early childhood education to address issues of diversity in culture and language has never been greater. The larger forces at work include globalization, which tends to promote educational practices that deny the place

Language and Cultural Diversity in Early Childhood Education, pages 147–165

of local cultures and languages (Spring, 2008), as well as the U.S. push for universal preschool, which tends to reduce the options available to families of diverse backgrounds (Sarsona, Goo, Kawakami, & Au, 2008). The exception occurs in cases, such as that of Hawai'i, where state legislation provides support for a variety of early childhood efforts, including home visits, family care, parent-participation preschools, and center-based preschools.

We argue in this chapter for the importance of building early childhood education programs for indigenous students on the foundation of indigenous perspectives, using the Native Hawaiian perspective as our example. We believe that traditional Hawaiian educational values and methods should be adopted for the education of Native Hawaiian students, including the very youngest. In our view, it is not enough to infuse culture into education; culturally based values and methods need to drive how education is delivered. A proper honoring of the family, community, land, and indigenous language have the potential to revitalize education for young Native Hawaiian children, and in the process offer program innovations beneficial to teachers and students of many ethnic groups in Hawai'i and around the globe.

We begin by defining what we mean by an indigenous perspective, with a specific application to Native Hawaiians. We provide conceptual overviews of culture as framework versus culture as ingredient, and of culturally responsive instruction. We introduce Keiki Steps, a parent-participation preschool (also referred to as a family–child interaction learning program) for Native Hawaiian children, as an example of a program that uses Hawaiian culture as its framework. To make clear how Keiki Steps has been shaped by Hawaiian culture, we discuss two key values that should inform early childhood programs designed for Native Hawaiian children: *'ohana* (family) and *kaiāulu* (community).

AN INDIGENOUS HISTORICAL PERSPECTIVE

We use the term *indigenous* to refer to peoples who inhabited an area before it was colonized or annexed, who continue to observe their own cultural practices and values, and who regard themselves as a nation (Castagno & Brayboy, 2008). Native Hawaiians qualify as an indigenous group within the United States because they were the first to inhabit the Hawaiian archipelago, and did so for nearly 2,000 years before the arrival of the British explorer James Cook in 1778; maintained their distinct, non-Western culture in the face of unrelenting efforts to stamp it out; and have long sought recognition by the U.S. government as a nation with a status comparable to that attained by Native American tribes.

Native Hawaiian children of today are descendants of the original Polynesian inhabitants of the Hawaiian Islands. As with other indigenous populations in the U.S. and around the world, Native Hawaiians have experienced tremendous disruptions to their well-being and traditional way of life during more than 200 years of Western contact and colonization (Benham & Heck, 1998; Kame'eleihiwa, 1992). Chief among the tools of colonization has been a system of Western schooling, introduced to the islands by Congregational missionaries from New England, beginning in the 1820s, rooted in Protestant values of discipline and individualism (Nāone, 2008). Reports have long documented the unfortunate effects of conventional Western schooling for many Native Hawaiian children. The poor outcomes of this system are plainly seen at all levels of schooling, beginning with the elementary grades and reaching to the university. Results indicate that, as a group, Native Hawaiian students in the public schools of Hawai'i have reading and math scores below those of students in other groups (Kamehameha Schools Office of Program Evaluation and Planning, 1993). Not surprisingly, rates of college graduation are significantly lower (Hagedorn, Tibbetts, Kana'iaupuni, Moon, & Lester, 2004), limiting life opportunities, such as employment in fields requiring advanced education.

A paradox raised by these statistics is that, prior to the advent of Protestant missionary schooling, Native Hawaiians were a technologically and socially advanced society with an education system that allowed for a complex and deep level of knowledge, ranging from food and sustenance in an island environment to all aspects of the arts (Kanahele, 1986). Furthermore, 20 years after Hawaiian became a written language, literacy rates among Native Hawaiian equaled or exceeded those in other societies (Nāone, 2008). In the second half of the nineteenth century, while the missionaries and their descendants used literacy to position Native Hawaiians as inferior heathens, Native Hawaiians were able to appropriate literacy as a tool for their own purposes, namely, cultural preservation and political resistance (Au & Kaomea, 2008).

CULTURE AS FRAMEWORK

We believe that the solution to improving the educational futures and lives of Native Hawaiian students lies in applying traditional aspects of Native Hawaiian education in the context of the modern world. As implied in our remarks about literacy and Native Hawaiians, we do not believe in retreating to the past, but rather in creating educational pathways where Native Hawaiians may appropriate Western technologies for their own purposes and prosper in a globalized world, while holding firm to their cultural identity as an indigenous people.

Specifically, from the perspective of early childhood education, what can be done to help young Native Hawaiian children prosper in school and later in life? What are the characteristics of a successful early childhood education program with the dual goals of giving children a firm grounding in their own culture, while preparing them for academic success according to Western standards? Our position is not to elevate Native Hawaiian cultural knowledge over Western knowledge, or vice versa. We believe that children can benefit from acquiring both types of knowledge, and that each has its place in Native Hawaiian early childhood education programs. Yet, given the dominance of Western knowledge in schooling in modern Hawai'i, we must be aware that our challenge will almost always be to secure a proper place for Native Hawaiian cultural knowledge.

We argue that an early childhood education program capable of reaching these dual goals must utilize Hawaiian culture as its very framework. Such a strategy is a departure from conventional efforts to bring Hawaiian culture into schooling by treating culture as an ingredient. Culture is typically treated as an ingredient in what Banks (1995) has called the contributions and additive approaches to multicultural education. An example of the contributions approach would be to read children a storybook about the life of Kamehameha I (the ruling chief who united the islands under one government). An example of the additive approach would be to add several lessons on the life of Kamehameha I, but without changing the structure of the overall curriculum or classroom, for example, to permit analysis not only of this one great historical figure, but also of other accomplished Hawaiian leaders. As these examples imply, when culture is treated as an ingredient, superficial adjustments are made to the content of the curriculum, absent a reframing of the curriculum or classroom itself.

How do we begin to make Hawaiian culture the framework for an early childhood curriculum or program? The answer is that we must start by building on the foundation of Hawaiian values and the worldview from which these values come. These values can and should inform our decisions about all aspects of a program, from its goals, participants, and location, to its social and academic content, to the nature of interactions between adults and children.

Our position is consistent with those of researchers who have called for culturally responsive schooling for indigenous youth, with a clear emphasis on "sovereignty and self-determination, racism, and indigenous epistemologies" (Castagno & Brayboy, 2008, p. 941). In terms of sovereignty and self-determination, the main idea is for Native Hawaiians to take control of their own destiny by deciding which aspects of Western culture and schooling they should accept, and which they should reject. Nāone (2008) writes, "Ultimately, I say that we have the right, the will and the responsibility to say yes to what we can use and no to the things that threaten us and our people" (p. 3).

With respect to indigenous epistemologies, a key question for the education of Native Hawaiian children is what counts as knowledge that should be taught in school and, therefore, included in the curriculum. Beginning with the introduction of Western schooling, the curriculum for Native Hawaiian children has been based on knowledge valued from a Western or mainstream point of view. In this regard, we must remember that, despite their centuries-long subjugation, indigenous peoples and indigenous knowledge systems have existed for millennia. We do well to focus our energies on creating a new system of education by drawing upon the knowledge of millennia, rather than fighting against the subjugation of past centuries. As Mignolo (2000) argues, "Alternatives to modern epistemology can hardly come from modern (Western) epistemology itself" (p. 9).

Several recent studies point to the benefits to Native Hawaiian students of schooling emphasizing Hawaiian culture and language. Although these studies did not specifically address early childhood education programs, they are indicative of the potential of approaches rooted in Hawaiian culture. In the first study, Warner (1996) highlighted the differences between Native Hawaiian students who attended Hawaiian immersion schools and those who attended mainstream public schools. After the Hawaiian language was brought to the brink of extinction in the early 1980s, a small group of dedicated Native Hawaiian educators and parents established the Hawaiian immersion schools as a state-funded alternative to conventional public schools. In these schools, students receive instruction exclusively in the Hawaiian language until grade 5. When the immersion program was founded in 1987, its core curriculum was to be the same as that in other public schools, with the difference being only in the language of instruction. Over time, however, the curriculum has placed an increasing emphasis on Hawaiian culture, as Native Hawaiian scholars, such as Warner, argued for a curriculum based on Hawaiian epistemology and foundations. Warner (1996) noted of students in Hawaiian immersion schools:

> They do not appear to suffer the identity crises of the past three generations. They are not ashamed of being Hawaiian and are not ashamed of speaking their language. They are generally motivated to learn the language, and it appears that they tend to be less alienated from school than their monolingual, ethnic Hawaiian, or part-Hawaiian peers. (p. 10)

Kanaʻiaupuni and Ishibashi (2005) compared the academic achievement and engagement levels of Native Hawaiian students enrolled in Hawaiian-focused charter schools to those of Native Hawaiian students enrolled in mainstream public schools. They found that charter school students achieved higher scores on standardized tests of reading and math achievement at grade 9 than did those enrolled in mainstream public schools. Furthermore, reinforcing the conclusions of Warner (1996), charter school students tended to be more engaged in school and to show significantly higher attendance rates.

One of the few studies to examine possible effects of Hawaiian culture in early childhood settings was conducted by Kana'iaupuni (2004). She measured various cultural inputs in early childhood education at 14 public and 15 private preschool sites. The study followed children from preschool through grade 1. Kana'iaupuni found that the practice of Hawaiian cultural customs in the home had a beneficial effect on children's development. These practices might include experiential activities, such as hula, fishing, and surfing, and oral, academic, and artistic activities, such as genealogy and music. Specifically, children who knew their given Hawaiian name and had a solid understanding of its meaning scored higher on measures of vocabulary, social skills, and language skills than children who had little or no understanding of their Hawaiian name, or who did not have a Hawaiian name. These preliminary findings offer tantalizing hints of the positive effects that a focus on Hawaiian culture may impart to young, Native Hawaiian children.

CULTURALLY RESPONSIVE INSTRUCTION FOR NATIVE HAWAIIAN CHILDREN

Culturally responsive instruction is not a new idea. However, reviews show that almost all of the early research on this approach was conducted in elementary and secondary classrooms (e.g., Osborne, 1996; Au & Kawakami, 1994), with a few studies set in early childhood education settings appearing more recently (Genishi & Goodwin, 2008). Application of the principles of culturally responsive instruction offers the promise of narrowing or closing the gap between the educational achievement of Native Hawaiian students and their mainstream peers at all levels of schooling, including early childhood (Sarsona, Goo, Kawakami, & Au, 2007).

Culturally relevant pedagogy (Ladson-Billings, 1995; Osborne, 1996), culturally responsive teaching (Gay, 2000), and culturally congruent instruction (Au & Kawakami, 1994) are slightly different terms for approaches grounded in the same set of beliefs. One belief is that the purpose of using culturally responsive instruction should be to increase the school success of children of diverse cultural and linguistic backgrounds, so that they can achieve at the same high levels as their mainstream peers. Another belief is that school success is to be achieved by drawing upon children's experiences in the home culture, so that school experiences become meaningful. The idea is to promote children's competence in the heritage culture and language, not just mainstream culture and language. Schooling is reconceptualized as a means of immersing children in the cultural traditions of their people, rather than as a means of separating them from these traditions. Indigenous groups, including Native Hawaiians, often give high priority to the preservation of their language and culture because they have come close to having both intentionally and completely eradicated through colonialism.

From a conceptual point of view, we can outline two different theoretical paths for improving the school achievement of students of diverse cultural and linguistic backgrounds. These two paths are shown in Figure 7.1 (adapted from Au, 2007). Au labels the first path the *direct* or *assimilationist* approach. Advocates of this approach think that early childhood and other educational programs should immerse children of diverse backgrounds in mainstream content and interactional processes from the very beginning. An assimilationist approach is reflected in most early childhood education programs, in which children are taught basic concepts such as colors and numbers, and are socialized according to mainstream norms of behavior. The curriculum is generally limited to knowledge and experiences that children are believed to need so that they can be successful in school, with success being defined in terms of readiness and vocabulary tests, as well as other mainstream criteria, all within the confines of middle-class American values and ideals. Educators who follow an assimilationist approach often are unaware that they are doing so, and may believe simply that there is only one right way to "do school," which is independent of the cultural and linguistic backgrounds of their students. When educators place too great an emphasis on mainstream knowledge and skills, and assess children only in these terms, they can easily fall into the pattern of thinking in terms of deficits, rather than differences. In addition, this ideology is based on the premise that children are not able to learn vast and diverse amounts of knowledge. For example, in the U.S., bilingual education may be denigrated because children are not thought to have the ability to gain command of one language, much less two or more, without becoming confused. This assumption is belied by the millions of young children growing

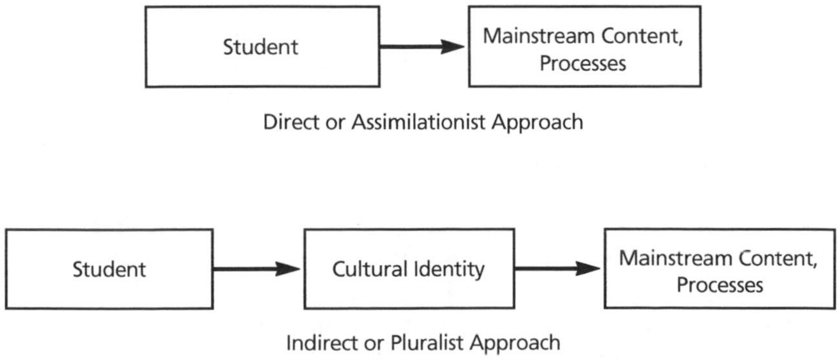

Figure 7.1 Two approaches to early childhood education.

up in other parts of the world who readily learn to speak two, three, or even four languages.

Au labels the second path the *indirect* or *pluralist* approach. This is the path endorsed by advocates of culturally responsive instruction, one that sees children and their families in terms of difference, rather than deficit. Early childhood education programs that follow this second path take the stance of affirming, reinforcing, and building the cultural identity of young children of diverse backgrounds. Educators working in these programs believe that children who have a strong cultural identity, based on a firm grounding in the traditional culture and language of their people, will have a solid foundation upon which to add mainstream knowledge. Children will more readily acquire mainstream knowledge when it can be connected to what they already understand and value. Furthermore, children are educated to become contributing members of the family and community, rather than being alienated from them, and can be active participants in efforts to preserve and perpetuate the language and culture. This second, pluralist path is the one we have chosen to follow with the Keiki Steps curriculum, which seeks to celebrate Native Hawaiian culture.

In keeping with a pluralist path, we must be alert to the assimilationist assumptions frequently underlying efforts to implement conventional, center-based preschools in diverse settings, such as Native Hawaiian communities. Center-based preschools are sometimes regarded as the gold standard, the best solution for preparing young children for success in school and later in life. We urge caution before jumping to this conclusion. Center-based preschools may be the appropriate solution for some families, but, as Sarsona (2004) argues, Native Hawaiian families may not prefer this option. Native Hawaiian families may prefer to have grandparents or other members of the extended family care for the children while the parents are at work. The advantages are that grandparents can pass on traditional knowledge, secure the bonds of family, and give young children richer, more varied experiences than those typically encountered in the classroom. Time with grandparents can be part of the process of integrating children into Native Hawaiian culture, rather than educating them away from it.

Evolution of Keiki Steps

Keiki is one of the common Hawaiian terms for *child*, and Keiki Steps is a parent-participation preschool program for young Native Hawaiian children. From its origins, Keiki Steps has been a grassroots, community-based effort. Keiki Steps came about through the initiative of Michelle Mahuka, a mother of two young children and resident of the Hawaiian homestead community of Nānākuli. In 1998, Mahuka saw a television ad about parent-participation preschool programs (also called play morning programs and, more recently, family–child interaction learning programs), and she decided that she wanted her own children to participate in this kind of program. She called the agency whose name appeared in the ad, only to be informed that there was no parent-participation preschool program serving her rural community. One had been available, but it had closed three years earlier (Roberts, 1993). Mahuka found out that the nearest available program was located in a suburb several miles away, along Farrington Highway. This location did not appeal to Mahuka. She wanted to see if a parent-participation preschool program could be started in Nānākuli, to serve the many families with young children there.

The agency suggested that Mahuka contact Sherlyn Goo, then the executive director of the Institute for Native Pacific Education and Culture (INPEACE), a nonprofit, Native Hawaiian educational services organization (www.inpeace-hawaii.org). Goo heartily endorsed the idea and set about approaching possible funders. In the meantime, Mahuka secured donations from businesses and organizations in the community. Soon after, Goo was approached by parents in the Hawaiian homestead community of Waimānalo who also wanted a parent-participation preschool program for their community. Because funding for the Waimānalo second project fell into place quickly, the first Keiki Steps site began operations there six months before the Keiki Steps site in Nānākuli.

By 2009, Keiki Steps has grown to 13 sites for parent-participation preschools in Native Hawaiian communities, on three of the six main islands in the state of Hawai'i. Keiki Steps to Kindergarten (KSTK), a three-week summer program, was added for the purpose of easing the transition of young children from Keiki Steps into kindergarten. In the summer of 2008, 40 KSTK classrooms at 33 public elementary schools engaged 617 children and their families.

Overview of Keiki Steps Program and Curriculum

As a parent-participation preschool program, Keiki Steps operates four mornings a week, Monday–Thursday, from 7:30 to 11:30 a.m. On two Fridays a month, either a field trip or parent education class is held. Each site can accommodate up to 25 children and their caregivers per session. Elementary schools are the preferred location, because parents or other caregivers can see that the older children arrive safely at their classrooms and then bring the younger children to Keiki Steps. This arrangement significantly contributes to creating seamless transitions from early childhood programs to elementary schools for children and families.

Several major differences may be noted between a Keiki Steps parent-participation preschool and a mainstream center-based preschool, where children are dropped off and picked up. The first is that every child has a teacher present with them at all times, in the sense that the caregiver attends the preschool with the child. One of the goals of Keiki Steps is to help caregivers understand that they are teachers of young children, whether they see themselves in that role or not, and to provide them with support in that role. Although Keiki Steps is called a *parent*-participation program, young children often attend with other family members, such as grandmothers, grandfathers, aunts, and uncles.

A second difference is that Hawaiian culture is weighted equally as a curriculum area, along with literacy, math, science, social studies, and the arts. Keiki Steps has a written curriculum for children from ages 1 through 4, built, in part, on the foundation of Hawai'i's state preschool content standards, and Keiki Steps classrooms are set up just like any other high quality preschool classroom in the U.S., with centers for all aspects of child development. Mainstream curriculum content and best practices are understood and recognized. At the same time, a significant shift has taken place, from treating culture as an ingredient to viewing culture as the framework for the program, in keeping with the concepts discussed earlier in this chapter.

A third difference is that Keiki Steps classrooms use multi-age grouping. While there is a curriculum with activities geared for infants and toddlers, plus a curriculum with activities geared for 3- and 4-year-olds, the children and their teachers—Keiki Steps staff and caregivers—mingle freely. As a result, Keiki Steps classrooms have a warm, inviting feeling, with multiple generations gathered to learn together in the same place.

A final difference between Keiki Steps and conventional early childhood education programs is seen in the comprehensive professional development training program designed for its staff. Nearly all staff members are Native Hawaiian women who reside in the communities served by Keiki Steps, and many are in the workplace for the first time. As a condition of employment, staff members are required to participate in certificate or degree programs to prepare themselves for careers in early childhood education. INPEACE pays for tuition, books, and 4 hours a week of professional development time to support the educational progress of Keiki Steps employees.

Key Hawaiian Values Foundational to the Program

We now discuss key values in Hawaiian culture and traditional education that can be used to frame an early childhood education program. After discussing these values, we will show their application in the Keiki Steps program.

'Ohana and kaiāulu: *'Ohana* is the Hawaiian word for *family*, immediate and extended. In the 'ohana, older siblings care for the younger ones, aunties and uncles care for nieces and nephews, and grandparents and parents all raise children. So seamless are the relationships in 'ohana that the words for niece and nephew did not exist prior to foreign influence; the same words one would use for son and daughter or siblings were used for niece and nephew.

Kaiāulu is the Hawaiian word for *community*, and community is seen as the natural extension of families within Native Hawaiian culture. Native Hawaiians turn to their community for validation, advice, comfort, and safety. They feel responsible to their community, and the community, in turn, accepts responsibility for them. They gain strength from their community, which, in turn, challenges them to become even stronger. Native Hawaiians are vested in the well-being of their community and are called to ensure that every member is held accountable and kept safe.

According to Pukui, Haertig, and Lee (1972), and others (Kamakau, Barrere, Feher, & Pukui, 1991; Kamakau & Hawai'i, 1996), education in the Native Hawaiian tradition was specific to the strengths of the child and performed in a mentoring fashion by kūpuna (*elders*, plural form). Children were encouraged to experience the environment and roam freely until the age of 6 or 7, sometimes older, when they were then selected to be trained in a particular skill (Pukui, Haertig, & Lee, 1972). For example, a child who demonstrated an uncommon memory and strong verbal skills might be watched for some time to determine if indeed that child might become a chanter or story keeper. The kupuna (*elder*, singular form) who was the keeper of that talent, ability, or skill would then accept that child as a student, and the child would become the recipient of the kupuna's specialized knowledge. All children learned to care for the land and serve as stewards of the natural resources around them, but certain children had talents best suited for particular types of environments (such as the ocean or mountains) or work (such as ceremony, reading the natural environment, hula, or combat). In this way, individuals were selected to have a particular skill set passed on to them, based on their strengths and natural talent.

Kūpuna were the teachers, a role for which they were perfectly suited, for several reasons. First, kūpuna possessed the detailed knowledge and expertise that comes as a result of extensive life experience, practicing and testing a particular body of knowledge time and time again over the course of many decades. Secondly, their older bodies, however fit, were not as strong and agile as those of the mākua (*adults*, plural form) who were responsible for raising and harvesting food. In a society where each individual's contribution was needed and valued, it made sense for younger adults, those with stronger bodies, to take on the jobs requiring physical strength and stamina, while the older ones utilized their years of experience and the patience that comes with age. Thirdly, kūpuna, as teachers, perpetuated the value of ʻohana and kaiāulu, where everyone was responsible for the well-being and care of each child. Native Hawaiians have any number of poetical expressions and sayings to express their love and regard for children and the importance of raising children correctly, and children's behavior—proper and improper—is seen as a reflection of the ʻohana. In traditional society, it was important that each child become successful, because the future of the community depended on it. Children were responsible to their elders, and this fostered strong relationships across generations and among community members.

Strengths-based model: Nāone (2008) explains that Native Hawaiians followed a strengths-based model that fostered high levels of self-esteem. As mentioned earlier, individuals were well suited to their roles by both ability and training. They practiced skills necessary for the sustenance, betterment, and very survival of the family and community, and they could be recognized for their expertise and their contributions. It was understood that one did not need to become an expert in all areas, because one could rely on the expertise of others.

Each person had a role and responsibility to family and community that balanced life. The mahiʻai (*farmer*) and family shared the food they grew, the lawaiʻa (*fisherman*) and family shared their catch from the ocean, the aliʻi (*chief*) shared the ability to protect the land base, the ʻōlapa (*hula dancer*) and hoʻopaʻa (*chanter*) re-enacted and passed on stories so that all would remember the lessons learned generation after generation. The elders from each area of expertise were the teachers of the next generation and remembered for their guidance. Even today, students of traditional hula are taught a particular style of dance according to the teachings that are passed down from each kumu hula (*hula teacher*) to the next, generation after generation. Should they become teachers, they are expected to perpetuate the same style of dance by teaching others to dance and chant following the traditions that were passed on to them.

In the Native Hawaiian system of teaching and learning, young children are given the opportunity to develop and experience the world around them at their own pace. This approach allows children to engage with the environment, both material and interpersonal, in a wide variety of ways, shaped by their own interests and curiosity. When placed in an environment rich in material and human resources, children have many opportunities to build the skills necessary for school and gainful employment. Those experiences include touching, feeling, and exploring a variety of textures (such as sand, dirt, water, and oil), and manipulating objects to learn about cause and effect (such as putting a cap on a bottle, picking leaves or flowers, playing with pots and pans, and pouring water from one size cup to another).

Learning in context: The Native Hawaiian way of learning is not based on lectures and abstract discussions taking place in sterile environments. Instead, learning takes place within the actual cultural context with which the child is expected to engage. Often, the appropriate context is the natural world and great outdoors. Music and hula may well be taught indoors, but, even then, the rhythm and beat of drums and other instruments provides a supportive environment. There is a fundamental and profound assumption that every single cultural activity provides young children with opportunities for learning. Compellingly, the contextualized and exploratory approach to learning favored in Native Hawaiian culture is consistent with the recommendations of experts in brain development (Halfon, Shulman, & Hochstein, 2001).

It is critical to understand the differences between the Hawaiian system of education and the mainstream system prevalent in U.S. classrooms and other Western-dominated locations. Despite the rhetoric of differentiated instruction and the movement toward Response to Intervention (Fuchs, Fuchs, & Vaughn, 2008) in many American classrooms today, all children are expected to learn at the same rate and meet the same end-of-grade expectations for academic achievement. No Child Left Behind (NCLB) (2001), the recent reauthorization of the U.S. Elementary and Secondary Education Act, has exacerbated the push toward normative performance, as measured by large-scale tests. Although educators acknowledge that children develop at different rates in physical, mental, and emotional terms, NCLB fosters the assumption that children can and should progress at the same rate, in terms of academic learning. Obviously, this model does not take account of the child who develops skills in an order other than that specified in the curriculum, who learns at a slower pace, or who has interests and talents beyond those shared by mainstream classmates. In contrast, in the traditional Hawaiian system, children were allowed to mature at their own rate, so late bloomers were not subject to inappropriate expectations that might cause a sense of inadequacy. Children were selected for participation in formal learning when they were developmentally ready, and an age range of several years for the timing of entry into formal learning was accepted and expected.

As implied, depending on their evident abilities and interests, children might be taught by immediate family members, usually grandparents, as well as by kūpuna unrelated by blood. This practice meant that children might be chosen for specialized training in fields beyond those known to immediate family members. The effect was to create closer relationships within the community, as young and old were connected through the bonds of occupation and expertise. Furthermore, everything a child learned had immediate application and practical value to the community, with contributions increasing in magnitude as the child grew older. For example, if a young person had been selected to be a canoe builder, the kupuna teacher might start lessons with planting and caring for the koa tree (a type of acacia, noted for the durability and beauty of its wood) that would ultimately become the canoe. The next step might involve having the youth carry heavy items, to gain the strength necessary to bring a massive koa tree down from the mountains when that time came. Another step might be learning to make carving tools and to carve small items such as bowls, in preparation for the laborious task of shaping an entire canoe. Learning would continue in this fashion until the youth became an expert.

Key to the Native Hawaiian approach was that learning was always initially done with the eyes. An often repeated saying among Native Hawaiians is "E pa'a i ka waha, e hana i ka pepeiao," which advises learners to close their mouths and use their ears. To this day, children are expected to learn by carefully observing their elders' every action, without questioning or interrupting, unless invited to do so. Nāone (2008) recalls, "I can remember watching how to make lei [flower garlands] for what seemed like forever, always waiting in excited anticipation for when I would be ready to make my own."

Once the kupuna judged a young learner to be ready (that is, to have the necessary degree of knowledge, physical skill, patience, and listening ability), the student was assigned a specific task. The learner had to complete the first task successfully before being given another task. New skills were acquired on the basis of skills already mastered, and learners advanced to the next step at their own individual rates.

Tēnā system: Beniamina (personal communication, cited in Nāone, 2008), a mānaleo (*native speaker of Hawaiian*) and kupuna from Ni'ihau (a remote, privately owned island, where Hawaiian remains the language of everyday communication) refers to learning in the tēnā system. The literal meaning of *tēnā* is *to command, give an order,* or *send on business.* In this system, the child is given a task when the teacher believes that child is ready. If the child completes the task successfully, the child is deemed ready to move on to a more challenging task. If the child does not complete the task successfully, the child is thought not to be ready and to require more time and support for learning. No dire consequences or negative implications are involved; the child will simply be given another chance to complete the same task later on, when better prepared.

Here is an example of how the tēnā system works. A child might be sent down the road to gather palapalai (a lacy fern prized by hula dancers). If the child comes back with a fern other than palapalai (an easy mistake to make, as other ferns may look quite similar), then the child has demonstrated a lack of readiness to identify the proper materials for making a lei. A related task that also requires a discriminating eye would involve the picking of medicinal plants, and the kupuna would know that the child should not yet be sent on such an errand alone.

Where the tēnā system continues to be applied, children show high rates of success in accomplishing tasks, because children have been chosen for learning a particular expertise based on their strengths relevant to that pursuit. Also, kūpuna are adept at watching and assessing children closely, so that children are not tested until the kupuna judges them to be ready to perform well. Children often feel that they are ready much earlier, but with the wisdom gained through years of experience, kūpuna always seem to know when the time is right. With high rates of success and low rates of failure, the tēnā system engenders and preserves passion for life and ensures the perpetuation of a vibrant array of specialized knowledge and skills within Native Hawaiian society. Many of these specialties or cultural practices continue to be perpetuated (for example, featherwork, hula, fishing, and martial arts).

At present, Native Hawaiian families are often given the impression by educators and early childhood providers that the best route is to send their young children to center-based preschools, to be taught by non-family members who are usually outsiders to the community and who may have little knowledge of Hawaiian culture. This route is in marked contrast to the tēnā system, which relies on the values of ʻohana and kaiāulu, and on elders within the family and community who develop close and lasting ties to young children, who customize learning experiences to each child's talents and interests, and who prefer to judge children's efforts on their own merits, rather than in terms of normative expectations.

AN EXAMPLE OF CULTURE AS FRAMEWORK

We believe that Native Hawaiian traditions of learning, including the tēnā system, can and should provide the framework for early childhood education programs for Native Hawaiian communities. We propose dismantling the four walls of the classroom to take education outdoors to the natural environment, where children can become connected to land and place.

In the move from culture as ingredient to culture as framework in Keiki Steps, we built upon a solid foundation by putting ʻohana (*family*) and kaiāulu (*community*) at the very core of the program's philosophy and design. Keiki Steps was enhanced with the advent of Kupu Ola (literally, *to sprout forth life*), an initiative that serves not only the families and children of Keiki Steps, but kindergarten students and their teachers as well. The initiative is being piloted on land at two elementary schools on the Waiʻanae coast of the island of Oʻahu. The coast is home to the state's largest concentration of Native Hawaiians. In Kupu Ola, parents, caregivers, children, and teachers come together to create and maintain a native plant outdoor classroom. Traditionally, Native Hawaiians followed a moon calendar of 29–30 days to ensure the success of their planting and cultivation. Each day in the cycle has its own name, beginning with *hilo,* the new moon, and centuries of trial and error have produced a system in which fruits, vegetables, medicines, roots, and flowering plants are planted according to the lunar cycle to give each type of plant the opportunity to flourish.

In the design phase, we determine where each type of plant will be located, according to the climate of the area and the practical use of the plant (for example, whether it needs to be easily accessed so its flowers can be picked). The participants learn not only how to plant, but the best conditions for each plant (soil, depth, light, wind, and rain), how to maintain each plant, how to gather the plant materials for cultural use (for example, for medicine, a lei, or an imu [*underground oven*]), and then how to prepare the materials for consumption. Children work at their ability level alongside their parents, grandparents, and teachers. Everyone works together, utilizing the strengths of the group, in order to have the highest level of productivity. For example, the stronger adults dig the holes, the older children carry the plants and potting soil and help put the plants in the hole, and the younger children scoop the dirt into the hole and carry the small rocks. In addition to engaging in the physical activities of planting, all participants hear, learn, and practice the stories and songs of place, including the names of the winds, rains, mountains, and waterways of that particular community, along with traditional chants associated with planting.

The goals of the Kupu Ola initiative are consistent with the Native Hawaiian perspective, which treats children and their learning as inseparable from ʻohana and kaiāulu. Children learn science, math, literacy, and music, as well as traditional Hawaiian knowledge, in the culturally appropriate setting of the outdoor classroom, through hands-on experiences that draw upon all five senses. Parents and caregivers are empowered with cultural knowledge that might otherwise have been suppressed or forgotten. Through participation in Kupu Ola, these adults can have their understandings reinforced or developed, putting them in a stronger position to pass on Hawaiian cultural knowledge to their children and grandchildren. Keeping the flame of Hawaiian tradition burning within families enhances the vitality of the community, as children and adults gain confidence and feel pride in their cultural identity as Native Hawaiians. Finally, native plants, many of them rare and endangered, are preserved to enrich the environment for future generations.

Most important of all from a Native Hawaiian perspective, the Kupu Ola initiative links young children and their families back to the *ʻāina,* a term that refers to the land and all that sustains the people. Native Hawaiian tradition holds that there is profound knowledge stored in ʻāina (Nāone, 2008).

In Native Hawaiian tradition, children were taught the names and stories of the places in their home communities, as well as of the places where their ancestors and the ali'i (*chiefs*) came from. Kupu Ola perpetuates these traditions through its outdoor classroom curriculum and is a solid example of utilizing culture as a framework versus ingredient. Field trips will not suffice, because these occasional events keep children in the status of visitors and do not build either the deep knowledge of place or the strong sense of responsibility for place foundational to a Hawaiian worldview. Children must feel their ties to the land on an ongoing, daily basis.

CONCLUSION

The overarching theme of this chapter is that young children of indigenous backgrounds can benefit from, and, indeed, are entitled to, early childhood education programs that treat culture as framework versus ingredient. It is not enough to infuse culture into education; cultural values and knowledge need to drive how early childhood education is delivered. We argue that treating culture as framework versus ingredient requires a deep rethinking of the assumptions inherent in early childhood education programs designed to serve indigenous groups.

In exploring this theme, we focused on the example of early childhood education for a particular indigenous group, Native Hawaiians. We presented the conceptual basis for culture as framework by reviewing research on culturally responsive instruction, including studies showing the benefits of culturally-focused education for Native Hawaiian students. We outlined the basic elements of a Native Hawaiian perspective toward young children and their learning by referring to two key cultural values: 'ohana (*family*) and kaiāulu (*community*).

We then showed the application of a Hawaiian worldview to a parent-participation preschool program called Keiki Steps. This program is based in Hawaiian communities and run by Native Hawaiian women who reside in these same communities. By moving beyond the confines of the classroom to an outdoor environment, Keiki Steps and the Kupu Ola initiative allow children, parents, caregivers, and teachers to engage together in the creation and maintenance of a cultural garden. As they explore and help in the garden, children are given the opportunity to engage in tasks at their own level and to gain Hawaiian cultural knowledge, as well as mainstream academic knowledge. By building on the foundational concepts of 'ohana, kaiāulu, and 'āina (*land*), Keiki Steps strengthens families and prepares children for successful lives within Native Hawaiian communities and beyond. The example of Keiki Steps suggests that culture as framework, versus culture as ingredient, may well serve as a powerful and generative concept in the design of early childhood education programs not only for Native Hawaiians, but for other diverse and indigenous groups as well.

A well known ʻōlelo noʻeau (*poetical saying*) among Native Hawaiians is "ʻAʻohe pau ka ʻike i ka hālau hoʻokahi" (Pukui, 1983). The literal translation of this saying is, "All knowledge is not taught in the same school," and the meaning is that we can and should learn from many sources. For too long, the knowledge used to formulate educational policies and programs for Native Hawaiians and other indigenous peoples has come from Western, colonial sources. We think the time has now come to build early childhood education efforts for young children of indigenous backgrounds upon the rich cultural traditions that are their heritage.

REFERENCES

Au, K. (2007). Culturally responsive instruction: Application to multiethnic classrooms. *Pedagogies, 2*(1), 1–18.

Au, K., & Kaomea, J. (2009). Reading comprehension and diversity in historical perspective: Literacy, power, and Native Hawaiians. In S. Israel & G. Duffy (Eds.), *Handbook of research on reading comprehension* (pp. 571–586). New York: Routledge.

Au, K., & Kawakami, A. (1994). Cultural congruence in instruction. In E. Hollins, J. King & W. Hayman (Eds.), *Teaching diverse populations: Formulating a knowledge base* (pp. 5–23). Albany: State University of New York Press.

Banks, J. A. (1995). Multicultural education: Historical development, dimensions, and practice. In J. A. Banks & C. A. M. Banks (Eds.), *Handbook of research on multicultural education* (pp. 3–24). New York: Macmillan.

Benham, M. A., & Heck, R. H. (1998). *Culture and educational policy in Hawaiʻi: The silencing of native voices.* Mahwah NJ: Erlbaum.

Castagno, A., & Brayboy, B. (2008). Culturally responsive schooling for indigenous youth: A review of the literature. *Review of Educational Research, 78*(4), 941–993.

Fuchs, D., Fuchs, L., & Vaughn, S. (Eds.). (2008). *Response to intervention: A framework for reading educators.* Newark DE: International Reading Association.

Gay, G. (2000). *Culturally responsive teaching: Theory, research, and practice.* New York: Teachers College Press.

Genishi, C., & Goodwin, A. L. (Eds.). (2008). *Diversities in early childhood education: Rethinking and doing.* New York: Routledge.

Hagedorn, L., Tibbetts, K., Kana'iaupuni, S., Moon, H., & Lester, J. (2004). Factors contributing to college retention in the Native Hawaiian population. *Research conference on Hawaiian well-being.* Honolulu: Kamehameha Schools.

Halfon, N., Shulman, E., & Hochstein, M. (2001). Brain development in early childhood. In N. Halfon, E. Shulman & M. Hochstein (Eds.), *Building community systems for young children.* Los Angeles CA: UCLA Center for Healthier Children, Families and Communities.

Kamakau, S., Barrere, D., Feher, J., & Pukui, M. (1991). *Tales and traditions of the people of old (Na mo'olelo o ka poe kahiko).* Honolulu: Bishop Museum Press.

Kamakau, S., & Hawai'i, A. Ō. (1996). *Ke kumu aupuni : Ka mo'olelo Hawai'i no Kamehameha ka na'i aupuni a me kāana aupuni i ho'okumu ai. Honolulu, HI,* . Honolulu: 'Ahahui 'Ōlelo Hawai'i.

Kame'eleihiwa, L. (1992). *Native land and foreign desires.* Honolulu, HI: Bishop Museum Press.

Kamehameha Schools Office of Program Evaluation and Planning. (1993). *Native Hawaiian educational assessment 1993.* Honolulu, HI: Kamehameha Schools Bernice Pauahi Bishop Estate.

Kana'iaupuni, S. (2004). Ola ka inoa (the name lives): Cultural inputs and early education outcomes of Hawaiian children, *Research Conference on Hawaiian Well-being.* Honolulu: Kamehameha Schools.

Kana'iaupuni, S., & Ishibashi, K. (2005). *Hawai'i charter schools: Initial trends and select outcomes for Native Hawaiian students.* Honolulu.

Kanahele, G. H. S. (1986). *Ku kanaka, stand tall: A search for Hawaiian values.* Honolulu HI: University of Hawaii.

Ladson-Billings, G. (1995). Toward a theory of culturally relevant pedagogy. *American Educational Research Journal, 32*(3), 465–491.

Mignolo, W. (2000). *Local histories/global designs: Coloniality, subaltern knowledges, and border thinking.* Princeton NJ: Princeton University Press.

Nāone, C. K. (2008). *The pilina of kanaka and 'aina: Place, language and community as sites of reclamation for Indigenous education—the Hawaiian case.* Unpublished doctoral dissertation, University of Hawai'i, Honolulu.

No Child Left Behind. (2001). *Public Law No. 107–1110, 115 Stat. 1425, 2002,* 2004. Available from http://www.ed.gov/policy/elsec/leg/esea02/beginning/html

Osborne, A. B. (1996). Practice into theory into practice: Culturally relevant pedagogy for students we have marginalized and normalized. *Anthropology & Education Quarterly, 27*(3), 285–314.

Pukui, M. (1983). *'Olelo No'eau: Hawaiian proverbs and poetical sayings.* Honolulu: Bishop Museum Press.

Pukui, M., Haertig, E., & Lee, C. (1972). *Nānā i ke kumu (Look to the source).* Honolulu: Hui Hānai, an auxiliary of the Queen Lili'uokalani Children's Center.

Roberts, R. N. (1993). Early education as community intervention: Assisting an ethnic minority to be ready for school. *American Journal of Community Psychology 21*(4), 521–535

Sarsona, M. (2004). *Early education choices key to family well-being.* Retrieved July 12, 2005, from http://starbulletin.com/2004/12/02/editorial/commentary.html

Sarsona, M., Goo, S., Kawakami, A., & Au, K. (2008). Equity issues in a parent-participation preschool program for Native Hawaiian children. In C. Genishi & A. Goodwin (Eds.), *Diversities in early childhood education: Rethinking and doing* (pp. 151–165). New York: Routledge.

Spring, J. (2008). Research on globalization and education. *Review of Educational Research, 78*(2), 330–363.

Warner, S. (1996). *I ola ka 'ōlelo i nā keiki : ka 'apo 'ia 'ana o ka 'ōlelo Hawai'i e nā keiki ma ke Kula Kaiapuni.* Honolulu Department of Hawaiian and Indo-Pacific Languages and Literatures, University of Hawai'i.

CHAPTER 8

MIGRANT AND REFUGEE CHILDREN, THEIR FAMILIES, AND EARLY CHILDHOOD EDUCATION

Susan Grieshaber and Melinda G. Miller

ABSTRACT

One of the effects of globalization is the increasing movement of people around the globe. Transnational migration brings demographic changes that produce challenges for education and social services. While there is a growing body of literature about educational concerns associated with migrant and refugee children, young migrant and refugee children are not often included in this research because it concentrates on secondary and primary schooling. In this chapter we review the literature that relates to young migrant and refugee children, their families and early childhood education. More specifically, we synthesize the state of knowledge relating to curriculum, parents and teacher education. Following the analysis of recent research, the chapter concludes with some suggestions for further research, policy makers and practitioners.

Language and Cultural Diversity in Early Childhood Education, pages 167–190

POPULATION TRENDS

One of the effects of globalization is the increasing movement of people around the globe. Whether it is due to migration by choice or matters connected to war and persecution that produce refugees and asylum seekers,[1] the transitional displacement of people in the early twenty-first century has meant that 200 million people are living away from their country of birth (Global Commission on International Migration, 2005). According to Adams and Kirova (2006c), Australia, Canada and the U.S. are "three major receiving nations for transnational migrants" (p. 199). The estimated net migration rate for the U.S. for 2009 is 4.32 migrants per 1000 of the population. For Canada it is 5.63/1000 of the population and Australia 6.23/1000 (Central Intelligence Agency [CIA], 2009). These countries also accept quotas of refugees from refugee camps and have long histories of immigration. The U.S. census of 2000 indicated that nearly 46 million people (18% of the population) spoke a language other than English as their first language and of these 29 million (about 60%) speak Spanish (Nieto & Bode, 2008). This diversity is reflected in public school enrolments in the U.S. The school-age population (5–17 years) increased by 17 percent from 1990–2000 and the percentage of English language learners increased by 46 percent during this same time (Nieto & Bode, 2008). However, as Nieto and Bode point out (2008), immigration is one of the "most contentious issues" (p. 7) in the U.S.

Unlike the U.S. which has a long history of immigration, some of the Nordic countries have recently experienced a change in the composition of their population. In Denmark for instance, migrants now constitute 4.1% of the population and in Norway it is 3%, while in Finland there are over 100 different migrant groups, with most coming from Russia and Somalia (OECD, 2006).

Globalization has also produced changes in the population of several European countries, with an estimated net migration rate in 2009 of 2.19/1000 population for Germany and 2.16/1000 for the UK (CIA, 2009). Australia, which has a much smaller population than the U.S. has recently experienced societal transformation due largely to changes in the source countries of Australia's permanent arrivals since the mid 1990s. In accordance with United Nations priorities, the Australian Humanitarian program resettled approximately 24,000 refugees from the Horn of Africa (notably Sudan and Somalia), the Middle East and South West Asia in 2005 and 2006, and expects to settle a similar number each year for the next few years (Department of Immigration and Multicultural and Indigenous Affairs (DIMIA), 2005). The number of new migrants settling permanently in Australia in 2007–8 increased by 7.3% (Australian Human Rights Commission, 2008).

New theorizing about issues of migration that includes refugees has moved from cultural deficit models, through economic and social reproduction models and explanations of cultural incompatibilities, to current understandings of the complexities of cultural globalization. Such perspectives recognize that overlooking the rich cultural, social and cognitive resources that come with migrants and refugees is counterproductive to all facets of society (Cummins, 2004, p. xv). In his study of the socio-economic environment in the United States, Florida (2004) detailed the conditions under which new migrants contribute critically and creatively to the vibrancy of society. Significantly, feeling safe and valued were paramount and correlated with areas of greatest growth and vitality.

In this chapter we review literature that relates to young migrant and refugee children from birth to age eight, their families and early childhood education. Migrants and refugees are those who have settled permanently in a new country. Having said that, for the most part when reviewing literature, we have used the same descriptors as the authors. For instance, because Adair and Tobin (2008) use the term "immigrant" to describe the parents in their study, we follow suit. This accounts for the variations in use of the terms migrant and immigrant throughout the chapter. We concentrate on literature published between 2000 and 2009, although we do move outside these years on occasion. Our preference was to restrict the literature to empirical research only, but given the small amount of research undertaken in the area of our focus, we draw on a range of publications, some of which relate to primary and secondary education. We do this because of the relevance of certain issues about primary and secondary schooling to young migrant and refugee children and early education contexts.

Initial scans of the literature revealed that most empirical studies have used qualitative methodologies such as case studies. Interview and observation studies have also been undertaken. We draw on a range of literature from around the globe but concentrate on studies from the U.S. and Australia (because we are Australian and the 2009 estimated net rate of migration to Australia is the highest of the countries cited above [CIA, 2009]). Examples are used to illustrate key points and there is no intention of generalizing these to all countries. For the purpose of this chapter we have chosen to focus on three areas of literature: curriculum; relationships with parents, and teacher education. Curriculum was selected because more research has been undertaken in primary and secondary schools about migrants and refugees than in early childhood settings. In addition, little has been written about the education of refugee children (Hamilton & Moore, 2004), and there is "little research about refugee children's educational experiences" (Rutter, 2005, p. 5). Curriculum is an area in which practitioners can make a difference when working with migrant and refugee children. A small section about different approaches to the use of the arts to support migrant and refugee children is included because art therapy is one approach often used as a technique with refugee children who have experienced trauma situations.

The second focus of our review of literature is relationships with parents. Like curriculum, this area of research is small and growing. Relationships with parents is a key focus of most early childhood programs. Developing positive relationships with migrant and refugee parents is an important part of the daily work of early childhood educators because there is a very real likelihood that migrant and refugee parents may hold different views about early childhood education than what their children experience in the programs they are attending (Adair & Tobin, 2008). Teacher education is the third topic of our review of literature. We have selected it because teacher preparation and in-service programs can not only teach about the importance of drawing on the rich cultural, social and cognitive resources that come with permanent new settlers, but also appropriate ways of going about this. As Florida (2004) pointed out, feeling safe and valued is paramount to migrants being able to contribute critically and creatively to their adopted society. However, feeling safe and valued requires understandings of culture that are "multidimensional and complicated and not simply [about] ... artefacts, food, and music" (Nieto, 2004, p. xxvii).

After reviewing the literature and considering relevant theoretical positions for each of these three topics, we discuss implications for researchers, policy makers and practitioners. The chapter concludes with some recommendations about young migrant and refugee children, their families and early childhood education. While research studies about refugee children are dominated by what Rutter (2005) calls the trauma literature, our focus remains educational and encompasses children of migrants and refugees, their families and the early childhood contexts in which they are engaged.

TRANSNATIONAL MIGRATION

Transnational migration brings demographic changes that produce challenges for education and social services. Children from immigrant families have been described as "at-risk" due to the difficulties their parents can experience in finding employment and because, often, they have little knowledge of the official language and culture of their adopted country (OECD, 2006). According to the Australian Research Alliance for Children and Youth (ARACY) (2008) other reasons that make life difficult include "... being part of a minority group in Australia ... experiences prior to migration (for example refugee trauma), the different values and practices ... the problems ... face[d] having qualifications and experience ratified, and the various forms of racism ... experience[d]" (p. 1). Poverty is another issue often faced by immigrant families (Adair & Tobin, 2008; OECD, 2006). Conditions for migrants and refugees are made more difficult when a number of these factors act in combination.

Racism seems to be something experienced by many migrants and refugees. In the UK, particular conceptualizations of 'race' are integral components of media and public debates about refugees and historically, about migrants (Rutter, 2005). Rutter argues that "older phenotypic notions of 'race' have survived in the popular imagination, as well as among some policy makers" (p. 10). She cites the British National Party as continuing to promulgate "ideas of distinct races, racial separation and repatriation of those who are not white" (p. 10). In Australia, addressing racism has attracted increased media attention and assumed heightened significance since the Sydney 'race' riots in December, 2005, and various other incidents such as a university professor making statements that "Sub-Saharan Africans have an average IQ of 70 to 75" and that "...an expanding black population is a surefire recipe for an increase in crime, violence and a wide range of other social problems" (Roberts, 2005). Like the UK, Australia has historically rooted conceptions about 'race' that transferred to assimilation policies and multicultural approaches to education. However, the more contemporary approach of anti-racist education was not adopted as fervently in Australia as it was in the UK, the U.S. and Canada. Much like the UK, current policies in Australia promote social cohesion and integration; expressions of which, in our view, are really assimilation by another name (see Ho, 2007).

There is a large body of literature about educational concerns associated with migrant children, but young migrant children are not often included in this research because it concentrates on secondary and primary schooling. For parents who have recently migrated, enrolling their child in an early childhood program can be the definitive moment when cultural values of their home and the adopted culture come into contact and, often, conflict (Multicultural Health Brokers Co-op [MHBC], 2004). This means that early childhood settings are often the first context in which migrant parents and their young children come face to face with differences between the culture of home and the public culture of their new country. The potential for tension between families and early childhood settings can arise when curricula are not responsive to children's cultural values and practices (see Adair & Tobin, 2008). In Western countries such as the UK, U.S., Canada and Australia, early childhood curricula have a history of being primarily Eurocentric or monocultural because they are based on developmental psychology, which means that young children from migrant backgrounds are likely to experience forms of marginalization in their early education experiences.

CURRICULUM

There is a distinct lack of relevant research identifying the educational needs of young children of migrant families (see Adams & Kirova, 2006a), and a growing and serious concern that simply providing regular mainstream education for these young children is not enough (Ariza, 2006).

In this section we consider literature that identifies refugee and migrant children as having special needs and provide field examples from research to illustrate how this notion is produced by teachers' actions and curriculum choices. In the literature, special needs tend to be associated with pre-migration experiences such as trauma. However, as Adams and Kirova (2006c) point out, relocation can also be traumatic, especially if the new arrivals are a "visible minority" (p. 199) in their new community. What follows considers literature about trauma; teachers, practitioners and children in early childhood settings; the use of the arts as curriculum initiatives, and transformational approaches to education.

That refugee children have special needs, especially those who have experienced trauma, is a point that continues to be made in regard to education generally, as well as early education. A corpus of literature addresses the social, medical, political, linguistic and educational issues of refugees, but little has been written about refugee children (see Hamilton & Moore, 2004). In the few studies that have investigated the needs of refugee children, the focus has been on children's traumatic experiences rather than their educational experiences (Rutter, 2005).

One approach to the inclusion of refugee children in early years classrooms is to provide practical strategies and advice for teachers, such as making classrooms more responsive to those who have experienced trauma (Szente, Hoot, & Taylor, 2006). In line with this approach, others have argued for refugee children to be considered as distinct from those who have migrated for other reasons, on the basis that the experiences of refugee children often involve trauma and therefore they have special needs (Waniganayake, 2001). In support of this, strategies put in place by teachers have also been examined, with one study investigating how teachers and practitioners responded to coping behaviors of children who have been traumatized—the results of which concluded that a range of appropriate strategies was developed that supported healing and provided a safe environment (see Sims, Hayden, Palmer, & Hutchins, 2000).

Common initiatives in early childhood settings include providing information about school policies and expectations, and parents' rights being translated into parents' native language. Well planned buddy programs have also met with success, particularly as social isolation and loneliness seem to be experienced by young immigrants irrespective of their racial, ethnic, and linguistic backgrounds (Kirova & Wu, 2002). Appropriate materials for children at various levels of knowledge should always be available and it is essential to provide teachers with adequate professional development opportunities to prepare them to be successful in working with migrant and refugee children and their families. One form of professional development proven to be a productive way to assist teachers to use effective strategies with newly arrived children is mentoring (Adams & Shambleau, 2006).

The extent to which children receive appropriate support can be impacted by the amount of information a teacher receives (or is willing to find out) about children's prior experiences. For example, by law in the U.S., teachers and administrators are not able to ask about immigration status (Szente & Hoot, 2006). These circumstances create particular difficulties for teachers in light of repeated cautions in the literature concerning assumptions about refugee children that can lead to further isolation in interactions and curriculum choices (Szente & Hoot, 2006). While a lack of information about children's backgrounds is problematic for staff, attempts should be made to find out about children's home and previous lives. This aligns with Adams and Shambleau's (2006) reminder about the well known teaching strategy of building on the knowledge and strengths that children bring to the classroom to ensure more inclusive practices are implemented. It is similar to learning about "families' funds of knowledge" (Gonzalez, Moll, & Amanti, 2005), which also refers to their strengths and resources, and how learning occurs in family contexts. This knowledge is then used to create teaching approaches that are linked to children's lives, local histories and community contexts. Nieto and Bode (2008) suggest vigorous family outreach and provide an example of a teacher who visits every family in the two weeks prior to school beginning to learn about the children who will be in her class.

Despite good intentions and effective strategies, the immigrant experience for children remains highly problematic because of learning a new language, the disruption to family life, and learning to live in another culture where things may be very different from home cultures and values (Suárez-Orozco & Suárez-Orozco, 2001). Regardless of the variance in cultural differences, isolating practices can and do occur as seen in a study of children who migrated from mainland China to Hong Kong with their families. The findings revealed that the children experienced segregation, prejudice and marginalization because of their accents and dialects, despite their ethnic similarity to Hong Kong Chinese (Rao & Yuen, 2006). This experience is consistent with migrants who are racially different from the dominant group (Li, 2001; Moreau, 2000). As in Rao and Yuen's study, the approach of school staff in the adjustment process for children is highly significant to educational outcomes for young children. One key difficulty is teachers' unchanging and monocultural conceptualizations of how schooling should be conducted in particular locations regardless of the changing demographic of the student population and the increasing complexity of society generally (see Chong, 2005). Recent research in primary schools in Hong Kong highlights why a monocultural approach is problematic, with reports from teachers working with newly arrived children from mainland

China indicating that traditional approaches to teaching and learning are ineffective (Chong, 2005). One implication is that teachers are challenged to move beyond monoculturalism and adopt teaching and learning approaches that are successful with newly arrived children.

These examples show how personnel in early childhood settings may engage in practices that can lead to the marginalization of migrant and refugee children. While these practices can be extensions of the broader curriculum and may be inadvertent, it draws attention to the need for regular professional learning opportunities, appropriate resources and ongoing support for all staff. In an Australian study in before school contexts, Robinson & Jones Díaz (2006) reported that children were judged by staff according to their proficiency with English: "...children's ability to mix effectively with other children...is measured against the ability to speak English...what counts as cultural capital for these children is the ability to 'fit' into the monolingual 'English only' setting" (p. 115). Robinson & Jones Díaz found that the majority of long day care practitioner participants "constructed bilingual children's lack of English as a deficit and located children in discourses of 'need'" (p. 115). Accordingly, such children are marked as different (deficit) by practitioners. As Adams and Kirova (2006b) note, practitioners do not always have a correct understanding of children's language abilities and competence. Most migrant children act as language brokers for their parents and other family members and these skills are not always reflected in the classroom or academic achievement (Adams & Kirova, 2006b). McBrien (2003) advised against making assumptions that "students are slow or need special education services because they do not speak fluent English" (p. 78). This advice is exemplary in that it acts as a reminder of how easy it is to fall into deficit approaches, that is, equating a lack of English proficiency with cognitive or other inability.

Other relevant Australian research has shown how a boy (Nate) who had migrated from the Pacific Islands and was in Year 3 (aged 8 years) was categorized by his teachers as performing at a low level and struggling with literacy and numeracy (Grieshaber, 2008a). Nate completed a set computer task of making a maze at a more sophisticated level than all other children in the class. At the same time he engaged in an unsanctioned practice on another window, drawing one of the characters from *Mortal Kombat*, which resulted in a small group of boys watching in awe and discussing what he was drawing, as *Mortal Kombat* was unknown to them. Nate was astute enough to switch back to the maze window when the research assistant moved near him. Despite his multiliteracy talent, the teachers did not see or acknowledge his efforts at the maze, nor did they come to know about the complex digital artefact that he created at the same time as completing the set task. There is a high probability that he remained known by the teachers as a child who was struggling with literacy and numeracy.

Other research in secondary and primary school shows that when teachers do interact with students, the questions they ask provide migrant and refugee students with limited ways of responding, which means that they are prevented from becoming actively involved in classroom discussion (Lee, 2002; McBrien, 2005).

The Arts and Children "In Need"

As a specific curriculum area, the arts have received attention in relation to young migrant and refugee children. Art therapy has been used as a technique for refugee children who have experienced trauma situations and are seen as having special needs because of their emotional and psychological fragility (Brunick, 1999). Being mindful of the conditions that enable migrants to flourish in their adopted country (Florida, 2004) means taking care that well intentioned humanitarian discourses do not continue to construct refugees as helpless and in need of support (Rutter, 2005).

In contrast to using art-as-therapy, McArdle and Spina (2007) used art as a language with refugee children aged about eight years in an attempt to move beyond positioning them as deficit because of their differences in "language, culture and social capital" (p. 50). Using art as a language is aimed at building children's identities and social capital as it enables children to communicate with each other and adults without the barrier of language. Art as a language may also be able to help children with language acquisition and other academic achievements, as well as build connections between the worlds of school and family. The children engaged in three visual arts workshops with a practising artist over a three-week period. They experienced the language of art, specific skills, techniques and artistic processes, and an appreciation of particular artists' works. The idea was to provide "exposure to, and experience in the arts as well as an avenue for creative expression" (p. 51). In contrast to popular views about the purpose of art-as-therapy, the children did not represent traumatic experiences that may have been part of their past. Instead they engaged in the set task with the resources and processes required for art-making, and communicated with each other, the artist and the researchers through sharing the art-making. The workshops enabled the teachers, children, artist and researchers to establish meaningful connections and for the children to produce unique three-dimensional portraits. Several of the children were able to communicate that they had hope for the future.

In a slightly different approach, Campey's (2002) suggestion is to use the expressive arts in whole class or whole school approaches in ways that have particular benefit for immigrant and refugee children coping with trauma. The claim is that the coping and resiliency skills of all children would be enhanced in a climate of reducing resources, more curriculum demands, and the increasing difficulty of providing programs for individual children. The strategies about which Campey talks are not unique. What is being suggested is that strategies promoted for migrant and refugee children (such as buddy programs, ensuring that all children can see themselves in the curriculum, recognizing celebrations, providing translations and opportunities for children's self-expression and so on), may benefit all children if used as part of a whole school approach. This idea has merit and is worth considering as others have made similar suggestions. For example, one line of argument that has been pursued by some authors is the transformation of schooling so that it is oriented to the diversity of educational needs of all students, and in the process respects their social and cultural origins, and the abilities they bring to the setting (Blanco & Takemoto, 2006; Neito & Bode, 2008).

To many people, transformation means something monolithic (or systemic) and even revolutionary, which also suggests the idea of significant events that cause change in a relatively short amount of time. Contrary to this idea, Nieto and Bode (2008) locate educational transformation as something that is ongoing and "in progress", which takes time and is firmly within the province of those who work with children and families in classrooms on a daily basis. Globalization has resulted in the presence of migrant and refugee children in many early childhood contexts. While cultural, linguistic and ethnic diversity is not uncommon in early childhood settings, what might be different is the increasing diversity of the source countries of migrants and refugees. Such changes present ongoing challenges to early childhood practitioners, classrooms and schools; curriculum, pedagogies and assessment; organization and management, and the socio-political context in which schools are located.

The idea that transformation is part of what happens on a daily basis in classrooms is a vote of confidence in practitioners but requires sustained hard work. Nieto and Bode (2008) provide many practical strategies for classroom practitioners which are related to all facets of classroom life. These include focusing on human differences and similarities in the preschool years, having high expectations of all children, using the curriculum critically, using pedagogies that engage children in meaningful ways, and using inclusive disciplinary strategies. Among other ideas, Nieto and Bode also suggest respecting student differences, and making differences and similarities an explicit part of the curriculum. This includes talking about skin colour, hair texture and other physical differences to teach children that it is unacceptable to laugh at new class members who speak with an accent; that dark-skinned children can be the princess in role plays, and that it is objectionable for children to refuse to play with dark-skinned dolls because they are "dirty" (see Derman-Sparks & Ramsey, 2006). Many of these strategies are not part of everyday practice in early childhood settings, particularly those that are prefaced on notions of developmental psychology and normative understandings of children's development (these are discussed further in the section about Teacher Education). The presence of migrant and refugee children in early childhood settings is also a unique opportunity to learn about and work with their families.

RELATIONSHIPS WITH PARENTS AND FAMILIES

There is much emphasis in early childhood education about parents as partners in the education process and about transition to school. However, both these bodies of literature (parents as partners and transition to school) do not deal comprehensively or specifically with developing relationships with migrant and refugee parents. Because of this, early childhood programs that serve children of migrants and refugees though generally well intended, may not consider perspectives of the parents. Little research has involved parents of young immigrant and refugee children (see MHBC, 2004; Pryor, 2001) and even less has consulted migrant parents about their values, beliefs, expectations and concerns regarding their young children's education.

The small but growing body of research about migrant parents, their children and early childhood education employs mostly qualitative approaches. On the whole, migrant families tend to value education (Suárez-Orozco & Suárez-Orozco, 2001) even though they may have different opinions and beliefs about specific aspects of it. For example, immigrant parents may be unfamiliar with being involved in their child's educational experiences and may have low levels of schooling themselves (Hernandez, 2004). It is possible that some migrant parents may have had no prior contact with educational settings, while others choose not to become involved in their child's education. Others may not be familiar with the style of instruction (Li, 2006) and some may not be able to communicate with staff or speak openly with them. Some may believe that teachers are the education experts and there is no need to become involved, and others may disagree with testing and assessment procedures (Adams & Kirova, 2006a). Conversely, migrant parents may be familiar with school routines and procedures in the country of settlement such as testing and a competitive academic environment. There are wide parental differences and they are attributable to "culture, prior experiences, and individual personalities" (Adams & Kirova, 2006a p. 9). The teachers in the study undertaken by Adams and Shambleau (2006) recognized the importance of reaching out to newly arrived parents because of cultural differences, and the significance of families and schools working together. However, the case study of a Sudanese refugee family in Buffalo, NY depicted the way in which parents, who were already marginalized because of their 'race' and refugee status, were positioned as powerless by the school their children attended (Li, 2006). The parents were unable to effect any changes to the programs their children experienced and were also excluded from decisions made about their children's education. Canadian research has concluded that too often, programmatic reforms for young children are initiated without input from parents (Pacini-Ketchabaw & Scheter, 2003), and this is particularly true when the parents are migrants.

One approach that has taken parental perspectives into account is the work comparing ideas about preschool held by teachers and immigrant parents (Adair & Tobin, 2008; Tobin, 2004; Tobin, Arzubiaga, & Mantovani, 2007). Tobin (2004) argues that preschool programs are able to serve immigrants better when parents, teachers and other stakeholders talk to each other. The aim of comparing ideas held by immigrant parents and others is to act as "a catalyst for dialogue among parents, practitioners, scholars and policymakers about the problems and possibilities of creating preschool programs that reflect the values and beliefs of both immigrant communities and of the societies to which they have immigrated" (Adair & Tobin, 2008, p. 137). This research is still underway but some ideas that have emerged to date include:

- In many cases immigrants parents hold different views about quality and best practice;
- The technique of watching and discussing a video of a day in the preschool is helpful for facilitating ongoing discussion between staff and parents, and with careful structuring adversarial and contentious situations can be avoided;
- The idea that "We need to learn to hear immigrants' parents expressions of desire for their children to become Americans as something other than assimilationism or capitulation to the agenda of the right" (Adair & Tobin, 2008, p. 149);
- Many teachers of immigrant children do not fully understand the experiences of poverty or the "racism and the discrimination they face, and the feeling of alienation they experience in response to the racism" (p. 149). Even when aware, early childhood staff often do not know what to do about it.

Experiences of racism and discrimination occur inside early childhood educational settings as well as outside them. For staff, dealing with these issues means "working consciously against their own biases and those of the students" (Kirova & Adams, 2006, p. 324). It also means understanding how identity, difference, power and privilege are all interconnected within the socio-political context of society and that decisions about education are never neutral (Nieto & Bode, 2008).

TEACHER EDUCATION

In teacher education programs course work related to the education of children from culturally and linguistically backgrounds can be limited (see Early & Winton, 2001). When coursework about children from diverse backgrounds is present, it is often located in content about developmental psychology or child study, generally as an adjunct to the topic of "inclusion". For over 15 years critiques of developmental psychology have revealed how normative understandings about children's strengths and areas of need are constructed from uncontested, Eurocentric ideas of developmentalism. Against developmentalism, elements of "difference" are interpreted as developmental delay or deficit (see Burman, 1994; Lubeck, 1996; Ryan & Grieshaber, 2005).

For refugee children in particular, perpetuations of trauma or "at-risk" discourses position them as helpless and traumatised and in need of support from "mainstream" agencies and services including education. The positioning of refugee children as in-need is also evident in the contemporary humanitarian discourse which perpetuates notions of culture as different to that of the mainstream (Rutter, 2005). When this occurs, notions of culture and difference are attached to deficit models rather than being viewed as a resource in mainstream channels (Kalantzis, 2005).

Despite the corpus of work that critiques normative understandings of education and children's development, pre-service teacher education programs often present course work that is grounded in normative or Eurocentric models of teaching and learning (Hickling-Hudson, 2004). Normative models do not offer pre-service teachers extended explorations about curricula that attend to intersections of 'race,' ethnicity, gender, class and sexuality. In early childhood degree programs in particular, subjects about children's development and the inclusion of children with additional needs (of which 'cultural needs' are an adjunct) and which are premised on developmentalism, are more often core or compulsory units, while subjects focussed on cultural diversity are elective and located in broader faculty offerings separate to the early childhood degree program. In instances whereby critiques of developmental psychology are included in course work, pre-service teachers may still have little access to exemplars of practice that illustrate transformative approaches to responding to cultural diversity in early childhood curricula (Ryan & Grieshaber, 2005).

Identity Work in Teacher Education

One growing component of teacher education course work related to cultural diversity is 'identity work'. The growth of this field is evident from the plethora of studies conducted since the 1990s that have investigated how and why teacher education courses should prepare pre-service teachers (completing 3–4 year bachelor degrees or graduate diplomas) to teach diverse student populations (for examples see Aveling, 2006; Bernhard, 1995; Brandon, 2003; Cockrell, Placier, Cockrell, & Middleton, 1999; Duesterberg, 1998; Hickling-Hudson, 2004; Jones, 1999; Lawrence & Bunche, 1996; Lin Goodwin & Genor, 2008; Obidah, 2000; Rosenberg, 2004; Santoro & Allard, 2005; Siwatu, 2007; Sugrue, 1997; Tatum, 1992; Vavrus, 2002). These studies generally focus on the need for pre-service teachers to be supported to challenge cultural assumptions in a range of contexts and critically examine their personal beliefs and positioning in society using a cultural framework. These studies vary in their aims, goals and successes. For us, the issue with racism, discrimination and pre-service teachers remains teacher identity formation, or, as Kirova and Adams (2006) have pointed out, "working consciously against their own biases and those of the students" (p. 324). This is by no means easy and requires ongoing work and support.

The focus on teacher identity formation draws from a cultural approach taken up by theorists and researchers interested in understanding how pre-service teachers' cultural backgrounds influence their attitudinal stance and ideas about pedagogical practices they intend to employ in the classroom. Because the demographic of the pre-service teaching population in many Western nations comprises white, middle-class females (as seen in the Australian context), identity work has focused largely on how white teachers develop an understanding about their own ethnicity and its impact on how they view and (will) interact with people of a cultural background different to their own. As Graue (2005) states, "the cultural perspective works to identify the tacit, normative, socially developed conceptions of identity and affiliation that shape meaning making for individuals within groups" (p. 159). In this growing body of work, meaning making relates to white individuals' conceptions of identity within the mainstream group.

For pre-service teachers, cross-cultural identity work is important because it creates the likelihood of crisis and confrontation - or "spaces" of confusion and doubt from which possibilities for critical explorations and change are produced (Schick, 2000). In some teacher education programs, ethnicity related course work may be undertaken in conjunction with explorations of interrelated identity constructions that frame individuals' understanding of self including class, gender and sexuality. Combined, all of these perspectives allow for important autobiographical work, although it is critical for this work to be famed sociologically as well as psychologically to ensure that as individuals, pre-service teachers develop understandings of self *in relation to* connections and interactions with others and institutions in their personal and professional lives (Phillips, 2005). This is particularly important for white identity construction work as findings from research in this area often report on the extent to which individual bodies acknowledge their white ethnic status, not inclusive of the ways in which awareness of the influence of their cultural background is also embodied in pedagogical actions and interactions with children and families in specific educational contexts.

Teacher Education and Parental Involvement

When identity construction work focuses on interactions with others as well as self, autobiographical explorations can also support pre-service teachers to explore their disposition toward, and images of, children and families. Of particular salience is their ideas, wonderings and fears about interacting and 'partnering' with children and families from cultural backgrounds different from their own (see Flanigan, 2007). As 'partnership' discourses are given much space in early childhood education course work and literature, pre-service teachers' beliefs about parental involvement and the positioning of parents in the teacher/parent relationship should align with explorations of notions of self in relation to others.

In two recent studies about pre-service teachers' beliefs about relationships with families conducted by Flanigan (2007) and Graue (2005), findings provide insight into how pre-service teachers' beliefs and ideas about partnerships with families contribute to the fragility of home/school relations. While many factors combine to produce a fragile state, including institutionalised practices, both studies call for greater involvement from faculty to provide components in degree programs that afford pre-service teachers opportunities to develop relationships with families in the local community throughout their degree program. It is real-world interactions between pre-service teachers and families that "can provide broader awareness of the issues families face in schooling" (Graue, 2005, p. 183). When faculty commit to parent and community involvement as part of students' clinical experiences (Flanigan, 2007), students have increased opportunities to make links between families' experiences and theoretical concepts that underpin understandings about home/school links (Graue, 2005). This approach to collaborations with families aligns with a service learning model that focuses as much on students as people as potential teachers—a key component also seen in autobiographical work.

While a focus on autobiographical work is critical to pre-service teachers' identity development (Lin Goodwin & Genor, 2008), there will always be a need to be wary of imbalances in the extent to which pre-service teachers' notions of self are disrupted and the extent to which the content they are offered in a degree program comes under greater scrutiny. In drawing from the example provided earlier, it is pertinent to consider Heyning's

(2001) viewpoint that "scientific knowledge" (such as developmentalism) provides spaces for pre-service teachers to construct themselves as [future] "experts"—able to make claims about and act as experts in their professional role. The notion of expert is linked to broader discourses of professionalism in which there is an expectation that professional knowledge is located in scientific or standardised realms (Osgood, 2006). In the role of expert, teachers are positioned to rely on objective forms of knowledge that reduce notions of family involvement to that of secondary forms of interaction centered on the idea of parents as clients rather than partners. As stated by Graue (2005), "objective decisions come at the cost of separation from clients and a devaluing of the knowledge of families" (p. 178).

For pre-service teachers autobiographical work can be undermined by overriding influences in course content that create opposing notions of what it is to be and do as an early childhood professional. For children and families from migrant and refugee backgrounds, pre-service teachers' preparation and resulting constructions of self/other and their professional role will impact significantly the foundation on which home/center relationships are forged and how they work (or not) in the interests of both parties. If foundations for relationships devalue the knowledge and participation of families, then "teachers have little to draw on but their own experiences" (Graue, 2005, p. 183). Given that the majority of early childhood teachers are socialised within Eurocentric frameworks, and autobiographical work in teacher education is most often limited to singular subject offerings, these circumstances will contribute to oppressive forms of interactions between teachers and families from diverse backgrounds as well as approaches to teaching and learning afforded to children in early childhood contexts in the future.

IMPLICATIONS

Many nations are affected by transnational migration and educational systems and must respond to these changes and offer the best education possible. That educational institutions and staff have been, and remain challenged by transnational migration is undeniable. The research and examples presented here demonstrate that while early childhood practitioners may require new strategies for dealing with diverse populations who bring a varying range of pre-migration experiences, they should also be aware of the effect of humanitarian discourses. As Rutter (2005) acknowledges about refugees, pity is the "outcome of humanitarian discourses" (p. 9) and succeeds in strengthening the idea that refugees are different from the rest of the population because they are traumatized and dysfunctional. A key understanding about migrant and refugee children is that they do not represent a homogeneous group: "Diversity exists in every group, whether refugees or nations, whether of a single ethnic or cultural group or of a multicultural group" (Kirova & Adams, 2006, p. 323). And while educational settings alone cannot be held responsible for the socialization and acculturation of immigrant children, it is practitioners, educators, early childhood and school contexts that are the "key to facilitating the socialization and acculturation of immigrant children" (Adams & Kirova, 2006a, p. 2). Increasing fundamental theoretical and professional knowledge about the learning needs of particular populations of young children and their families will help to develop high quality and high equity education that aims for success for all students (Luke, Weir & Woods, 2008). We conclude the chapter with suggestions for researchers, policy makers and practitioners, which are not exhaustive.

Suggestions for Researchers

- Invite migrant/refugee parents to be active participants in research;
- Invite migrant and refugee children to be active participants in research;
- Focus on very young children because of the importance of the early years for children's identity and overall development;
- Research the types of professional development that suit early childhood practitioners when exploring cultural diversity;
- Research curriculum, pedagogy, assessment and disciplinary practices that practitioners find successful;
- Research the factors that create successful experiences for young migrant children and their families in early childhood settings.

Suggestions for Policy Makers

- Provide greater scope in coursework about children from diverse backgrounds in curriculum in teacher education;
- Involve, advocate and endorse the involvement of migrant and refugee parents in local and broad policy decisions;
- Advocate for and endorse the involvement of migrant and refugee parents in decision-making at all levels about the curriculum, pedagogy and assessment, as well as in decisions that involve their children;
- Acknowledge the real life experiences of migrants and refugees in terms of the poverty, racism, discrimination and alienation that

many face on a daily basis and provide suggestions for how early childhood practitioners might work productively with these factors;
- Recognise that migrants and refugees are not homogeneous and that diversity and difference exist in any group;
- Identify examples of individual and institutional racism and provide suggestions for non-racist practices.

Suggestions for Practitioners

- Learn about individual and institutional racism and discrimination;
- Learn about deficit theories and how they position difference of any sort;
- Learn about your own biases and those of the children in your class, and work conscientiously against them (Kirova & Adams, 2006, p. 324);
- Recognize that migrants are not homogeneous and that diversity and difference exist in any group;
- Focus on strengths and abilities that children and families bring so that culture is viewed as a resource rather than a deficit (see Gonzalez et al., 2005; Kalantzis, 2005);
- Make differences and similarities an explicit part of the daily curriculum (see Nieto & Bode, 2008);
- Recognize that there is no one 'right' way of teaching migrant and refugee children and that a variety of approaches and resources are needed;
- Identify children's learning preferences and use them pedagogically;
- Take up relevant professional development opportunities;
- Share what works with other practitioners;
- Involve and consult meaningfully with migrant and refugee parents in localised practices.

CONCLUSION

This chapter has reviewed literature about migrants and refugee children and their families, and early childhood educational settings. It has pointed to significant demographic changes to early childhood education contexts that have arisen because of changed global circumstances. At the same time, challenges to the early childhood field provided by these changed circumstances have been highlighted, as have examples of responses in the areas of curriculum, relationships with parents and families, and teacher education. Curriculum and relationships with parents and families are tangible and within the jurisdiction of those who work with children and families on a daily basis. We have faith that practitioners working at the interface with children and families in these unique conditions are more likely to create responsive practices that are potentially transformative, simply because pedagogy and curriculum are shaped by the context as well as the specific children and families with whom practitioners are working (Grieshaber, 2008b). As much of the literature reviewed in this chapter has suggested, starting small is the key. However, there are no easy solutions or recipes to follow that will produce guaranteed results, mainly because the socio-political context of society (and therefore education) has altered.

The socio-political environments in which many early childhood practitioners and teacher educators were raised are monocultural. These circumstances underscore the need for practitioners and teacher educators to learn more about the lives and educational needs of migrants and refugees, and also confront their own racism and biases. Teacher education provides a context in which current and future early childhood professionals can commit to learning about a variety of perspectives in order to recognize and acknowledge that there are many ways of seeing and understanding the world. The road for early childhood teacher education is paved with good intentions but these alone cannot engender the changes required in pre-service teacher education. New theorizing about migrant and refugee children and families that affords a view of difference as a resource must permeate content areas in teacher education in place of developmental discourses. When new theorizing is given adequate space in teacher education, current and future early childhood professionals can learn about the ways in which they frame and respond to the educational needs of migrant and refugee children, and how these responses can impact the experiences of migrant and refugee children and their families in early childhood settings.

NOTE

1. A refugee has been assessed by a relevant national government of international authority such as the United Nations Office of the High Commissioner for Refugees and meets the criteria set out by the *Convention Relating to the Status of Refugees 1951* (Refugee Convention). Asylum seekers claim refugee status but have not been assessed.

REFERENCES

Adair, J., & Tobin, J. (2008). Listening to the voices of immigrant parents. In C. Genishi & A. Lin Goodwin (Eds.), *Diversities in early childhood education: Rethinking and doing* (pp. 137–150). New York: Routledge.

Adams, L. D. & Kirova, A. (2006a). Introduction to Part I: Global migration and the education of children. In L. D. Adams & A. Kirova (Eds.), *Global migration and education: Schools, children, and families* (pp. 1–12). Mahwah, NJ: Lawrence Erlbaum.

Adams, L. D. & Kirova, A. (2006b). Introduction to Part II: They are here: Newcomers in the schools. In L. D. Adams & A. Kirova (Eds.), *Global migration and education: Schools, children, and families* (pp. 83–86). Mahwah, NJ: Lawrence Erlbaum.

Adams, L. D. & Kirova, A. (2006c). Introduction to Part IV: Far from home with fluctuating hopes. In L. D. Adams & A. Kirova (Eds.), *Global migration and education: Schools, children, and families* (pp. 199–202). Mahwah, NJ: Lawrence Erlbaum.

Adams, L.D., & Shambleau, K.M. (2006). Teachers' children's and parents' perspectives on newly arrived children's adjustment to elementary school. In L.D. Adams & A. Kirova (Eds.). (2006). *Global migration and education: Schools, children, and families* (pp. 87–102). Mahwah, NJ: Lawrence Erlbaum.

Ariza, E.N.W. (2006). *Not for ESOL teachers.* Sydney: Pearson.

Australian Research Alliance for Children & Youth (ARACY). (2008). *Achieving outcomes for children and families from culturally and linguistically diverse backgrounds.* Centre for Social Research, Edith Cowan University, Western Australia.

Aveling, N. (2006). 'Hacking at our very roots': Rearticulating white racial identity within the context of teacher education. *Race, Ethnicity and Education, 9*(3), 261–274.

Bernhard, J. K. (1995). Child development, cultural diversity, and the professional training of early childhood educators. *Canadian Journal of Education, 20*(4), 415–430.

Blanco, R., & Takemoto, C.Y. (2006). Inclusion in schools in Latin America and the Caribbean: The case of the children of Haitian descent in the Dominican Republic. In L. D. Adams & A. Kirova, (Eds.), *Global migration and education: Schools, children and families* (pp. 53–66). New Jersey: Lawrence Erlbaum.

Brandon, W. W. (2003). Toward a white teachers' guide to playing fair: Exploring the cultural politics of multicultural teaching. *Qualitative Studies in Education, 16*(1), 31–50.

Brunick, L. L. (1999). Listen to my picture: Art as a survival tool for immigrant and refugee students. *Art Education, 52*(4), 12–17.

Burman, E. (1994). Deconstructing developmental psychology. London: Routledge. *Childhood, 7*(1), 5–14.

Campey, J. (2002). Immigrant children in our classrooms: Beyond ESL. *Education Canada, 42*(3), no page range.

Chong, S. (2005). The logic of Hong Kong teachers: An exploratory study of their teaching culturally diverse students. *Teaching Education, 16*(2), 117–129.

Central Intelligence Agency (CIA). (2009). The world factbook. Accessed 7 June 2009. https://www.cia.gov/library/publications/the-world-factbook/geos/ca.html

Cockrell, K. S., Placier, P. L., Cockrell, D. H., & Middleton, J. N. (1999). Coming to terms with "diversity" and "multiculturalism" in teacher education: Learning about our students, changing our practice. *Teaching and Teacher Education, 15*, 351–366.

Cummins, J. (2004). Foreword. In S. Nieto, *Affirming diversity: The sociopolitical context of multicultural education.* (4th ed.) (pp. xv–xvii). Boston, MA: Allyn and Bacon.

Department of Immigration and Multicultural and Indigenous Affairs [DIMA]. (2005). *Fact sheet 60: Australia's refugee and humanitarian program* [Online]. Retrieved February 4, 2009, from: http://www.immi.gov.au/facts/60refugee.htm

Derman-Sparks, L., & Ramsey, P. G., with Edwards, J. O. (2006). *What if all the kids are white? Anti-bias and multicultural education with young children and families.* New York: Teachers College Press.

Duesterberg, L. M. (1998). Rethinking culture in the pedagogy and practices of preservice teachers. *Teaching and Teacher Education, 14*(5), 497–512.

Early, D. M., & Winton, P. J. (2001). Preparing the workforce: Early childhood teacher preparation at 2- and 4-year institutions of higher education. *Early Childhood Research Quarterly, 16*, 285–306.

Florida, R. L. (2004). *The rise of the creative class : and how it's transforming work, leisure, community and everyday life.* New York: Basic Books.

Flanigan, C. B. (2007). Preparing preservice teachers to partner with parents and communities: An analysis of college of education faculty focus groups. *The School Community Journal, 17*(2), 89–109.

Global Commission on International Migration. (2005). *Final report: Migration in an interconnected world: New directions for action.* Retrieved March 5, 2009, from: http://www.gcim.org/en/finalreport.html

Gonzalez, N. E., Moll, L. C., & Amanti, C. (2005). (Eds.). *Funds of knowledge: Theorizing practices in households and classrooms.* Mahwah, NJ: Lawrence Erlbaum.

Graue, E. (2005). Theorizing and describing preservice teachers' images of families and schooling. *Teachers College Record, 107*(1), 157–185.

Grieshaber, S. (2008a). *Marginalization, making meaning and mazes.* In C. Genishi & A. Lin Goodwin (Eds.), *Diversities in early childhood education: Rethinking and doing* (pp. 83–101). New York: RoutledgeFalmer.

Grieshaber, S. (2008b). Interrupting stereotypes: Teaching and the education of young children. *Early Education and Development,* 19(3), 505–518.

Hamilton, R. & Moore, D. (2004). *Educational interventions for refugee children: Theoretical perspectives and implementing best practice.* London: RoutledgeFalmer.

Hernandez, D. (2004). Children and youth in immigrant families: Demographic, social, and educational issues. In J. A. Banks & C. A. McGee Banks (Eds.), *Handbook of research on multicultural education* (pp. 404–419). San Francisco: Jossey Bass.

Heyning, K. E. (2001). Teacher education reform in the shadow of state-university links: The cultural politics of texts. In T.S. Popkewitz, B.M. Franklin & M.A.

Pereyra (Eds.), *Cultural history and education: Critical essays on knowledge and schooling* (pp. 289–312). New York: Routledge.

Hickling-Hudson, A. (2004). Educating teachers for cultural diversity and social justice. In G. Hernes & M. Martin (Eds.), *Planning for diversity: Education in multiethnic and multicultural societies* (pp. 270–307). Paris: International Institute for Education Planning (UNESCO).

Ho, C. (2007). *Father still knows best: The new paternalism and Australian multicultural policy.* Paper presented to the Social Justice in Early Childhood conference: Curriculum as activism. Sydney. 24 March.

Jones, R. (1999). *Teaching racism or tackling it: Multicultural stories from white beginning teachers.* London: Trentham.

Kalantzis, M. (2005). Conceptualising diversity—Defining the scope of multicultural policy, education and research. *Australian Mosaic, 10*(2), 6–9.

Kirova, A. & Adama, L. D. (2006). Lessons learned and implications for the future. In L. D. Adams & A. Kirova (Eds.), *Global migration and education: Schools, children, and families* (pp. 321–326). Mahwah, NJ: Lawrence Erlbaum.

Kirova, A., & Wu, J. (2002). Peer acceptance, learning English as a second language and identity formation in children of recent Chinese immigrants. In A. Richardson, M. Wyness & A. Halvorsen (Eds.), *Exploring cultural perspectives, integration and globalization* (pp. 171–190). Edmonton, AB: ICRN Press.

Lawrence, S. M., & Bunche, T. (1996). Feeling and dealing: Teaching white students about racial privilege. *Teaching and Teacher Education, 12*(5), 531–542.

Lee, S. (2002). Learning "America": Hmong American high school students. *Education and Urban Society, 34,* 233–246.

Li, G. (2006). Crossing cultural borders in the United States: A case study of a Sudanese refugee family's experience with urban schooling. In L. D. Adams & A. Kirova (Eds.), *Global migration and education: Schools, children, and families* (pp. 237–249). Mahwah, NJ: Lawrence Erlbaum.

Li, P. (2001). The racial subtext in Canada's immigration discourse. *Journal of International Migration and Integration, 21*(1), 77–97.

Lin Goodwin, A., & Genor, M. (2008). Disrupting the taken-for-granted: Autobiographical analysis in preservice teacher education. In C. Genishi & A. Lin Goodwin (Eds.), *Diversities in early childhood education: Rethinking and doing* (pp. 201–218). New York: Routledge.

Lubeck, S. (1996). Deconstructing 'child development knowledge' and 'teacher preparation'. *Early Childhood Research Quarterly, 11*(2), 147–167.

Luke, A., Weir, K., & Woods, A. (2008). *Development of a set of principles to guide a P–12 syllabus framework: A Report to the Queensland Studies Authority, Queensland, Australia.* The State of Queensland (Queensland Studies Authority): Brisbane.

McArdle, F., & Spina, N. (2007). Children of refugee families as artists: Bridging the past, present and future. *Australian Journal of Early Childhood, 32*(4), 50–53.

McBrien, J. L. (2003). A second chance: Helping refugee students succeed in school. *Educational Leadership, 61*(2), 76–79.

McBrien, J. L. (2005). Educational needs and barriers for refugee students in the United States: A review of literature. *Review of Educational Research, 75*(3), 329–364.

Moreau, G. (2000). Some elements of comparison between the integration politics of Germany, Canada, France, Great Britain, Italy and the Netherlands. *Journal of International Migration and Integration, 1*(1), 101–120.

Multicultural Health Brokers Co-op (MHBC). (2004). *Mapping the life experiences of refugee and immigrant families with preschool children: A research report presented to the Early Childhood Development Initiative*, Edmonton, Alberta, Canada. Multicultural Family Connections Project.

Nieto, S. (2004). *Affirming diversity: The sociopolitical context of multicultural education.* (4th ed.). Boston, MA: Allyn and Bacon.

Nieto, S. & Bode, P. (2008). (5th ed.). Affirming diversity: The sociopolitical context of mukticultural education. Boston, MA: Pearson.

Obidah, J. E. (2000). Mediating boundaries of race, class, and professional authority as a critical multiculturalist. *Teachers College Record, 102*(6), 1035–1060.

OECD. (2006). *Starting strong II: Early childhood education and care.* OECD: Paris, France.

Osgood, J. (2006). Deconstructing professionalism in early childhood education: Resisting the regulatory gaze. *Contemporary Issues in Early Childhood, 7*(1), 5–14.

Pacini-Ketchabaw, V., & Scheter, S. (2002). Engaging the discourse of diversity: Educator's frameworks for working with linguistic and cultural difference. *Contemporary Issues in Early Childhood, 3*(3), 400–414.

Phillips, J. (2005). Exploring the possibilities. In J. Phillips and J. Lampert (Eds.), *Introductory Indigenous studies in education: The importance of knowing* (pp. 1–8). Frenchs Forest, New South Wales: Pearson Education Australia.

Pryor, C. B. (2001). New immigrants and refugees in American schools: Multiple voices. *Childhood Education, 77*(5), 275–283.

Rao, N., & Yuen, M. (2006). Listening to children: Voices of newly arrived immigrants from the Chinese mainland to Hong Kong. In L. D. Adams & A. Kirova (Eds.), *Global migration and education: Schools, children, and families* (pp. 139–150). New Jersey: Lawrence Erlbaum.

Roberts, G. (2005). 'Racist' professor cautioned, but launches new attack. *The Australian.* 21 July.

Robinson, K. H., & Jones Diaz, C. (2006). *Diversity and difference in early childhood education: Issues for theory and practice.* Maidenhead, UK: Open University Press.

Rosenberg, P. M. (2004). Color blindness in teacher education: An optical delusion. In M. Fine, L. Weis, L. Powell Pruitt & A. Burns (Eds.), *Off white* (pp. 257–272). New York: Routledge.

Rutter, J. (2005). *Refugee children in the UK.* Maidenhead, England: Open University Press.

Ryan, S. K. & Grieshaber, S. (2005) Shifting from developmental to postmodern practices in early childhood teacher education. *Journal of Teacher Education 56*(1), 34–45.

Santoro, N., & Allard, A. (2005). (Re)Examining identities: Working with diversity in the pre-service teaching experience. *Teaching and Teacher Education, 21*, 863–873.

Schick, C. (2000). 'By virtue of being white': Resistance in anti-racist pedagogy. *Race, Ethnicity and Education, 3*(1), 83–102.

Sims, M., Hayden, J., Palmer, G., & Hutchins, T. (2000). Working in early childhood settings with children who have experienced refugee or war-related trauma. *Australian Journal of Early Childhood, 25*(4), 41–46.

Siwatu, K. O. (2007). Preservice teachers' culturally responsive teaching self-efficacy and outcome expectancy beliefs. *Teaching and Teacher Education, 23*(7), 1086–1101.

Suarez-Orozco, C., & Suarez-Orozco, M. (2001). *Children of immigration.* Cambridge, MA: Harvard University Press.

Sugrue, C. (1997). Student teachers' lay theories and teaching identities: Their implications for professional development. *European Journal of Teacher Education, 20*(3), 213–225.

Szente, J. & Hoot, J. (2006). Rxploring the needs of refugee children in our schools. In L. D. Adams & A. Kirova (Eds.), *Global migration and education: Schools, children, and families* (pp. 219–235). Mahwah, NJ: Lawrence Erlbaum.

Szente, J., Hoot, J., & Taylor, D. (2006). Responding to the special needs of refugee children: Practical ideas for teachers. *Early Childhood Education Journal, 34*(1), 15–20.

Tatum, B. D. (1992). Talking about race, learning about racism: The application of racial identity development theory in the classroom. *Harvard Educational Review, 62*(1), 1–24.

Tobin, J. (2004). *Children of immigrants in early childhood settings in five countries: A study of parent and staff beliefs.* Unpublished paper submitted to the Bernard van Leer Foundation.

Tobin, J., Arzubiaga, A., & Mantovani, S. (2007). Entering into dialogue with immigrant parents. *Early Childhood Matters, 108,* 34–38.

Vavrus, M. (2002). *Connecting teacher identity formation to culturally responsive teaching.* Paper presented at the National Association of Multicultural Education Annual Meeting, Washington, DC, October 30 - November 3, 2002.

Waniganayake, M. (2001). From playing with guns to playing with rice: The challenges of working with refugee children. An Australian perspective. *Childhood Education, 77*(5), 289–294.

CHAPTER 9

THE CULTURAL AND SYMBOLIC "BEGATS" OF CHILD COMPOSING

Textual Play and Community Membership

Anne Haas Dyson

ABSTRACT

Even as the population of school children becomes more diverse in sociocultural and linguistic experience, the curricular trend is toward more regulated, uniform literacy programs for young children; within such programs, child writing is an individual act dependent on skill mastery. Moreover, the increased emphasis on literacy has engulfed times and spaces once allowed to dramatic and constructive play, including drawing. As a response to such trends, in this chapter I consider child composing as itself a form of symbolic play on paper. Drawing on the theoretical and empirical literature, I focus on two critical "begats" of young school children's writing: experience manipulating, or playing with, the symbolic stuff—the voices and images—of their everyday lives; and a community of peers within which and for which children

Language and Cultural Diversity in Early Childhood Education, pages 191–211

compose. In the process, I illustrate that, far from uniform, children's diverse experiences as cultural beings inform the ways in which they make sense of and take some control over the written medium.

Your mother told you I'm writing your begats, and you [my young son] seemed very pleased with the idea. Well, then. What should I record for you? I, John Ames, was born in the Year of Our Lord 1890.... At this writing I have lived seventy-six years, seventy-four of them here in Gilead, Iowa....

So writes the Reverend Ames in his journal, the entries of which comprise Marilynne Robinson's novel, *Gilead* (2004, p. 9). The Reverend Ames' "begats" for his little boy are themselves produced from the cultural stuff—the daily practices and meaning-infused artifacts—of his daily life. Among the textual artifacts are passages from books, bits of sermons, passed-on family stories, and mulled-over utterances voiced by those with whom he shares history and community. His "begats" are not just a recounting of "what happened," but are themselves crafted from these artifacts, which may be appropriated, in turn, by his son.

Reverend Ames' narration is a fitting introduction to this chapter's focus on the "begats"—the foundational experiences—that give rise to and sustain our diverse children as they become writers. Writing, be it an old man's or a young child's, is situated within, and energized by, some sort of community membership; a writer gives voice, but it is a dialogic voice written in response to, and in relation to, others (Bakhtin, 1981). Indeed, in the view of the language philosopher, Bakhtin, one's "own" voice is made from, and sounds against the backdrop of, the voices of others. Among such voices might be those of doting fathers, sermon-giving reverends, rambunctious young sons... or, to move beyond Reverend Ames' world to a child's, rapping singers, humankind-saving superheroes, and guiding (and disciplining) teachers.

Situated voices and their textual artifacts are crafting material for adult authors (Bakhtin, 1981), and they are *also* the cultural stuff—kinds of "textual toys" (Dyson, 2003)—with which children make imagined worlds. Children's use of such voices to make a world are evident when they play; they appropriate ways of talking and acting, and thereby become, for example, a mom trying to discipline her child, a counter clerk shouting an order in a fast food restaurant, a minister preaching to the congregation, or a superhero doing battle with a villain (Dyson, 2005; Fromberg & Bergen, 2006; Garvey, 1990). These imagined worlds can provide a context for children's play with written graphics (e.g., ticket-writing by police officers, order-taking by a waiter [Christie, 2006]). The interest herein, though, is how children find a symbolic playground on the blank space of a page itself.

In this chapter, I focus on two critical "begats" of young school children's composing: a community within which and for which children compose; and experience manipulating, or playing with, the symbolic stuff—the voices and images—of their everyday lives. These two foundational concepts are particularly important in contemporary times.

Even as the population of school children becomes more diverse in sociocultural and linguistic experience, the curricular trend is toward more regulated, uniform literacy programs for young children (Genishi & Dyson, 2009); within such programs, child writing is an individual act dependent on skill mastery. Moreover, the increased emphasis on literacy has engulfed times and spaces once allowed to dramatic and constructive play, including drawing (Bergen, 2006). As a response to such trends, I discuss child writing as itself energized and supported by children's experiences as social participants and playful symbol users; moreover, far from uniform, children's diverse experiences as cultural beings inform the ways in which they make sense of and take some control over the written medium.

Below, I introduce the basic conceptual tools for this discussion of community membership and textual play in childhood composing. That backdrop is woven from a sociocultural view of language, a Vygotskian perspective on the prehistory of writing, and a childhood studies view of children's agency in a community of peers.

DIVERSITY AND POSSIBILITY IN CHILDHOOD COMPOSING

You and Tobie are on the porch steps sorting gourds by size and color and shape... assigning names. Some of them are submarines and some of them tanks, and some of them are bombs.... [You and your friend] make those sounds of airplanes and bombs and crashing and exploding. We did the same things, playing at cannon fire and bayonet charges. There is certainly nothing in that fact to reassure.

—Robinson, 2004, p. 192

Reverend Ames' vignette about dramatic play might seem beside the point in a discussion of child writing. Surely, to understand writing, common sense would say to focus on children's marks on paper and on how those marks change over time. But common sense is often wrong. Moreover, "common sense" might block from educators' view the capacity of many of our children. In this section, I suggest an alternative view.

A Soiocultural Stance

From a sociocultural perspective, written language is a mediator of a social event, an event itself being a kind of cultural practice (Heath, 1983; Street, 2000). Literacy practices vary because of cultural, linguistic, and socioeconomic factors, along with personal interests and dispositions (Barton & Hamilton, 1998; Clay, 1998; Heath, 1983; Levinson, 2007; Street, 1993). For this reason, young children come to school with different experiences with, and knowledge and know-how about, print.

For example, children who may have had limited experiences with school-valued literacy practices, like adult/child picture book reading, may have engaged in print-mediated activities like playing school with siblings, sending birthday cards or thank you notes, watching videos with captions in a heritage language, or engaging in home language Bible study (Kenner, 2005; Long, Volk, & Gregory, 2007; Zentella, 2005). Even a walk through a downtown displays signs and announcements on buildings, streets, and cars, as does watching a sports show, with its labeled people (on uniforms), spaces (on playing fields), and time (on scoreboards). These activities do not all yield the same degree or kind of knowledge, nor is explicit attention to written graphics necessarily an aspect of all; nonetheless, when children are encouraged to pay attention to written language, these daily activities offer demonstrations of written language in use.

Moreover, whatever children's experiences with print, all bring some symbol-producing predilection to school. The ability to share symbols and, thereby, to organize and express inner feelings and experiences is a part of all children's human heritage. Across cultures, children orally represent and, thereby, shape and invent experiences through their storytelling, playing, and drawing (Ochs & Capp, 2001; Lancy, 2008; Matthews, 1999). Comfortable symbolic tools, like familiar communicative practices, offer resources with which teachers and children can build new possibilities.

Cultural Tools and the "Prehistory" of Written Language

Early in the last century, the Russian psychologist Vygotsky (1978) theorized the developmental "prehistory" of children's writing. In his view, learning to write differs in an important way from learning to speak. When they learn to talk, children *spontaneously* appropriate words used by other people. These meaning-saturated symbols, born in dialogue (Bakhtin, 1981), are the basis for children's capacity to think with words (see Vygotsky, 1962). In learning to write, however, children have to *deliberately* reflect on and choose words (i.e., spoken symbols) that then will be represented through graphic symbols.

Vygotsky (1978) argued that writing (as the deliberate representation of spoken ideas) happens first through gesture, play, and drawing. For example, in play, children rename themselves and objects as other than what they are (e.g., a mom, a baby, a kitty); they use their own gestures, movements, and voices to symbolize a pretend world. In drawing, young children name their lines, curves, and spaces, transforming them into objects, people, and actions; in fact, they learn to use speech to plan, monitor, and, indeed, to narrate their graphic symbol-making. Thus, their drawings become, quite literally, a way of writing, that is, a way of graphically negotiating and rendering a spoken world.

Written language, then, is another medium, albeit a more abstract one, for negotiating and representing a world. Its "prehistory" is found in, builds on, and, indeed, is interwoven with, other kinds of symbolic activity. Young children will learn to communicate through manipulating written language if they find that symbolic tool "relevant to life" (Vygotsky, 1978, p. 118). And, in school, young children may find symbolic tools relevant if those tools enable them to interact and play with their peers.

Child Agency in Communities of Children

Children's formal instruction in written language occurs within school literacy practices that are organized for, and guided by, teachers. But practices, as contexts for participation, are actively constructed, not simply provided (Bauman, 2004). From their first experiences in educational institutions, children both conform to institutional rules and transform them; they use their experiential, linguistic, and symbolic resources not only to negotiate official practices, but to construct unofficial or hybrid ones. Configurations of such practices constitute a local peer world (Corsaro, 2005; Sutton-Smith, Mechling, Johnson, & McMahon, 1995).

Corsaro (2005), for example, illustrates how preschoolers draw on shared cultural storylines to develop imaginative, playful routines, like racing to the top of a climbing structure in order to be "bigger than everyone." As children grow older, speech plays an increasing role in organizing and collaboratively constructing imagined worlds (Franklin, 1983, 2008; Vygotsky, 1978). In their play, children describe and negotiate ongoing action, and they assume complementary roles and represent their enactment through the use of qualities of their voices, including volume, pitch, and duration of sound (Anderson, 1990; Corsaro, 2005; Garvey, 1984). For example, becoming an upset baby involves a different voice than becoming a worried mother. Children may even manipulate different languages, as in Long,

Volk, and Gregory's (2007) description of young, bilingual Puerto Rican children playing minister and church-goers.

Similar verbal and interactive processes can occur during children's drawings in group settings; through such processes, a child's individual activity becomes communal in nature (Dyson, 1989, 2007; Fineberg, 2006; Matthews, 1999). As they sit side-by-side, children's verbal monitoring and narrating of drawn actions may alert others to their symbol-making. Those others may respond or even coordinate their drawings with a peer's voiced graphic play. This coordination is supported by community membership and shared cultural knowledge, including that of popular culture (Thompson, 2006).

With experience and official school expectations for "writing," children's speech can also transform writing into a new medium for peer social relations and play. In the next sections, I illustrate how a blank page can become a playground, linked to writing, drawing, and dramatic action in a community of peers. I consider first the potentially productive interplay between teacher agency and children's agency, then I turn to forms of textual play that may be undervalued, including those involving popular culture and sociolinguistically diverse voices.

COMPOSING AT THE CURRICULAR CROSSROADS OF OFFICIAL AND UNOFFICIAL PLAY

In the Reverend Ames' journal entry about war play, Reverend Ames' young son and his friend appropriated the cultural narratives and symbolic images of their local and historical times and spaces. With their talk, they transformed the meaning of common objects in their rural community (from gourds to submarines), and, then, with talk mixed with sound effects, gesture, and movement, they narrated an action-filled adventure. At times, they sprawled on the floor drawing these detailed figures, as the meanings they were examining were rearticulated within the possibilities of different media (Kress, 2003).

It is not so hard to imagine that, in time, those same boys might have action-packed adventures at least in part through the written medium, in which submarine captains might give voice to their orders in more extended ways than they would inside a gourd-like submarine propelled through invisible waters by a child's arm and engine sound-effects.

In this section, I illustrate teachers' official efforts to formally introduce children to composing by building on their symbolic play, and I also illustrate children's *un*official efforts to reframe their writing within playful peer relations. Both of these phenomena involve a critical interplay between school and childhood worlds.

Teacher Organized Play

The centrality of play to the social, intellectual, and language lives of children has led to deliberate pedagogical efforts to situate child composing within children's storytelling and play. Over the last 30 years, the early childhood educator Vivian Paley (e.g., 1981, 2004) has strongly influenced such efforts. Her own books are narrations of her teaching life, in which she listens to children's play and then helps them draw on that play for public storytelling. Through the process of writing down their stories, Paley helps the children engage in the deliberate process of choosing words, that is, in composing. She explains:

> Our kind of storytelling is a social phenomenon, intended to flow through all other activities and provide the widest opportunity for a communal response. Stories are not private affairs; the individual imagination plays host to all the stimulation in the environment and causes ripples of ideas to encircle the listeners.
>
> My role [is] ... to enable others to hear the storyteller by repeating each sentence as I write it down ... [and to] question any aspect of the story I might misinterpret—any word, phrase, sound effect, character, or action that does not make sense. ... Throughout the day I may refer to similarities between a child's story and other stories, books, or events. (Paley, 1990, pp. 21–22)

These written narratives are transformed into a kind of author's theater: Mrs. Paley reads each dictation aloud, as child authors act out their words with and for their peers. In this way, the dictated stories, grounded in children's play, are transformed and brought to dramatic life once again, at a slower pace and in a public situation where teacher and peers might offer new perspectives on the stories or question their meaning.

Paley's pedagogy is consistent with Vygotsky's view of writing as entailing reflection on language, as linked to other symbolic media, and, also, as learned through participation in social practices valued in communities. Even if dictation is not a familiar practice to all children, play and storytelling are likely to be. Moreover, it is clear from Paley's examples that children draw on situated voices from varied experiences as they construct and discuss their stories. For example, in the following dictating activity, when 5-year-old Reeny is narrating her story, her speech has features of African American English (e.g., optional variants of the verb *be,* optional third person singular present tense *s* ["he say"] [Rickford & Rickford, 2000]); when she becomes a character in her story, her speech has features of fictional royalty (e.g., the form of address ["Your Highness"]):

> "Once there was a little princess...And a mother and father. They was the king and queen."
>
> "Do you want to say 'They *were* the king and queen'?" [asks Mrs. Paley.]
>
> "They *is* the king and queen." She hurries on lest I [Mrs. Paley] interrupt again.
>
> "And the princess was walking in the forest deeply and she got lost."
>
> "*In the forest deeply is nice,*" I offer, to which Reeny says:
>
> "Thank you.... Then the princess sees the opening and there is a prince."
>
> "And he says, 'Hi baby'?" [her peer] Bruce snickers.
>
> "Uh-uh," Reeny replies with great dignity, "'cause, see, a prince don't talk that way. He say,'Good morning, madam. How is Your Highness today?'" (1997, pp. 3–4)

Bruce, in fact, had been greeting Reeny by assuming the voice of a cool dude greeting a girl. In the vignette, he is bringing that playful greeting into the textual space of her story. But Reeny had already told him that that greeting was for his girlfriend ("and I'm not your girlfriend"), and most certainly it was not a royal greeting for a princess. Reeny knew how to negotiate identities with others and how to orchestrate voices to make a world, as Bakhtin (1981) would say.

Influenced by Paley, the team of Nicolopoulou, McDowell, and Brockmetyer (2006) introduced storytelling and acting in McDowell's Head Start classroom. The researchers traced the changing nature of children's dictations, which became longer and more coherent over time. Even though the children's stories drew on daily experiences, they were overwhelmingly fictional, as in Damian's on how "me and Spiderman and Batman" watched movies when they weren't busy fighting bad guys (p. 132)

Interestingly, the children's participation in public composing and acting seemed to influence another child composing activity, a "journal" for child-initiated drawing and writing. As the school year progressed, children narrativized their journal drawings, telling stories about them, and even made their own approximations of writing, behaviors that had not been common in previous years. As is consistent with the argument being developed in this chapter, the children grew as composers in ways that involved the support of other symbolic media and participation in a community in which composing had interactive and public dimensions. Moreover, the composing activities were open to children's appropriation and use of everyday voices and textual toys, like superhero characters and their exploits, both heroic and humble.

Child Organized Play

As already noted, literacy programs for young school children (K–2) are increasingly structured and paced (e.g., particular lessons are to occur district-wide at particular points in the year). In programs so prescribed, composing is organized strictly as an individual activity, not a collaborative or communal one; "true" narratives may be required, imagined ones discouraged (except when "fiction" is taught); and children's tendency to draw during composing countered as soon as possible by requests for "quick sketches" before writing. Nonetheless, this does not mean that children's playful practices, symbolic repertoire, and social relations do not figure into their early efforts to write.

During writing periods, children typically spend a significant amount of time sitting side-by-side at their desks, as teachers circulate or work in one-to-one conferences with children. Whether they "should" or "should not," young children tend to be drawn to other children and to play. Indeed, even in highly structured literacy activities, children may engage in playful banter and spontaneous competitions (Glupcynski, 2007; Sahni, 1994). Children's textual productions, then, may begin to mediate familiar peer relations and childhood practices.

Children's talk about each others' productions may be first evident during drawing (Dyson, 1989). With time and experience, and given some interactional space, written language, too, may become more central to the goings-on, in ways at first modest and then more elaborate. In the following vignette, kindergartener Latrez and his peers Ervion and Charles, all African American, illustrate the humble beginnings of a potential child practice involving planned but not necessarily held parties. (The vignette is drawn from an ongoing ethnographic study [Dyson, in progress] of an evolving composing culture):

> Ervion, Latrez, Patrice, and Charles are sitting (in roughly that order) near the end of a long worktable as writing time begins. Latrez is looking for the pencil cup, when Ervion says that he has drawn 3 kids who are coming to his sleep-over (a kind of birthday celebration in the discourse of this class). Latrez loses interest in the pencil cup and looks intently at Ervion, who is needing some help:
>
> **Ervion:** Hey Charles, how you spell your name?...
> **Charles:** C, H
> **Ervion:** (to Charles) How you write a H?

Latrez: (piping up) H is like this. (moving his finger straight up) It's up—(finishes making the letter in the air)
I'm gonna have a birthday party.

Just as Latrez makes that declaration of his own party, the children's teacher, Mrs. Bee, sits down by Ervion to help him write his message. As Latrez listens, Ervion explains to her that he is trying to write that "Charles come over to my sleepover."

Latrez: Put my name in there [in your text]!

Mrs. Bee calls Latrez's attention to his own paper, on which he has drawn a snowman and, in block letters, written SNO; he now adds *Ervion* (a word easily visible on Ervion's paper; Charles too eventually writes *Ervion*).

Latrez: (to Ervion) I'm gonna have a birthday party. On March 4. [It's now December.] And somebody can come over. Only 5 people.
Patrice: Can I?
Latrez: Only boys coming over... Ervion, on March 4, you want to come over to my birthday, on March 4?

Ervion is still being guided by Mrs. Bee. Latrez looks elsewhere.

Latrez: Charles, when you have your birthday party can I come over?
Charles: Yeah.
Latrez: Thanks.

Latrez then erases his whole page and draws a "castle" he lived in "long, long away." In his picture, he goes through the castle door all by himself and there, in the castle:

Latrez: ...I had a birthday party. And I got a surprise.

In such modest ways, child interactions may transform an official written production into a valued symbolic space ("Put my name in there!"). Moreover, evident in this nascent birthday planning practice is the expectation of reciprocity, that is, the sense that participants should respond in kind to each other, given their relationship, the particular practice, and the societal ideologies so embedded (Dyson, 1997, 2006). For example, given gender ideologies, Latrez engages in no social work to include, or gain inclusion from, a girl; indeed, he actively excludes her.

Finally, Latrez's decision to change his writing topic from a snowman to a "long, long away" time and place illustrates both the potential fluidity of children's composing—the movement among media and among worlds—and the playful intentions that undergird it (Dyson, 2003; Kress, 2003; Matthews, 1999; Pahl, 2003). Through his dynamic relationship with his peers and his paper, Latrez enacts a space of "utopian longings and notions" (Vygotsky, 1978; Zipes, 2004, p. 3); that space happened "long, long away" when he lived in a castle and had a birthday party.

At this point in Latrez's developmental history as a composer, drawing lent itself best to positioning himself on the cusp of a party just behind the door in a long away world, even as Ervion's name, stretched out linearly in its official place on a page, best suited his strategic efforts to get his own name on his friend's paper. Such movement among media allows children to invent new meanings and new selves, as Pahl (2003) illustrates in an analysis of a child's multimodal play with Pokemon creatures.

In a classroom serving socioculturally diverse children in a low-income urban neighborhood, I observed first graders using talk, drawing, and writing to develop classroom-wide but unofficial practices, including planning pretend parties (Dyson, 2007). Although, initially, many such parties were not co-ed, children who were writing about planned parties, whether girls or boys, came under intense pressure for inclusion from tablemates (i.e., if you do not write me in your party, I won't write you in mine). Thus, composers wrote into their plans the names of peers across the usual playmate lines of gender and race. Moreover, party planning gave rise to many related practices, including ones occurring mainly during inside activity time or "recess" on bad-weather days (e.g., issuing oral invitations, making lists of invitees [or crossing people off lists], and negotiating who would pick up whom on the way to the party); in this way, the children evidenced their knowledge of the interrelated communicative practices associated with get-togethers of varied kinds.

In a related way, other sorts of child practices evolved, as children met official expectations to write with texts that had unofficial social meanings; these practices were at least partially linked to common, out-of-school experiences with multi-modal texts. For example, during composing time, children used drawing and, eventually, writing to enact dramatic battles with their peers (inspired by cartoons and, also, a playground chase-game); and they re-created sports games seen on TV or at neighborhood venues. None of these practices, though, gave rise to any official discussions of composing decisions, discursive conventions, or ideological tensions (e.g., those associated with the gender of warriors and with the differing perceptions of the "fun" of battle).

Similarly, child practices contained graphic conventions of varied kinds, particularly in the drawings they entailed, but none were included in the official curriculum (Dyson, 2008). For example, drawn narratives of sports scenes necessitated abbreviations, initials, and numbers on sports jerseys, helmets, scoreboards, and sports fields. Coaches could yell in dialogue bubbles, their voices loud in all capitals or stretched out in repeated letters ("Nooo... [33 o's]"). Scenes related to video games entailed particular kinds of represented fonts, and cartoon-inspired battle scenes necessitated visuals related to movement (e.g., arrows) or chaotic action (e.g., dense scribbles).

In sum, young composers appropriate situated voices and visuals from familiar practices and appealing texts, whatever their medium. As these become the center of peer attention, they may give rise to new ways of playing on paper. The "begetting" knowledge of communicative practices and their symbolic conventions, the intensity of peer interest—all may be invisible in the official curriculum.

Narrow notions of how and what young children should write have consequences for children's learning and, also, for their public acknowledgement as good students (Siegel, Kontovourki, Schmier, & Enriquez, 2008). Indeed, if children's writing is evaluated only in relationship to teacher assignments, and if play, drawing, and talking are not recognized as linked to child composing, then potential pathways to official literacy participation and growth are closed. Without some official recognition, children's experiential resources, grounded in their everyday experiences, cannot be acknowledged, extended, or problematized (e.g., as potential tools of inclusion or exclusion; for pedagogical counter-examples, see Marsh & Millard, 2000). In brief, as the following section underscores, narrow visions of children's resources work against equity for our socioculturally diverse children (Clay, 1998).

CURRICULAR INEQUITIES: (UN)POPULAR TEXTUAL TOYS AND SILENCED VOICES

In this section, I emphasize two important, but often undervalued, aspects of children's cultural and symbolic resources: textual knowledge and know-how linked to children's participation in popular culture; and the talk and situated voices of children's everyday language, when it is other than a standardized English.

Writing in Media-Saturated Childhoods

You liked the movie. [Your friend] Tobias isn't allowed to go to movies, so you brought him almost half your box of Cracker Jacks, which I thought was decent of you.

—Robinson, 2004, p. 214

In Reverend Ames' view, it makes little sense to forbid his own son from the cartoons and movies he enjoys, given the pervasiveness of media in his child's life—and the good Reverend lived in the middle of the last century!

Indeed, at least since post World War II, American childhoods have been thoroughly saturated with the media (Goodenough, 2008; Kline, 1993; Seiter, 1993). Television, movies, the radio, and, more recently, video games provide children with a range of cultural stuff—textual toys—for their own play; that is, they provide models of communicative genres, conceptual content like storylines, appealing characters, repeatable lines, and, as noted above, varied kinds of symbolic conventions, as well as powerful underlying ideologies, like those of gender, race, power, and beauty. For these reasons, children's sociocultural identities may lead them to play with certain media material more than others, based, perhaps, on gender, race, cultural connections or language used (Dyson, 1997, 2003; Kenner, 2005).

This pervasive media material lacks the social "distinction"—the cultural value—of more socially and economically removed forms of symbolic material (Bourdieu, 1984). Children of socioeconomic means have access to alternative forms of consumption, like "educational" toys, "artful" movies and picture books. Indeed, media material may bring to mind passive children, who replay (and compose) unoriginal stories built on stereotypes and stereotypical action (the brave superhero who saves the beautiful damsel in distress). Teachers may thus feel that children should not use such material in school (Marsh, 2003).

There is no need, though, to construct an oppositional relationship between forms of perceived "popular" and "high" culture. In their play, and in their composing, children may actively remix material from varied multimodal sources, adapting it to the social situation and symbolic media to hand. For example, through a year-long ethnographic study in an urban, multiracial first grade, I focused on a group of African American friends (the self-designated "brothers and sisters"), documenting their reliance on nonacademic social worlds to negotiate their entry into school literacy (Dyson, 2003). Those worlds provided these San Francisco Bay children with agency and meaningful symbols, including those from popular music, films, animated shows, and sports media. The children had experience manipulating this material in their dramatic play, narrative talk, and drawing; moreover, the material had social cache among friends and peers. In this way, it helped "begat" child writing.

To illustrate, during the daily free writing time, children who imagined themselves members of a professional football team initially drew appropriately labeled sports fields and players, TV-screen layouts of sports scores, and, eventually, fictional replays of imagined games and fact-oriented recounts of football statistics. Their play even led to learning the names of teams' cities and states and locating them on maps—and, for one child, to an interest in television weather reports, which, like sports reports, detailed movement of "characters" (e.g., tornadoes) across cities and states. To further illustrate, some children imagined themselves as popular singers, which led to drawn and labeled concert scenes, collaborative song writing (and singing)—and an interest in classroom poetry, with its rhythm and rhyme.

As in earlier studies conducted in urban classrooms (Dyson, 1993, 1997), the teacher made the curriculum permeable to children's appropriation of everyday textual knowledge and, thereby, broadened the genre material considered within school, linked the children's material to school-introduced genres, and raised critical issues for discussion among children. Indeed, even as the literacy curriculum is narrowing for our children, educators in many locations are investigating ways to use children's pleasures and interests to construct new pathways to school-valued knowledge (e.g., Evans, 2005; Kamler & Comber, 2005; Marsh, 2003).

In an older but particularly vivid example, Marsh (1999) set up a Batman and Batwoman Headquarters as a role-play center for two classes of 6–7-year-olds; the classes were culturally, economically, and linguistically very diverse. The center was stocked with all manner of literacy materials, from varied kinds of paper products and writing instruments to a computer. (The children themselves made props, like a Batmobile and maps.) Marsh discussed with the children some of the reasons Batman and Batwoman might decide to write and the products that could ensue, like letters to the police and to the Joker, maps for use in the Batmobile, newspaper reports, and comics. The children wrote all manner of literacy products, so motivating was the idea of entering and exerting some control in the powerful world of well-known superheroes.

Teachers who observe children's play and listen to their talk may discover a wealth of textual knowledge and symbolic experience they had not known existed. That material, whether introduced by children themselves or their observant teachers, may allow more children to find engaging, appealing pathways to writing.

Writing in a Sociolinguistically Complex World

Your mother... sits at the kitchen table and copies poems and phrases.... This is mainly for you. It is because I'll be gone and she'll have to be the one to set an example. She said, "You'd better show me what books I got to read." So I pulled down old John Donne... "One short sleepe past, wee wake eternally".... Your mother's trying to like him.

—Robinson, 2004, p. 77

The Reverend's wife was not an educated woman, and she worried that, when her elderly husband was gone, she would not be a proper example, a fitting language-user, for her son. What is a "proper" example? Are young children's voices, in this socially, culturally, and linguistically complex society, "fitting" resources for entering into school composing? Many curricular guidelines for early schooling would say "no," particularly those associated with federally funded literacy programs; in such guidelines, even young children are to write the variant of English considered standard (see Genishi & Dyson, 2009).

This is a problem. Our children tell stories and dream their utopian tomorrows in many Englishes and other languages. It is these familiar ways with words that children rely on as they learn to draw their speech, in Vygotsky's sense. Thus, all young children deserve equal access to comfortable voices for entering into literacy, a point frequently made by scholars focusing on our multilingual student population (e.g., Genishi, Stires, & Yung-Chan, 2001; Reyes & Halcon, 2001).

Moreover, as argued throughout this chapter, the voices of children's families and communities, of their popular pleasures and beloved stories, all echo in children's own voices; in this way, they are children's resources for enacting worlds on paper. If our goal in child composing is to further the sort of communicative flexibility evident in children's play—their capacity for adapting their voices to communicative roles and situations—then we would do well to further young children's storytelling voices and playful enactments on paper. Children, after all, do not learn language, oral or written, through correction, but by appropriating and playing with new kinds of voices (Nelson, 2007) and even new languages (Long, Volk, & Gregory, 2007; Reyes, 2001).

As brief closing examples, consider two texts by six-year-old Tionna, a speaker of African American Language (and a focal child in an ethnographic study of children's interpretation of "basic" instruction [Dyson, 2006, 2007]). In the first, Tionna, like her good friend Mandisa, anticipates the activity for the day in the afterschool care program—the garden club:

> Today me and Mandisa have garden club....
> I think Addy [the garden club volunteer] will check are garden/she will be madd
> because people was stepping in it
> every time we go to garden clud
> we have two snaks and choclit mike
> the other kids have one snack and white mike

In the above text, Tionna has chosen a topic to match her friend Mandisa's. She becomes a "we," a "me and Mandisa," whose garden has suffered the indignity of people's steps and, yet, whose garden club treat sets them apart from the others with their bland white milk. In terms of the "basics" stressed in her class, Tionna had varied "problems," including the "me and

Mandisa" and the "people was" (both constructions corrected in her class, in anticipation of a mandated standardized test).

Tionna, though, wrote vividly and with an evaluative flair. And this surely was in part because her everyday performative style with her peers found its way into the textual space of a page. She knew something of manipulating words to get others' attention. (As an example of that performative style, note the closing two lines' parallel structure and evaluative twist.) Moreover, in her classroom community, she could share writing topics with her friends, just as she did oral ones, and she looked forward eagerly to the end of official writing time, when she could read her work to her classmates. In other words, Tionna had experience as a manipulator of words and a writing community with and for whom to write. These are the foundation—the begats—of writing, not a standardized, generic voice.

Moreover, Tionna's alertness to appealing voices allowed her to assume new ways with written words. One day she sat making pop-up cards with Mandisa during in-classroom recess; Mandisa had learned to make the cards from her grandmother and was now teaching others. Tionna decided to make one for her mom for Mother's Day, and, in so doing, she appropriated a voice like that in a poem she had read in her reader that day (a poem with language that was a bit archaic, rather like John Donne's poem). She wrote:

> Out of all the moms there be
> you are the best one
> there is in live.
> Happy mothers day love mom.

Children are not experts in the analysis of sentence or discourse structure (as I expect many readers are not); nor do they understand the social and political significance of minor differences in ways of speaking (e.g., "the people was"). However, as they demonstrate in their play, children are sensitive to people using language, to situated voices. As they listen to and participate in new ways with words, they will appropriate new ways of speaking and writing—unless they have lost their sense of playfulness and agency in the manipulation of the symbolic stuff of language. (For an elaboration of how children learn new language variants and new ways with words, see Clark, 2003.)

TOWARD WRITING "BEGATS" WORTHY OF OUR CHILDREN

I think there must . . . be a prevenient courage that allows us to be brave—that is, to acknowledge that . . . precious things have been put into our hands and to do nothing to honor them is to do great harm.

—Robinson, 2004, p. 246

As the Reverend approaches the end of his begats for his child, and the end of his life, too, he decides that, in the end, what he wants most is to inspire his son to have the courage to appreciate the "precious" life around him and to serve that life in some way.

We, as educators, also have "precious things . . . put into our hands"—the children in our schools. And we, too, need courage. There is a persistent myth that is engulfing teachers of younger and younger children. This myth speaks of a curricular magical potion, which, when delivered in equal quantities, at a common pace, in a scripted manner to young children, will close achievement gaps between poor and minority children and the so-called mainstream children; as gaps disappear, literacy will reign over the land.

I have no ill will toward common skill teaching included in this magical potion; indeed, I have taught many children the letters of the alphabet and have also helped them become aware of sounds and how they manipulate them. But, as the child language scholar Katherine Nelson (2007) says so well, precisely because children's previous experiences are so varied, what they learn from any encounter "cannot be prespecified or predetermined" (p. 258); They "receive . . . the part that is meaningful to each individual . . . for further construction" (p. 265). The more constrained, the more scripted the writing activity, the less likely that children can make their resources relevant.

Moreover, a set of skills does not add up to the intention-driven act of writing. That act entails manipulating symbols in order to participate in some way in a social world. It begins with children's playful manipulation of movement, gesture, material props, graphic marks, and, above all, the human voice. Thus, in young children's literacy learning, true educational equity is promoted when all children have the right, and opportunities, to use what they know and can do to venture into new communicative and symbolic possibilities. That is, to learn to write, children must be able to make use of the voices, images, and texts of their everyday lives and their ways of playing with those resources. And they also must have a community in which their composing matters to others; they need support and guidance from teachers, who may deliberately couch writing in childhood play; and they need time and space to interact with peers, who will find their own ways of making writing relevant. In the interplay between the official world of teachers and the unofficial world of children, rich instructional possibilities abound.

It does take courage to work and argue against mandated tests and curricula, which narrow possibilities for teachers and children. In the particular case of writing, the argument in this chapter has been that we will not beget child composing by denying children the cross-cultural and, indeed, ancient human desires for play and companionship. These are needed even by our contemporary children, if they are to confidently go forward to compose the world anew.

REFERENCES

Anderson, E. S. (1990). *Speaking with style: The sociolinguistic skills of children.* New York: Routledge.

Bakhtin, M. (1981). Discourse in the novel. In C. Emerson and M. Holquist_(Eds.), *The dialogic imagination: Four essays by M. Bakhtin* (pp. 254–422). Austin, TX: University of Texas Press.

Barton, D. & Hamilton, M. (1998). *Local literacies: Reading and writing in one community.* London: Routledge.

Bauman, R. (2004). *A world of others' words: Cross-cultural perspectives on intertextuality.* Malden, MA: Blackwell.

Bergen, D. (2006). Reconciling play and assessment standards: How to leave no child behind. In D. P. Fromberg and D. Bergen(Eds.), *Play from birth to twelve: Contexts, perspectives, and meanings* (2nd ed.; pp. 233–240). New York: Routledge.

Bourdieu, P. (1984). *Distinction: A social critique of the judgment of taste* (R. Nice, Trans.). Cambridge, MA: Harvard University Press (Original work published 1979).

Christie, J.F. (2006). Play as a medium for literacy development. In D. P. Fromberg and D. Bergen (Eds.), *Play from birth to twelve: Contexts, perspectives, and meanings (2nd ed.)* (pp. 50–55). New York: Routledge.

Clark, E. V. (2003). *First language acquisition.* Cambridge, MA: Cambridge University Press.

Clay, M. (1998). *By different paths to common outcomes.* York, Maine: Stenhouse.

Corsaro, W. (2005). *The sociology of childhood* (2nd ed.). Thousand Oaks: Pine Forge Press.

Dyson, A. Haas. (1989). *Multiple worlds of child writers: Friends learning to write.* New York: Teachers College Press.

Dyson, A. Haas. (1997). *Writing superheroes: Contemporary childhood, popular culture, and classroom literacy.* New York: Teachers College Press.

Dyson, A. Haas. (2003). *The brothers and sisters learn to write: Popular literacies in childhood and school cultures.* New York, Teachers College Press.

Dyson, A. Haas. (2005). Crafting the humble prose of living: Rethinking oral/written relations in the echoes of spoken word. *English Education, 37,* 149–164.

Dyson, A. Haas. (2006). On saying it right (write): "Fix-its" in the foundations of learning to write. *Research in the Teaching of English, 41,* 8–44.

Dyson, A. Haas. (2007). School literacy and the development of a child culture: Written remnants of the gusto of life. In D. Thiessen & A. Cook-Sather (Eds.), *International handbook of student experiences in elementary and secondary school* (pp. 115–142). Dordrecht, The Netherlands: Kluwer.

Dyson, A. Haas. (2008). On listening to child composers: Beyond "Fix-Its". In C. Genishi & L. Goodwin (Eds.), *Diversities in Early Childhood Education: Rethinking and doing* (pp. 13–28). London, Routledge Falmer.

Evans, J. (2005). *Literacy moves on: Popular culture, new technologies, and critical literacy in the elementary classroom.* Portsmouth, NH: Heinemann.

Fineberg, J. (2006). *When we were young: New perspectives on the art of the child.* Berkeley, CA: University of California Press.

Franklin, M. B. (1983). Play as the creation of imaginary situations: The role of language. In S.W. & B. Kaplan (Eds.), *Toward a holistic developmental psychology* (pp. 197–220). Hillsdale, NJ: Erlbaum.

Franklin, M. B. (2008). Words in play: Children's use of language in pretend. In E. N. Goodenough (Ed.), *A place for play* (pp. 27–34). Carmel, CA: National Institute for Play.

Fromberg, D.P. & Bergen, D. (Eds.). (2006). *Play from birth to twelve: Contexts, perspectives, and meaning* (2nd. ed.). New York: Routledge.

Garvey, C. (1984). *Children's talk.* Cambridge, MA:Harvard University Press.

Garvey, C. (1990). *Play.* Cambridge, MA, Harvard University Press.

Genishi, C., Stires, S. & Yung-Chan, D. (2001). Writing in an integrated curriculum: Prekindergarten English language learners as symbol-makers. *Elementary School Journal,* 101, 399–416.

Genishi, C. & Dyson, A.Haas. (2009). *Children, language, and literacy: Diverse learners in diverse times.* New York: Teachers College Press.

Glupczynski, T. (2007). *Understanding young children's experiences with a scripted literacy curriculum.* Unpublished dissertation, Teachers College-Columbia, New York.

Goodenough, E. (2008). Introduction. In E. N. Goodenough (Ed.), *A place for play* (pp. 1–8). Carmel, CA: National Institute for Play.

Heath, S. B. (1983). *Ways with words: Language, life and work in communities and classrooms.* Cambridge, U.K: Cambridge University Press.

Kamler, B. & Comber, B. (Eds.). (2005). *Turn-around pedagogies: Literacy interventions for at-risk students.* Newtown, Australia: Primary English Teachers Association.

Kenner, C. (2005). Bilingual children's uses of popular culture in text-making. In J. Marsh (Ed.), *Popular culture, new media, and digital literacy in early childhood (pp.* 73–88). London: Routledge.

Kline, S. (1993). *Out of the garden: Toys, TV, and children's culture in the age of marketing.* New York: Verso.

Kress, G. (2003). *Literacy in the new media age.* London, Routledge.

Lancy, D. F. (2008). *The anthropology of childhood: Cherubs, chattel, changelings.* New York: Cambridge University Press.

Levinson, M. (2007). Literacy in English Gypsy communities: Cultural capital manifested as negative assets. *American Educational Research Journal, 44,* 5–39.

Long, S., Volk, D., & Gregory, E. (2007). Intentionality and expertise: Learning from observations of children at play in multilingual, multicultural contexts. *Anthropology & Education Quarterly, 38,* 239–259.

Marsh, J. (1999). Batman and Batwoman go to school: Popular culture in the literacy curriculum. *International Journal of Early Years Education, 7,* 117–131.

Marsh, J. (2003). Early childhood literacy and popular culture. In J.Larson, N. Hall, & J. Marsh (Eds.), *Handbook of early childhood literacy* (pp. 112–125). London: Sage.

Marsh, J. & Millard, E. (2000). *Literacy and popular culture.* London, Sage.

Matthews, J. (1999). *The art of childhood and adolescence: The construction of meaning.* London: Falmer Press.

Nelson, K. (2007). *Young minds in social worlds: Experience, meaning, and memory.* Cambridge, MA: Harvard.

Nicolopoulou A., McDowell, J., & Brockmetyer, C. (2006). Narrative play and emergent literacy: Storytelling and story-acting meet journal writing. In D. Singer, R. M. Golinkoff, & K. Hirsh-Pasek (Eds.), *Play = Learning: How play motivates and enhances children's cognitive and social-emotional growth* (pp. 124–144.). Oxford: Oxford.

Ochs, E. & Capps, L. (2001). *Living narrative: Creating lives in everyday storytelling.* Cambridge, MA: Harvard Press.

Pahl, K. (2003). Children's text making at home: Transforming meaning across modes. In G. Kress (Ed.), *Multimodal literacy* (pp. 139–154). New York: Peter Lang.

Paley, V. G. (1981). *Wally's stories.* Cambridge, MA: Harvard University Press.

Paley, V. G. (1990). *The boy who would be a helicopter.* Cambridge, MA: Harvard University Press.

Paley, V. G. (2004). *A child's work: The importance of fantasy play.* Chicago: University of Chicago Press.

Reyes, M. (2001). Unleashing possibilities: Biliteracy in the primary grades. In M. Reyes & J. Halcon (Eds.), *The best for our children: Critical perspectives on literacy for Latino students* (pp. 96–121). New York, Teachers College Press.

Reyes, M. & Halcon, J. (Eds.). (2001). *The best for our children: Critical perspectives on literacy for Latino students.* New York: Teachers College Press.

Rickford, J. R., & Rickford, J. R. (2000). *Spoken soul: The story of Black English.* New York: John Wiley.

Robinson, M. (2004). *Gilead.* New York: Picador.

Sahni, U. (1994). *Building circles of mutuality: A socio-cultural analysis of literacy in a rural classroom in India.* Unpublished doctoral dissertation. University of California, Berkeley.

Seiter, E. (1993). *Sold separately: Children and parents in consumer culture.* New Brunswick, NJ: Rutgers University Press.

Siegel, M., Kontovourki, S., Schmier, S., & Enriquez, G. (2008). Literacy in motion: The case of a shape-shifting Kindergartener. *Language Arts, 86,* 89–98.

Street, B. V. (Ed.). (1993). *Cross-cultural approaches to literacy.* Cambridge, UK: Cambridge University Press.

Street, B. V. (2000). Literacy events and literacy practices: Theory and practice in the New Literacy Studies. In M. Martin-Jones & K. Jones (Eds.), *Multilingual literacies* (pp. 17–30). Philadelphia: John Benjamins.

Sutton-Smith, B., Mechling, J., Johnson, T.W., & McMahon, F.R. (1995). *Children's folklore: A source book.* New York: Garland Publishing.

Thompson, C. (2006). The ket aesthetic: Visual culture in childhood. In J. Fineberg (Ed.). *When we were young: New perspectives on the art of the child* (pp. 31–44). Berkeley, CA: University of California Press.

Vygotsky, L. S. (1962). *Thought and language.* Cambridge, MA: MIT Press.

Vygotsky, L. S. (1978). *Mind in society.* Cambridge, MA: Harvard University Press.

Zentella, A. C. (Ed.) (2005). *Building on strength: Language and literacy in Latino families and communities.* New York: Teachers College Press.

Zipes, J. (2004). *Speaking out: Storytelling and creative drama for children.* New York: Routledge.

PART III

TEACHERS OF LINGUISTICALLY AND CULTURALLY DIVERSE CHILDREN

CHAPTER 10

TEACHERS TELLING STORIES

Inviting Children Into Imaginative and Diverse Worlds

Celia Genishi, Cara Furman, Julianne P. Wurm, Molly Cain, Laura Osterman, Aya Takemura, and Wei-Yee Angela Tsang

ABSTRACT

I can't hear the story because it's too loud right now!

So declared a 4-year-old to Angela Tsang, as the sounds of children preparing for yoga class made Angela's story inaudible. As a student volunteer, Angela wanted to tell stories to the class at every opportunity, in keeping with the guidelines of her college language and literacy class. After all, doesn't everyone need a story, the most compelling way of organizing and sharing the happenings of our lives (Dyson & Genishi, 1994)? In this chapter we discuss how complex the answer to that question is when stories are *told* and not read. Everyone may need stories, but we may not hear them as often—or as loudly—as we would like. An activity like yoga may push them off the curricular stage, or, more likely, early literacy activities may demand their star turns.

Language and Cultural Diversity in Early Childhood Education, pages 215–233

We begin with a brief summary of what is currently enacted in many early childhood classrooms for children from age 3 to 8. That is, we describe an educational context with an increasing focus on literacy and early reading, and decreasing attention to child-oriented events and activities, such as storytelling and play. We next review literature related to storytelling by teachers and children, as the two kinds are interrelated, and their significance in the curriculum. Finally, within the framework of a master's level course on language and literacy for prospective early childhood teachers, we introduce our own stories about our experiences as storytellers in the classroom. We close the chapter with our thoughts on the impact of stories on our own practices and their potential impact on prospective teachers of young children.

WHY WE NEED STORYTELLING: THE CURRENT PUSH TOWARD EARLY READING

In this section, we explain why teachers and children need to return oral storytelling to an audible, respected position on early childhood classrooms' stages. We do this by describing the current pressure on practitioners to emphasize literacy and, more specifically, early reading skills in the prekindergarten and kindergarten curriculum. Indeed, as we listen for storytelling in early childhood classrooms, we often hear, instead, the relative loudness of read-alouds of picture books and lessons about letters and sounds. When child experiences in schools and centers are limited to exposure to commercially published books and instruction in reading, adults have, in fact, defined the curriculum primarily in terms of literacy and have narrowly defined children as "readers." Opportunities for speaking, moving, listening, dramatizing, experimenting with drawing and writing, and playing begin to disappear, along with the broad goal of communicative flexibility. (See Genishi & Dyson, 2009, for elaboration of this goal for diverse young learners.) Before we present a critique of this narrow perspective on literacy, we emphatically state that we want all learners to become literate, to become fluent readers in every sense; and we acknowledge that occasional focus on reading skills can be valuable and, for some learners, necessary. However, we enthusiastically support broadly conceived curricula that invite all children into the world of books and words and into a full range of literacy practices.

The aim of this chapter is to invite—or re-invite—early childhood educators into a literacy practice based on talk, that is, the oral telling of stories with powers of their own, independent of the printed word. With modulated voices, eye contact, sound effects, movements, and imaginations, storytellers recreate known stories, invent their own, and thereby create stepping stones to printed texts. In the process, they often include revelations about themselves that strengthen relationships with children, who may reciprocate and share elements of their own lives, thus linking them in memorable ways with their teachers and peers. These personal links may go unformed when teachers are pressured to use recommended or mandated literacy curricula that ensure children's readiness for the next level of reader, test, or grade. Since the publication of *Becoming a Nation of Readers* (National Academy of Education, 1985) and, more recently, the passage of the No Child Left Behind Act of 2001 (NCLB), early childhood teachers have noted radical changes in their daily schedules that push events like storytelling off the list of activities. Kindergarten teachers in some school districts in the U.S., for example, now organize their days around 90-minute literacy blocks (Hu, 2008). Depending on the school district, those 90 minutes may incorporate storytelling and child play and invention—or they may not.

A further word about threats to child invention and stories: One of the most negative features of mandated scheduling and curricula is its selectiveness. Typically, only some school districts are required to use narrowly defined curricula, usually those whose students have performed poorly on standardized tests. Their schools receive federal or state funding for special programs to help students to "catch up." These students, then, are less likely to have opportunities to be inventive or to hear and tell frequent stories. Assumptions are made that all students in these schools are on the wrong side of the academic achievement gap, and in the U.S., the students tend to be of color and in under-resourced schools (Fennimore, 2000). Students are often seen as problems to be fixed, rather than as learners who bring their own resources and sense of agency with them to the classroom. In turn, their teachers, who are required to use "teacher-proof" mandated curricula, feel their sense of agency diminish as they are treated like technicians and not professionals (Cochran-Smith & Lytle, 2006).

Teachers who are required to teach their children in particular ways in 90-minute literacy blocks often focus narrowly on "reading," defined within the NCLB framework according to five components:

- phonological awareness (Sounds exist apart from words and can be manipulated.)
- alphabetic principle (There is a systematic relationship between letters and sounds.)
- fluency with text (Children should read with increasing speed over time.)
- comprehension (Children understand what they read.)
- vocabulary (Children know/can learn the meanings of words read.)

These are the five "big ideas" of reading derived from Reading First, the funding arm of NCLB, as articulated in the widely used standardized test called DIBELS, or Dynamic Indicators of Basic Early Literacy Skills (Good

& Kaminski, 2002). They are, indeed, big ideas, fundamental to reading, though defined in the most constraining ways (Goodman, 2006). In fact, adults giving DIBELS to young children use stopwatches to see how quickly they demonstrate ownership of these ideas! Note, however, that children's ability to engage in the play that could provide a context for them to draw or write, converse with peers, listen to or tell stories, and enjoy books is not included. Despite this exclusion, there is a growing literature focused on children as story tellers and skilled narrators from diverse sociocultural groups (Bloome, Champion, Katz, Morton, & Muldrow, 2001; Heath, 1983; Miller & Goodnow, 1995). At present, however, the big ideas folded into stories are drowned out by the loudness of phonics lessons or weekly spelling tests.

In sum, there is a jarring disconnect between current curricula for young children and what early childhood educators have long assumed are aspects of becoming literate and developing communicative flexibility. In this chapter, we rearrange the order and definitions of the big ideas of literacy learning to reclaim the primacy of oral language and storytelling within the broad range of skills and abilities of flexible child communicators. Next, we offer a selective review of literature, highlighting teachers as storytellers and illustrating influences of stories on children's learning.

LITERATURE ABOUT TEACHERS AND CHILDREN AS STORYTELLERS

We discovered that the literature about teachers and children as storytellers is not extensive. In particular, there are few research studies done on the topic. In this section, then, we include a combination of studies done "on" teachers and some done by teachers who are more accurately called teacher researchers. We begin with a focus on teachers telling their own stories, through the eyes of a researcher outside the classroom.

Teaching as Autobiography: Teachers Tell Their Own Stories

In *The Lives of Teachers,* Michael Huberman (1993) demonstrated the importance of teachers articulating their own stories about their lives in the career of teaching across the life cycle. Mixing quantitative and qualitative methods, Huberman and his collaborators carried out an exhaustive series of interviews of 160 secondary teachers in Switzerland at different points in their careers. While seeking trends across gender, age, and years of experience in the classroom, they also looked for a reflective narrative about teaching. (We would call this a story, although Huberman did not use the word.) For most teachers in the study, this kind of reflection on teaching and their lives felt foreign to them; yet, overall, they felt that reflecting upon their careers was both positive and helpful. Huberman inferred that, as teachers look at the trajectory of their lives (in other words, consider their stories), they have the potential to improve their teaching, because they understand better what they are trying to accomplish as teachers. By discovering the underlying theme or motivation of their teaching—for example, transmission of information within a discipline, relationships with students, or social justice—they may articulate new goals and act to achieve them.

According to Huberman, one's story is unavoidable in the classroom:

> As many informants remarked, a teacher negotiates in classes as much his [sic] person as his manner of instruction. When this person at the front of the class is unavailable, inefficient, less integrated, unsatisfied, there will be exerted a measurable influence on all the students, except, perhaps, for the three or four best ones, who somehow manage to succeed even in the most difficult conditions. (Huberman, 1993, p. 263)

Our stories enter the classroom and influence students, whether we mean them to or not. How this observation applies to our own group's stories in the language and literacy course is addressed later in the chapter.

Turning to a more focused study of 10 teachers, we see the notion of knowing one's story at the forefront of the elementary teacher education program at Teachers College, in which working successfully with learners of a wide range of social, cultural, and linguistic backgrounds is key. A. Lin Goodwin and Michele Genor (2008) explained that prospective teachers worked in multiple ways to analyze their own stories, with the emphasis less on telling and more on raising questions about how their stories might connect with those of their students. In articulating their personal stories, teachers from "minority" groups may gain confidence in the validity of their experiences, while teachers from mainstream cultural groups are pushed to question the universality of their experiences. If teachers do, in fact, "teach who we are" (Goodwin & Genor, 2008, p. 204), articulating, understanding, and sharing autobiographies may lead to owning who and where teachers are as they begin to help students grow, as well.

Similarly, in *Multicultural Strategies for Education and Social Change*, Arnetha Ball (2006) found that, when preparing teachers to work with people from diverse racial and economic backgrounds, teachers who felt comfortable sharing information about themselves in a protected and nonjudgmental environment were, ultimately, able to look at their own students with a more open mind. In working with teachers in the United States and South Africa, she found that as they explored their stories, often through writing, they became more effective teachers with lower income and "minority" students who often came from backgrounds different from their own.

Cindy Cohen (2007), also focusing on teachers as students, found that it was essential to welcome teachers' stories into the professional development classroom, so that teachers would, in turn, be ready to hear the stories of their students. Cohen quoted the work of Parker Palmer, a Quaker educator who wrote that we should encourage "our students to intersect their autobiographies with the life story of the world, so that they come to know intimately and passionately as well as objectively" (Palmer, cited in Cohen, 2007, p. 53). Without passing judgment, Cohen emphasized the need for teachers to write about their own experiences as learners. In allowing them, ultimately, to see themselves and their own experiences within an extensive dialogue, in the context of larger questions of social justice, she found that students could take ownership of their position of power in relation to others. Specifically, reflecting upon a working class Irish teacher's development, she wrote, "I think it's no coincidence that Jim honored his parents' suffering and celebrated their culture before he was able to think and write critically about the racism and sexism he had learned from them" (Cohen, 2007, p. 61).

Teachers as Storytellers

The brief review of literature so far shows how complex the act of telling stories is. In this section, we address the rich complexity of telling stories to children, beginning with the work of Vivian Paley, who is best known for her illuminating books about children's story creation and dramatization. As a nursery school and kindergarten teacher for 35 years, she developed an approach to early childhood curriculum grounded in children's stories (e.g., Paley, 1981, 1990, 1997, 2004). Our interest here, however, is in Paley's insights into the importance of *teachers* telling stories they themselves create, as a way of enhancing the storytelling and overall learning of children.

More than anything, the teacher as storyteller enables a common narrative to develop that reflects classroom members' experiences, as a whole. Unlike a read-aloud of a commercially published book or even the children's shared stories, Paley (1994) notes that when she tells or reads the story she created in response to particular classroom events, it is then owned by everyone: "When I read my chapter to the children, it joins all the other stories being told and played in every corner of the room. Together the children and I create an ongoing mythology that connects us to one another and establishes the continuity of our days" (p. 146). In an earlier book, *You Can't Say You Can't Play*, Paley (1992) told the story she referred to above, about a wise bird named Magpie, a princess, and her family and friends. The serialized story involved isolation, friendship, and community, to help her students reflect on those themes and, ultimately, build a more welcoming community, themselves. As the book's title suggests, the class worked together on the problems of rejection.

Further, shared experiences like Paley's are viewed as necessary to learning. For example, Susan Engel (1995), in her study of how children's stories develop, concluded that shared storytelling becomes a foundation for new learning. As if elaborating on Paley's insights, Engel explained that memory does not develop only within individuals; rather, it grows interpersonally within groups. She cited the psychologist, Frederic Bartlett, who said, "the telling of stories within a community constitutes a form of social memory" (cited in Engel, 1995, p. 124). Thus, through the collective processes of storytelling, children may remember and learn.

Storytelling does, indeed, provide lessons to be learned. Analyzing in depth Paley's ideas, Patricia M. Cooper (2009) discussed the significance of Paley's work for teacher educators. She argued that teachers like Paley have much to teach colleagues in early childhood classrooms, as well as teacher education programs. From Cooper's point of view, the lessons are not only pedagogical, including the "hows" of Paley's approach to storytelling, but also theoretical. And in Paley's work, the pedagogical and theoretical always overlap. Thus, Cooper described Paley's implicit theory of practice in terms of a pedagogy of meaning and a pedagogy of fairness: Stories told by children convey in myriad ways what is meaningful to them, and the telling and enactment of the stories embody their teacher's pedagogy of fairness. No child's story goes untold or unacknowledged, so that the developing curriculum of the classroom is truly inclusive and fair. Recall that Paley (1992, 1994) also included her own stories in the curriculum, extending the inclusiveness to herself.

Cooper (2009) not only theorized the work of Paley, but she also explained the practical implications of Paley's curricular approach. Cooper argued that current approaches to teaching literacy to young children ignore their capacity to create stories and build inclusive communities. Indeed, in earlier work, Cooper, Capo, Mathes, and Gray (2007) carried out a unique study of two public prekindergarten (pre-K), kindergarten, and multiaged classrooms, comparing the test performances of children who experienced a storytelling curriculum in the style of Paley's for one year to children who did not experience it. Children in the storytelling group scored significantly higher on the *Expressive Vocabulary Test* (*EVT-2*), the *Peabody Picture Vocabulary Test* (Dunn & Dunn, 2007), and the *Get Ready to Read!* screening test, suggesting that frequent storytelling may have had a more positive impact on measures of vocabulary and early literacy than skills-centered curricula. This kind of research is unlike anything Paley would have considered doing in her own classrooms, but the findings of Cooper et al. (2007) provoke thought about the potential impact of child-centered practices on early literacy learning. The findings also suggest the need for a rethinking of what methods might be included in literacy methods courses for preservice teachers.

Returning to the topic of teacher as storyteller, Nancy King (2007) wrote of the power of storytelling in classrooms of children and adults where stories can work "a kind of magic" (King, 2007, p. 204). She identified herself thus: "I am a storyteller, a teacher, a trickster, a shapeshifter who uses stories to engage the hearts and minds of the students with whom I work" (p. 204). In her role as professional developer, King found that the teachers she worked with wanted their students to develop creativity. She maintained that, in order for this development to occur, the teachers themselves needed to be confident and comfortable in their own creativity. King noted that, although adults often felt that they had lost the ability to create, what they had really lost was their access to that ability. For King, teaching teachers to engage in the process of storytelling helped them to redevelop their creativity and become better teachers.

The benefits for teachers of developing or regaining their storytelling abilities are multiple. For example, King used storytelling as a management device in her first teaching position as a 16-year-old junior counselor. She eventually took control of an uncooperative class by involving campers in an interactive play-like story. They began to pay attention to her and, like Paley's children, "were intrigued enough to enter into the imaginary world I had created" (King, 2007, p. 207). Later, when King became a teacher, she told stories and created stories with students, as a way of subtly establishing control and, at the same time, fostering engagement that helped to create classroom communities.

Summary of Literature

As you have seen, there is a small body of research or writing about teachers as storytellers. Those who wrote on the topic attributed great power to the content of stories, as well as to the telling of them. From different perspectives, Huberman (1993), Goodwin and Genor (2008), Ball (2006), and Cohen (2007) all illustrated the need for teachers to articulate their own stories, not just as a personally fulfilling reflective process, but as a potential way of improving their teaching. Paley (1992, 1994), Engel (1995), Cooper (2007, 2009), and King (2007) elaborated on the complex relationships among stories that teachers create, children's stories, memory, and varied ways of learning. In the next section, we shift focus to storytelling as an integral part of a teacher education course on young children's language and literacy.

TELLING OUR STORIES AND STUDYING OURSELVES: WORKS IN PROGRESS

We co-authors came together because of a required course at Teachers College, Columbia University, for master's students called "Language and Literacy in the Early Childhood Curriculum," for which Celia was the faculty instructor and Julianne (Julie), a doctoral student, was the co-instructor. Like most states, New York requires two methods courses in literacy for prospective teachers. Because the program in which Celia and Julie taught was the Integrated Early Childhood initial certification program, the course focused on children's language and literacy learning from birth to about age 4. Unlike the required course for literacy methods for kindergarten to grade 2, this one focused on the development of communication in very young children of diverse social and cultural backgrounds; the precursors of literacy; methods for enhancing language and literacy learning; and the resourcefulness of young language learners, including English language learners or, as we prefer to call them, emergent bilinguals (Garcia, Kleifgen, & Falchi, 2008). (See Genishi, Huang, & Glupczynski, 2005 for a fuller description of the course and an analysis of written assignments.)

We also came together because of Cara's deep interest in storytelling. Cara is a first/second grade teacher in a New York City public school who routinely incorporates in her language arts curriculum students' and her own stories. After Cara initiated an informal meeting with Celia about their mutual interest in stories, Cara visited the language and literacy class to hear some of the Teachers College students' stories and in turn tell about how she and her primary-grade students shared their stories. She also reviewed for us most of the literature just presented. Illustrating insights and recommendations from some of that work (Cooper et al., 2007; Huberman, 1993; King, 2007; Paley, 1994), Cara told us about how the stories she tells often come from her personal experiences. For instance, when her student, Michael, was upset because his mom could not afford to buy him a popular video game, Cara shared a story about how sad she was when her parents felt a coveted doll that her friends owned and brought to school was something her family couldn't afford. Her story led to students addressing the same theme, which Cara then said the class could write about during writing workshop. She concluded that the sharing of her own childhood experience was essential to moving her students from complaint to expression in print.

This may sound like an obvious use of story, but Cara noted that students' oral and written expression through storytelling developed in a particular social context with children of differing social and linguistic backgrounds and abilities, over time. In a narrative reflection about storytelling in her classroom, Cara wrote:

> In these cases storytelling served vital purposes. It helped to bring us together as a community, creating a place where we could share experiences and deal with issues without singling anyone out. It showed to the students, Michael in particular, that they weren't alone in their experiences and gave them some perspective and suggested ways out of feelings of frustration.

In her third year of teaching, Cara was in a public school where the administrators allowed some flexibility around literacy practices. She knew that her students needed to be able to read and write, but she was able to fit storytelling into a curriculum focused broadly on language arts, including children's spontaneous singing and dancing, as an accompaniment to their stories. Hardly passive, this community of learners was active and eager to perform what they were learning. (See Furman [in preparation] for the full, complex story.) In the next sections, we tell how four students initiated their professional storytelling lives, how, like Cara, they looked for spaces where stories might fit into daily schedules. Unlike Cara, they did not yet have their own classrooms, so that they were just stepping onto the storytelling stage in other teachers' classrooms.

Telling a Story to Grown-ups

In the college class where Cara spoke, storytelling was a part of the curriculum. In fact, the first assignment for Celia and Julie's course was to tell a story to the class. Some students commented that taking so much time to tell stories seemed rather odd, but the assignments were explained within the context of working with young children just entering the world of conventional literacy. The following were the guidelines included in the syllabus in the fall of 2008:

> *Story-telling (to be done individually, 3 groups of storytellers on 3 class days)*:
>
> Tell a story to the 4131 class that would be appropriate and engaging for *an audience of young children* (within birth through 4 or 5 age range). This may be a story you create, remember from childhood, or *adapt* from a book that you know. It should be *told* without any notes or props, and not read or recited or quoted from a book. On each story-telling day, we will have brief informal talks about the stories, their themes and cultural content, their impact on you as listeners, and so on. A *reflection* about the significance and cultural content of your story, of no more than one typed, double-spaced page, should be given to us, after you tell your story.
>
> You should choose a story that:
>
> - you consider to be a "good story" and that you really like and you think young children of a range of backgrounds and abilities will like;

- takes between 3 and 4 minutes to tell (since this is for an audience of young children and there are a large number of you in the class);
- reveals something about culture, broadly defined, either your own culture or another.

Try to tell the story to a group of prekindergarten children as a "rehearsal"; and consider audio taping yourself and classmates, so that you can begin a collection of stories to tell. (10% of course grade for storytelling and 5% for written reflection)

Celia and Julie told the class two kinds of stories as "models" to explain the assignment, one based loosely on a picture book and the other drawn from their own childhood experiences. They also recommended the use of storytelling for multiple purposes, for example, during transitions from one activity to another, or when attending to children who were not napping during "nap time." In addition, one of the required readings for the semester was Paley's *The Boy Who Would be a Helicopter* (1990), in which Paley described her approach to storytelling and story acting.

In short, storytelling was introduced early in the course as a "method of choice" that required no materials other than the teacher's voice and other means of communicating without props: memory and imagination. At the same time, to make our stories audible to a wider audience, we invited any class members to join us in the development of this chapter, which would focus on "teachers becoming storytellers." Seven students volunteered to become part of the storytelling and writing group, and four were ultimately in work sites or field placements that enabled them to tell their stories to the young children in their classrooms. In the next sections, we hear stories of storytelling, first, about the whole class as they completed the course assignment and, second, from Molly, Laura, Aya, and Angela, as they considered their learning over the course of the semester.

Stories as Diverse as Their Tellers

It will come as no surprise to you that the 30 students in the class (all women) told a wide range of stories, through which they brought their life experiences to the classroom stage in distinctive ways. The group of storytellers consisted of students of the following heritages: 1 South Asian, 1 Middle Eastern, 4 East Asian, 5 Latina, and 19 European American. Their ethnic, racial, and international backgrounds were often evident in their stories, as were their identities according to heritage and social class. Indeed, Celia invited these revelations when she identified herself in one of her stories as a Japanese American of working-class background.

Stories included personal experiences from childhood, for example, moving from one state to another or celebrating a religious holiday in repressive circumstances; combinations of personal experiences and fiction; folk tales from China or India, passed on by family members; stories with embedded or overt lessons or morals relating to equity and social justice; and stories, real or imagined, created for the purpose of engaging children by means of an appealing character, often an animal.

Also not surprisingly, storytellers varied in their levels of comfort as they told their stories. A number commented on how telling stories to their peers was completely different—nerve-wracking, really—from telling them to young children, whom they viewed as uncritical and easily mesmerized by stories. The children, of course, were not grading them on their performance and would be forgiving of a lapse in memory caused by stage fright. In reality, Celia and Julie found most of the student storytellers to be poised, prepared, and animated, as they would have been for prekindergartners. A number were clearly in their element, engaging their adult audience members just as they would pre-K children. Some had rehearsed their stories with their children and reported positive receptions. Whether anyone kept the storytelling alive after the assignment was completed is addressed in the next phase of our collective stories.

Four Storytellers: Drawing on the Diversity of Their Lives

Like their colleagues in the language and literacy course, Molly, Laura, Aya, and Angela told stories that drew upon their life stories. In fact, all four of them told stories involving at least one treasured family member who either told them stories or was a character in the story they told the class. Like all class members, after telling their stories, the four wrote reflections regarding the individual and cultural meanings of their story; and after the semester ended, these four wrote a summary reflection of their storytelling experiences. These latter reflections were written about 4 months after the semester started, so the history of their storytelling was brief and preliminary. Nonetheless, all four could look back at the way in which they were learning to tell stories and learning about themselves as storytellers. Next, we briefly summarize this look back and include excerpts from the reflections of the four students—presented in alphabetical order by last name—that reveal aspects of their life stories and of their teaching lives, within the context of the course and their field placement for the semester in New York City.

Molly: Once upon a time there was a little girl . Molly was completing her second semester of student teaching in an inclusive classroom for 2- and 3-year-olds in a private cooperative preschool where parents were required to participate in classroom activities and children with special needs were included in most classrooms. In her reflection on the story she told the language and literacy class, she revealed:

> The story that I chose to tell our class was inspired by tales my father told me when I was growing up. His stories always began the same way: "Once upon a time, there was a little girl named 'Molly Jones.' She was just like Molly Cain, except every once in awhile she would become as small as a mouse; and also, she could talk with animals." The story would also always end the same way: "And that was that." I would always cry, "No! One more story."

As she planned the story to tell her colleagues, she consulted with and learned from her father that he wove lessons into his stories about Molly Jones. This led Molly Cain to fold concepts into her stories for children, for example, friendship, information about animals, and colors. One girl, Tina, began to ask to hear stories routinely, particularly about animals: "Once upon a time, there was a little horse named Tina" became a typical way to initiate stories for her. Molly observed that when she told the story, Tina did not look at her, but stared past her with a slight smile, as if she were imagining what she heard. This led Molly to add "thought-provoking details" to be imagined in each subsequent story.

Although the curriculum of Molly's classroom was play-based, the schedule was set so that she had to be creative in weaving in these stories. She eventually fit them into the schedule by telling them at naptime to children like Tina who had trouble sleeping. This seemed especially appropriate, because she had heard the Molly Jones tales as bedtime stories. Looking to the future, Molly concluded in her end-of-semester reflection that storytelling is the most direct way for children to get lost in an imagined world, and that is key to eventually becoming readers of "picture-free books." She wrote that "children can best learn through stories when their imaginations are truly sparked and they are engaged in the narrative."

Laura: Revealing who you are. Laura was in her second semester of student teaching and also worked part-time in a private school with a curriculum that was play-based. She told a story to the language and literacy class that her mother told her:

> I selected a story that my mother created and told me when I was young. The story was about a young girl who mischievously disobeys her mother, paints her nails before bed, and wakes up only to discover that she is stuck to her bed. The details of the story are somewhat inconsequential and instead the true value lies in the experience and memory that I have of my mother and me sharing the story with one another. The power lies in the fact that the memory and story stayed with me for over 20 years and although I knew that the story was fictional, at times it felt as real to me as a true experience. This is a direct reflection of the power of storytelling and oral narrative.

Like Molly, as a child Laura heard stories before falling asleep at night. These were sometimes read and sometimes told. She remembered her father's tales of Claude and Charles, two spies who followed her family around the world just to make sure that she and her brother behaved. Evidently, her father mixed lessons with entertainment.

When Laura told the story about the girl with the painted fingernails to her 4-year-olds, the children were receptive and immediately wanted to tell stories about themselves. Sharing a story from her childhood seemed like a small event, but it created an opening for numerous child stories, which were ways of revealing what mattered to the 4-year-olds as people with real and sometimes invented histories to share. According to Laura, she was "often exploring and experimenting with my identity and my roles as a performer and as an observer." For her, storytelling was not only a method to use with young children, but it was also a means that enabled her to reflect on her values and culture. Storytelling, she said, "has helped me gain a clear picture of who I am and what I bring to the classroom." Further, "By creating a space for storytelling in the classroom additional ways of observing and interacting with the children were generated."

Aya: "Swimming Lesson" and the lessons of storytelling. Like Laura and Molly, Aya drew on experiences from childhood; but unlike Laura, she told a story to the class of adults based on an actual experience:

> This story, ""Swimming Lesson," is one of my favorites. The story takes place in a small Japanese town called Ikuno where my mother and grandparents lived. Ikuno has been my favorite place since I was a child and it has been the most important place too, impacting my life in many ways. I feel that my identity was formed there. Susan Engel says in the article we read, "Story telling is perhaps the most powerful way that human beings organize experience" (Engel, 1997, p. 3). It took me a long time while growing up to understand what kind of a person my grandpa was and how the culture of his generation was different from mine. In "Swimming Lesson" I organize my experience, my thoughts, and my feelings about this time in my life. Of all the people I had known my grandpa had the strongest spirit and never changed his beliefs. I learned a lot from him and my relationship with him influenced the kind of person I became.

Aya also told this story to the 3- and 4-year-old children she worked with as a weekly volunteer, but her experience was different from Laura's, in that the children seemed disinterested. Some of them had not swum before, and they did not seem to connect with the story. In her second and third stories to the group, Aya embedded messages or lessons, such as one on counting in the context of a loose retelling of *The Magic Pot* (Coombs, 1977). Children could imagine what to put into the magical pot that doubled whatever was put into it. She was able to tell a story once a week, trying out different kinds of stories and occasionally asking the children to enact part of a story. By the end of the semester, Aya was able to write, "When I was telling the story and everybody was quietly paying attention and listening, I felt the magic of storytelling."

Also, by the end of the semester, she was able to engage two boys in storytelling who had never participated in circle time or storytelling before. The teachers referred to one of them as having behavior issues, and the other seemed anxious. Aya later was gratified to learn that, one day when she was absent, this second boy began telling his own story during the class's theater activity. Her goal for the future is to experience what she calls "the next step," to have all the children tell their own stories.

Angela: Learning not to give up. Angela told a story that, like her three colleagues' stories, was rooted in her childhood experiences:

> The importance of family and community is emphasized in my story of Chinese siblings (based on my brother and me). Since both parents are busy with their work, the siblings take care of each other. The older sister takes care of the younger brother and sometimes even takes on the role of the mother: everyday. She makes sure he eats dinner and completes his homework, and when her brother gets hurt playing tennis, she gets help right away. On the other hand, the younger brother also takes care of his sister when she falls ill, and volunteers to stay with her in the hospital at night for an entire week.

Like Aya, Angela explained to the class the value placed on family relationships in her culture, something that Laura and Molly did not do, perhaps because they were not international students who felt the need to make their families' values explicit.

Here are some of Angela's insights from the written summary of her first steps in becoming a storyteller:

> I used to think that storytelling had to have a beginning, middle, and end, and it had to last at least 4 to 5 minutes. It took me an entire semester to learn that stories can be one or two sentences, and that I used to disqualify many stories . . . because I thought they were too short and ended too abruptly. One thing I learned from this project was to not give up.

And giving up was not what she did. She reported that, during the last week of the semester in a classroom in New York City:

> I finally enchanted the entire class with a story during lunch. Every child turned toward me, and for once, the only voice in the room was mine. No food was being thrown around, and when I finished the story, they asked for another story.

Because the classroom was not one in which talk was always encouraged, Angela was unsure about the future of storytelling there; but she believed her own stories were a success.

When Angela went home to Taiwan after the semester ended, she was in a contrasting setting: a large preschool with 35 classrooms and 20 to 25 children in each room. The 4- and 5-year-olds seemed unfamiliar with oral storytelling. When she explained in Mandarin that she was there to tell them a story, one boy asked, "So where's your book?" Angela proceeded to share two stories told by her colleagues in the language and literacy course, one about a young girl taking a test at a new school (told by Eileen Blanco), and another about a little girl whose favorite color was purple (told by Chelsea Miolee). Angela asked the children to add to the second story, and children began to respond; but story time ended, because it was time for lunch. Thus, she concluded that stories were probably not told at this school, rather, they were read. Despite the contrast in the organization and structure of the school, the focus on books was a notable similarity with the U.S. context.

TEACHERS TELL THE STORIES OF THEIR LIVES: STORYTELLING IN TEACHER EDUCATION

[C]onsider the potential of story, a form that can bridge two divided rivers, one full of centuries of cherished thinking and research, the other a communal river of memory, full of the ordinary events of daily life, in classrooms and out, sometimes written and often not.

—Genishi, 1992, p. 204

Although it happened outside the official context of our course, we include the story of Angela in Taiwan because it brings us back to a number of insights from our review of literature and our co-authors' stories: First, it is important to tell—and understand—the stories of our lives as teachers, to consider the content of our "communal river of memory" in order to see where we've been as teachers and where we might go next (Huberman, 1993; see also Jalongo, 1995). In agreement with Huberman and Jalongo, we co-authors argue that articulating and sharing our stories may help us understand the complexity of our teacher identities, one of Laura's aims. In addition, articulating and understanding our stories may, indeed, make us all better teachers, implying that the content of teacher education curricula might incorporate autobiographical and other stories (Cohen, 2007; Goodwin & Genor, 2008).

The second central insight is that if we focus only on learning to read and on reading stories in books, we and our children miss opportunities to imagine characters and events or entire stories, as Molly pointed out in her reflection. Moreover, stories spoken and heard can come to life or inspire at unexpected times, on unexpected classroom stages, as when the reportedly anxious boy in Aya's setting told his own story, after hearing many of Aya's. This boy may acquire a new identity of storyteller, since we have observed that, once started, the habit of storytelling is hard to break.

Third, creating communities through stories, as Vivian Paley has done for decades and Cara is doing in her first/second-grade class, has the potential to bridge the divided rivers referred to above. The centuries of research consisting of numbers that can now reduce learning to a single-digit test score may be mitigated and resisted by the stories of children and teachers, narrating the communal events of everyday life. At the same time, children may begin to understand how stories told are related to stories read. Thus, young children will learn not only the inescapable principle of how a letter is associated with a sound, but, more importantly, how a story about a friend is related to one's own story and can, in fact, be acted out and written down with words full of meaning for the child storyteller. The research of Cooper et al. (2007) suggests that by telling and acting out stories in the style of Vivian Paley, young children learn about new words and the foundations of early literacy. To join those divided rivers, then, we recommend, as Angela would, that we not give up on telling and retelling stories. We urge the expansion of research agendas in language and literacy to include the systematic documentation of the impact of storytelling on learning. And, finally, we urge the frequent and joyful exercise of our imaginations to create the stories that all of us need.

REFERENCES

Ball, A. (2006). *Multicultural strategies for education and social change: Carriers of the torch in the United States and South Africa.* New York. Teachers College Press.

Bloome, D., Champion, T., Katz, L., Morton, M. B., & Muldrow, R. (2001). Spoken and written narrative development: African American preschoolers as storytellers and storymakers. In L. Harris, G. Kamhi, & K. Pollock (Eds.), *Literacy in African American communities* (pp.45–76). Mahwah, NJ: Lawrence Erlbaum.

Cochran-Smith, M., & Lytle, S. (2006). Troubling images of teaching in No Child Left Behind. *Harvard Educational Review* (special issue), *76*(4), 668–697.

Cohen, C. (2007). The true colors of the new Jim Toomey: Transformation, integrity, trust in educating teachers about oppression. In E. Lee, D. Menkart, M. Okazawa-Rey (Eds.), *Beyond heroes and holidays: A practical guide to K–12 anti-racist, multicultural education and staff development* (2nd ed.) (pp. 57–69). Washington, DC: Teaching for Change.

Coombs, P. (1977). *The magic pot.* New York: William Morrow.

Cooper, P. M. (2009). *The classrooms young children need: Lessons in teaching from Vivian Paley.* Chicago: University of Chicago Press.

Cooper, P. M., Capo, K., Mathes, B., & Gray, L. (2007). One authentic early literacy practice and three standardized tests: Can a storytelling curriculum measure up? *Journal of Early Childhood Teacher Education, 28,* 251–275.

Dunn, L. M., & Dunn, D. D. (2007). *Peabody Picture Vocabulary Test (PPVT-4th ed.)* Upper Saddle River, NJ: Pearson.

Dyson, A. Haas & Genishi, C. (Eds.) (1994). *The need for story: Cultural diversity in classroom and community.* Urbana, IL: National Council of Teachers of English.

Engel, S. (1995). *The stories children tell: Making sense of the narratives of childhood.* New York. W.H. Freeman & Company.

Engel, S. (1997). The guy who went up the steep nicken: The emergence of storytelling during the first 3 years. *Zero to Three, 17*(3), 1, 3–9.

Expressive Vocabulary Test (EVT-2). (n.d.). Upper Saddle River, NJ: Pearson.

Fennimore, B. S. (2000). *Talk matters: Refocusing the language of public schooling.* New York: Teachers College Press.

Furman, C. E. (in preparation). Storytelling, the imagination, and identity in classroom communities (working title).

Garcia, O., Kleifgen, J., & Falchi, L. (2008). *From English language learners to emergent bilinguals.* Equity Matters: Research Review No. 1. Retrieved December 31, 2009 from http://www.tc.columbia.edu/i/a/document/6468_Ofelia_ELL_Final.pdf

Genishi, C., & Dyson, A. Haas. (2009). *Children, language, and literacy: Diverse learners in diverse times.* New York: Teachers College Press and Washington, DC: National Association for the Education of Young Children.

Genishi, C., Huang, S-y., & Glupczynski, T. (2005). Becoming early childhood teachers: Linking action research and postmodern theory in a language and literacy course. In S.Ryan & S. Grieshaber (Eds.), *Practical transformations and transformational practices: Globalization, postmodernism, and early childhood education* (pp. 161–192), in S. Reifel (Series ed.), *Advances in Early Education and Day Care* (vol. 14). New York: Elsevier.

Get Ready to Read! (n.d.). Screening tool for early literacy. Upper Saddle River, NJ: Pearson.

Good, R. H., & Kaminski, R. A. (2002). *Dynamic Indicators of Basic Early Literacy Skills* (6th ed.). Eugene, OR: Institute for the Development of Educational Achievement.

Goodman, K. S. (2006). *The truth about DIBELS: What it is, what it does.* Portsmouth, NH: Heinemann.

Goodwin, A.L. and Genor, M. (2008). Disrupting the taken-for-granted: Autobiographical analysis in preservice teacher education. In C. Genishi & A.L. Goodwin (Eds.), *Diversities in early childhood education: Rethinking and doing* (pp. 201–218). New York: Routledge.

Heath, S. B. (1983). *Ways with words: Language, life, and work in communities and classrooms.* New York: Cambridge University Press.

Hu, W. (2008, August 6). Where the race now begins at kindergarten. *New York Times,* p. B-1.

Huberman, M. (1993). *The lives of teachers* (trans. J. Neufeld). New York: Teachers College Press.

Jalongo, M. R. (1995). *Teachers' stories: From personal narrative to professional insight.* San Francisco: Jossey-Bass.

King, N. (2007). Developing imagination, creativity, and literacy through collaborative storymaking: A way of knowing. *Harvard Educational Review, 77*(2), 204–227.

Miller, P., & Goodnow, J. J. (1995). Cultural practices: Toward an integration of culture and development. In J. J. Goodnow, P. J. Miller, & F. Kessel (Eds.), *Cultural practices as contexts for development, No. 67, New directions in child development* (pp. 5–16). San Francisco: Jossey-Bass.

National Academy of Education. (1985). *Becoming a nation of readers: The report of the Commission on Reading.* Washington, DC: National Academy of Education/National Institute of Education; Champaign, IL: Center for the Study of Reading.

No Child Left Behind Act of 2001. (PL 107–110). www.ed.gov/nclb/landing.jhtml

Paley, V.G. (1981). *Wally's stories.* Cambridge, MA: Harvard University Press.

Paley, V.G. (1990). *The boy who would be a helicopter.* Cambridge, MA: Harvard University Press.

Paley, V.G. (1992). *You can't say you can't play.* Cambridge, MA: Harvard University Press.

Paley, V.G. (1994). Princess Annabella and the black girls. In A. Haas Dyson & C. Genishi (Eds.), *The need for story: Cultural diversity in classroom and community* (pp. 145–154). Urbana, IL: National Council of Teachers of English.

Paley, V.G. (1997). *The girl with the brown crayon.* Cambridge, MA: Harvard University Press.

Paley, V. G. (2004). *A child's work: The importance of fantasy play.* Chicago: University of Chicago Press.

CHAPTER 11

PREPARING EARLY CHILDHOOD TEACHERS TO ENACT SOCIAL JUSTICE PEDAGOGIES

Sharon Ryan and Nora Hyland

ABSTRACT

Educating early childhood teachers to be able to individualize instruction and respond to their students in ways that are equitable and culturally relevant is essential to good practice. National standards for initial licensure put forth by the National Association for the Education of Young Children (Hyson, 2003) assert that teachers must be able to link children's language and culture to the curriculum. Similarly, the Early Childhood/Generalist standards produced by the National Board for Professional Teaching Standards state that "accomplished early childhood teachers model and teach behaviors appropriate in a diverse society" (Hyson, 2003, p. 156). Yet, national studies of 2- and 4-year early childhood certification programs consistently find that most programs offer little coursework in diversity content of any kind (Early & Winton, 2001; Maxwell, Lim, & Early, 2006; Ray, Bowman, & Robbins, 2006). Thus, despite the fact that we are residing in a global world, it would seem that early childhood teacher education has made little progress toward providing teachers with the knowledge they need to be able to work adequately with the multiple cultures, languages, and abilities, of the children they serve.

Language and Cultural Diversity in Early Childhood Education, pages 235–249

This chapter reviews research on diversity and early childhood teacher preparation with the dual aims of both (1) trying to understand why teacher educators have not updated their programs to reflect the changing demands of the workplace, and (2) as a way of rethinking how to prepare teachers to enact social justice or more equity-oriented pedagogies. We begin by drawing on work in the K–12 sector to tease out the differences between terms used to describe what has often been labeled *multicultural* (Ramsey, 2006), with the aim of reasoning through shifts in the field from "beyond heroes and holidays" to more equity-focused pedagogies. We then review the empirical research that examines the preparation of preservice and inservice teachers to address issues of diversity. This chapter concludes with an argument for the development of a strategic research agenda that will lead to the reinvention of content and pedagogical approaches in early childhood teacher preparation. Our aim in asserting this research agenda is to ensure that diversity, difference, and social justice are viewed as foundational for every early childhood educator, no matter where they work and who they teach.

CONCEPTUALIZING TERMS AND APPROACHES

In reviewing the K–12 literature on preparing teachers to work with diverse student populations, there exists a myriad of terms to describe pedagogical practices: *Multicultural education, culturally responsive/relevant pedagogy, critical multiculturalism, critical pedagogy, teaching for social justice, anti-racist education,* and *anti-oppressive education* are all used broadly, often in ill-defined ways. To clarify what we call *equity or social justice pedagogies,* we group this diffuse list of terms into three broad categories: *Multicultural Education, Culturally Relevant Education,* and *Teaching for Social Justice.* In the following sections, we elaborate on each of these categories in order to frame our review of the research literature and our discussion on reinventing early childhood teacher education.

Multicultural Education

Multicultural Education (ME) was born of the U.S. civil rights movement of the 1960s, during which members of various ethnic groups demanded inclusion in the common curriculum of schools (Banks, 1993), and took hold in the field of education in the 1970s. As a result, the early years of ME took on an ethnic studies or single group studies approach, in which group-specific courses or units began to appear in the K–12 curriculum. This approach was primarily additive, and did little to fundamentally alter the cannon of what is considered valuable or important knowledge (McCarthy, 1993). For example, individual electives focused on African American Literature appeared in high school and college curricula, or elementary schools added a Black History month unit that was abstracted from the core curriculum.

As the field progressed through the 1980s, a number of writers and educators developed a wide range of pedagogical approaches to ME (Ramsey, 2006). Given the diversity of approaches to multicultural pedagogy and curriculum reform, leaders in the field began to differentiate and create a hierarchy of the various approaches to ME and the curricular reforms they proposed. Banks and Banks (1997) outline this hierarchy as having four levels: *The Contributions Approach, The Additive Approach, The Transformational Approach,* and *The Social Action Approach.* Sleeter and Grant (2002), identify five distinct approaches to multicultural theory and practice, which include: *Teaching the Exceptional and the Culturally Different, Human Relations, Single Group Studies, Multicultural Education,* and *Multicultural and Social Reconstructionist.*

Table 11.1 presents a side-by-side analysis of the Banks & Banks (1997) and Sleeter and Grant (2002) hierarchies emphasizing the ways that their categories converge and diverge. Clearly both recognize a broad range of

TABLE 11.1 Typologies of Multicultural Education

Banks & Banks (1997) Typology of Curricular Approaches to Multicultural Education	Sleeter & Grant (2002) Five Distinct Approaches to Multicultural Theory and Practice
The Contributions Approach: • Focus on heroes, holidays, and discrete cultural elements	*Teaching the Exceptional and Culturally Different:* • Guided by deficit ideology about cultural groups and "at-risk" populations; often include compensatory programs.
The Additive Approach:	*Human Relations:*
• Content, concepts and themes of various groups are added to the curriculum without changing its focus or structure. Focus on cultural awareness, prejudice reduction, and ethnic identity and pride.	
	Single Group Studies: • Focus on one group at a time—highlighting contributions, culture, forms of oppression, perspective, experience, etc. This approach is oriented toward a critical analysis of power and political action.
The Transformative Approach:	*Multicultural Education:*
• Incorporates prejudice reduction and the critical emphasis of single group studies, but emphasizes the study of multiple groups, total school and curriculum reform, and multicultural education for all students.	
The Social Action Approach:	*Multicultural and Social Reconstructionist:*
• Committed to developing critical thinking about issues of racism class, gender, sexual orientation, language, etc. Students make decisions on important issues of equity and justice and take action in an effort to reconstruct society and empower themselves.	

approaches to multicultural curricula and pedagogy. These approaches range from simplistic, uncritical additions to the curriculum, in which heroes and holidays of certain ethnic groups are celebrated and taught in isolation, to the bottom of the chart, which represents critical approaches to multicultural education, in which knowledge is thoughtfully critiqued and students engage in action toward positive social change.

Dominant multicultural literature tends to be focused on the lower levels represented by Banks and Banks (1997) and Sleeter and Grant (2002), and reflects a liberal multicultural paradigm of gaining information from multiple perspectives and generating better intergroup communications. These pedagogies are necessary as part of a concerted effort toward creating educational equity for all children; however, these alone fail to address power relationships or transform the existing social order. As a result of ME's early history of being exclusively concerned with race and ethnicity; its seemingly narrow focus on curriculum content; and its inclusion of, and focus on, low-level, liberal examples of pedagogy, curriculum, and practice, many educators, educational researchers, and theorists began to adopt and develop different terms for equity pedagogy in order to distinguish their work from liberal/mainstream ME. In the following sections, we describe two of these terms, *Culturally Relevant Pedagogy* and *Social Justice Pedagogy*.

Culturally Relevant Pedagogy

Culturally Relevant Pedagogy (CRP) became popular in the mid-1990s (Ladson-Billings, 1994; Gay, 2000). This approach focuses specifically on empowering pedagogies for students of particular historically marginalized racial and ethnic groups. Educational researchers have documented some of the ways that cultural dispositions, values, and traditions can be adopted in the classroom and positively affect the educational experiences of students of color (Au & Jordan, 1981; Heath, 1982; Moll, Amanti et al., 1992; Moll & Gonzalez, 1994). Advocates of CRP build on this perspective to argue that incorporating the cultural values and traditions of students is not enough. Rather, successful teachers of students of color must be able to understand and critique the oppressive relationship between the dominant US culture and the students' cultural group (Beauboeuf-Lafontant, 1999).

Ladson-Billings (1994), Gay (2000), Beauboeuf-Lafontant (1999), Klug and Whitfield (2003), and others have contributed to an understanding of the key philosophical, relational and political orientations, attitudes, beliefs, and related practices that mark CRP. For example, Ladson-Billings (1994) found that culturally relevant teachers strive for excellence with their students by assuming most, if not all, of the responsibility for their students' success. Culturally relevant teachers root learning in issues relevant to the students' lives and help students make connections between their home community and broader national and global issues. To help students make these connections, culturally relevant teachers view knowledge as socially constructed and teach their students to critically analyze information, so that it is possible for them to understand that Eurocentric views of knowledge and learning are not the only way of knowing.

CRP builds upon ME that is social reconstructionist (Sleeter & Grant, 2002) by emphasizing not only the curricular transformation of these teachers, but the beliefs, attitudes, and dispositions of successful teachers of students from historically marginalized groups. While much of the ME literature emphasizes curricular reform, the CRP literature emphasizes engagement with families and communities, high expectations, shared political struggle, and raising critical consciousness through critical literacy and knowledge deconstruction with students. However, the emphasis of this literature is on teachers working with homogeneous, albeit historically marginalized, racial or ethnic groups. This emphasis on particular ethnic groups makes it difficult to translate the tenets of Culturally Relevant Pedagogy to contexts in which there is a racial mix of students, or to one in which most students are White.

Social Justice Pedagogy

The theory and practice of teaching for social justice (or anti-oppressive education), while overlapping with theories and pedagogies of ME and CRP, is distinctly different. Teaching for social justice is aimed broadly at identifying injustice in many forms and working to dismantle that injustice through action. While other pedagogical and theoretical orientations operate with a specific focus on historically marginalized groups, teaching for social justice is essentially about identifying the dominant power structures that operate in and on the lives of people, in terms of race, class, gender, sexual orientation, ethnicity, and language, both nationally and globally.

Drawing on the critical theoretical tenet that knowledge, power, and agency are inter-related, and always present in schooling, a social justice orientation requires teaching to foster social consciousness in students and to encourage students to take action for social change (Ayers et al., 1998). As such, critical pedagogy and teaching for social justice form a theoretical and practical union aimed at creating schools and classrooms that center injustice and the quest for justice as the pedagogical and political purpose of schooling. Within this process, children are viewed as constructors of knowledge, and their lives, perspectives, communities, interests, language, concerns, and cultural resources become central to the educational endeavor (Apple, 2000). However, whereas CRP and ME approaches tend to focuses on particular oppressed communities or specific cultural groups, Social Justice Pedagogy (SJP) addresses multiple injustices and is appropriate to use with any population of students.

It is only a social justice orientation that requires teachers to critically analyze and address the ways in which their knowledge and actions can marginalize and limit children's learning, even if they are teaching in a predominantly White community. As SJP involves everyone, regardless of their background, in examinations of equity, justice, and social action, we believe it is the most informative approach for early childhood teachers. In what follows, we review the research base on early childhood teacher preparation to identify if and how this orientation is used to ready teachers for the classroom.

RESEARCH ON TEACHER PREPARATION AND DIVERSITY IN EARLY CHILDHOOD

To conduct our search of the literature, we first examined the most recent Handbooks on ME (Banks & Banks, 2004), teacher education (Cochran-Smith, Feiman-Nemser, McInyre, & Demers, 2008) and early childhood education (Spodek & Saracho, 2006) to see what was available. However, perhaps not surprisingly, aside from the text devoted to early childhood education, hardly any references were made to diversity of any kind, in relation to teachers of young children, although there is a chapter in the Spodek and Saracho text on ME (Ramsey, 2006), this chapter does not address teacher education. We then perused the specific journals dedicated to teacher education, namely, the *Journal of Teacher Education, Teaching and Teacher Education,* and the *Journal of Early Childhood Teacher Education.* Again, it was difficult to find empirical studies of early childhood teacher education in the more mainstream journals. While we did locate quite a number of articles addressing diversity in some way in the *Journal of Early Childhood Teacher Education,* unfortunately, most of the articles were not empirical studies of what teacher educators are doing in practice, but rather descriptive essays or reflections on their work. As we were interested in seeing if anyone had documented how they prepare teachers to enact SJP, to finalize our search we also examined journals that foreground critical approaches to the study of education and early childhood such as *Contemporary Issues in Early Childhood.*

Research on teacher education in general is a young field of inquiry (Cochran-Smith & Zeichner, 2005), and studies examining teachers and teaching in early childhood are relatively few in number (Ryan & Goffin, 2008). While it is possible to find studies that analyze teacher beliefs, attitudes, and dispositions toward cultural diversity (e.g., MacNaughton &

Hughes, 2007; Robinson, 2002) it was not so easy to locate empirical studies of how teacher educators are preparing future educators to address issues of diversity in their work. Most of the current research is also not from a social justice orientation. The research falls into two categories: studies of teacher preparation programs and smaller, often qualitative studies of strategies used by teacher educators in their own classrooms.

Studies of Teacher Preparation Programs

Over the past 8 years, there have been a number of policy reports articulating the recommended knowledge base and pathways for preparation of early childhood teachers (e.g., American Association of Colleges . . . , 2004; Bowman, Donovan, & Burns, 2001; Isenberg, 2000). Much of this policy interest has been catalyzed by the expansion of publicly funded preschool programs, as a way to ensure all children, regardless of background, enter school ready to learn. Federal and state mandates are now expecting teachers of 3- and 4-year-old children to have at least an Associate's degree, if not a Bachelor's degree, and some states have gone so far as to institute specialized early childhood teacher credentials.

This increased demand for qualified teachers, has prompted several studies to examine the kinds of programs of preparation available for teachers and whether existing programs are providing content and experiences that meet national standards and policies about what early childhood teachers need to know and be able to do. The first national study of this kind was conducted by Early and Winton (2001), and involved a survey of representatives (e.g., department chairs and program directors) at 438, two- and four-year institutions. While 60% of programs reported requiring an entire class or more in working with children with disabilities, only 40%, on average, required a class on working with children and families from diverse ethnic and cultural backgrounds. It was also found that only 10% of Bachelor's programs and 8% of Associate's programs offered content in working with bilingual students or English language learners (ELLs). A replication of this study conducted by Maxwell et al. in 2006 found that little had changed in the ensuing years.

These findings are supported by a series of state-level studies of preschool teacher preparation programs in New Jersey (Lobman, Ryan, & McLaughlin, 2005; Ryan & Ackerman, 2005). Although a specialized P–3 teaching certificate was created in 2002, when previously there had been none, both teacher educators and preservice teachers reported that preparation in addressing diversity issues in the classroom was less available than other content. When teachers were asked a series of questions about their efficacy to teach particular student populations, less than 50% of teachers felt skilled working with special needs students and ELLs.

The findings of these studies highlight the absence of coursework in diversity training. However, their focus has been more broadly about what kinds of content and field experiences are offered in programs that prepare early childhood teachers and whether this content matches what is being articulated in policy. There is only one national study that actually focuses exclusively on the kinds of diversity preparation offered to early childhood teachers.

Ray, Bowman, and Robbins (2006) surveyed the websites, syllabi, and program descriptions of 226 institutions' Bachelor's-granting programs, and found that, on average, these institutions offered 8.62 semester hours of coursework on special needs students and 8.37 hours on some diversity categories. Overall, these hours represent around 12% of a student's professional education hours. While most program materials referred to categories such as special needs, culture, and language learner characteristics, they were less likely to describe such issues as immigration status, race, minorities, and social class. Few institutions (7%) offered practical experience with diverse student populations. Ray et al. (2006) concluded that, while Bachelor's degree programs may recognize that diversity is an issue worthy of attention for early childhood teachers, "few hours of coursework and little practice is devoted to teaching early childhood teachers how to be effective educators of children of color, second language/dialect speakers and others" (p. vii).

These large-scale studies aim to inform policy and, therefore, tend to use either self-reports of program administrators or department chairs, coupled with examinations of documents such as web sites and syllabi. The limitation of these data sources is that they do not provide any sense of what teachers experience in the university classroom.

One exception to this group of studies is a study conducted by Kidd, Sanchez, and Thorp (2008), who documented qualitatively pre-service teachers' perceptions of their program experiences that contributed to their understanding of cultural differences and helped them acquire CRPs. The program studied was specifically designed to prepare students willing and competent to work with diverse students and their families. At the completion of the program, students were certified in early childhood education, early childhood special education, and English as a second language.

To elicit their perspectives on this program and its effectiveness, students were asked to write a 10-page "Guiding Principle Narrative" at the end of their final semester. Students were asked to reflect on their journey through the program and to use stories to illustrate how their assumptions about working with children and families from diverse backgrounds were challenged, changed, or reinforced. Analysis of the narratives showed that there were five types of inter-related experiences that helped students to acquire culturally responsive understandings and techniques. These experiences were (1) readings on issues of race, culture, poverty and social justice, (2) internships in diverse settings, (3) gathering family stories by interacting with families different to themselves, (4) critical reflection, and (5) dialogue and discussion. The authors conclude that the strength of the program is in its multi-faceted, rather than a single class, approach that provides preservice teachers with multiple opportunities to engage with issues of diversity.

While Kidd et al. (2008) show what might be possible from a programmatic perspective, the large-scale national surveys of early childhood teacher preparation programs suggest that early childhood teachers are more likely to get a class here and there than a focused series of experiences in addressing diversity and difference. Ray et al. (2006) assert that

> early childhood teacher education programs convey an unambiguous message to future teachers— professional competence requires weak and uneven knowledge and practice skills in educating children who have special needs, children of color, children who are low income, immigrants and second language/dialect speakers. (p. viii)

While this may be the case, studies where teacher-educators report on some of the strategies they are using to educate students about diversity issues offer some insights into how the field might begin to redress the current gaps in programs of preparation.

Studies of Strategies Used by Teacher Educators at Work

A number of teacher educators have written papers that provide descriptions of strategies they use to help preservice teachers consider issues of student identity, culture, and difference. The pedagogies described in these anecdotal and reflective accounts range from the use of postmodern approaches, such as multiple readings, situating knowledge (Ryan & Grieshaber, 2005), performance and improvisation (Lobman, 2005), as well as pragmatic suggestions, such as resources (e.g., picture books, films, activities) that teacher educators might use (Wolfe, 2006), and the incorporation of experiential learning opportunities that force students to interact with children and families from cultures different from their own (Hyland & Heuschkel, 2009; Wineburg, 1999).

Empirical studies that examine these kinds of strategies in action are few and far between. The studies that have been conducted tend to focus on pedagogies that raise students' awareness of different cultures. For example, Miller and Fuller (2006) describe how they used a Cultural Self-Analysis (CSA) project with 26, mostly White, undergraduate preservice Early Childhood teachers enrolled in a 5-week summer course called *Parent Involvement in Education.* The CSA project involved six steps: autobiography, biography, cross-cultural analysis, analysis of cultural differences, home-connection plan of action, and reflection. Using a constant-comparative method to analyze the projects, Miller and Fuller found that students developed greater confidence and comfort with families culturally different from themselves, and developed useful practical resources and strategies for facilitating connections between the school and family.

While Miller and Fuller (2006) focused on an in-class project, several researchers have set up and examined specific experiential learning opportunities on students' understanding, willingness, and effectiveness to respond to families and students from culturally diverse backgrounds. In a qualitative study using a service learning component, Szente (2008) describes how she required students in her Foundations of Early Childhood Education course to tutor culturally and linguistically diverse students in K–3 settings. After each visit, the students completed a log and reflective journal entry and wrote a case study about the experience at the completion of 15 hours of tutoring students. It was found that the tutoring experience improved students' self awareness and their understandings of general teaching techniques.

More explicit links between working with individuals from other cultures and student knowledge of working with cultural diversity is reported in a study conducted by Hooks (2008). Forty-four preservice teachers were partnered with adult ELLs and asked to conduct a mock parent–teacher conference. The students were also required to write pre- and post-conference reflections about the encounter. Qualitative analysis of the pre-conference data showed that students were anxious about conducting a conference with an adult who spoke limited English, as they were concerned about being able to communicate effectively with their ELL partner. After the conferences had been conducted, students reported feeling more confident and having more awareness and appreciation of diversity. Students also said that this experience improved their knowledge of what is involved in communicating with families and increased their commitment to involving parents in the classroom.

This small set of studies on pedagogies teacher educators have used to work with their students around cultural diversity, along with the anecdotal reports we found, would suggest that at least some teacher educators have begun to address diversity in their work. However, without more empirical studies that both describe the implementation of these strategies and their impact, the use of such pedagogies will remain the domain of those who develop them, rather than becoming more the norm in early childhood professional preparation. The problem of how to ensure that preservice teachers access adequate preparation to work with diverse student populations and their families is addressed next.

REINVENTING EARLY CHILDHOOD TEACHER EDUCATION

Preparation of early childhood teachers to address diversity issues has been examined at the macro-level of policy and program and at the more micro-level of the university classroom. The small body of research on pedagogy offers some examples of what teacher educators might do in their own classrooms, while most studies at the programmatic level illuminate the limited availability of diversity training in early childhood teacher education. From our perspective, it is not simply enough to add classes about diversity to the teacher education curriculum. While an additive approach will ensure that preservice teachers get some training in this important aspect of their work, it will not necessarily ensure that the kinds of training teachers receive will enable them to go beyond the lower levels of ME.

Currently, the research base primarily conceptualizes diversity preparation in relation to linguistic or cultural difference, and not on how difference is also named and enacted using other markers (e.g., class, gender, sexuality, immigrant status, special needs/ability, etc.). As a consequence, preservice teachers are more likely to learn about incorporating cultural differences as resources in the curriculum, but not how to disrupt and challenge the inequities that result in trying to assimilate diversity into what is already considered to be acceptable practice (Goodwin, Cheruvu, & Genishi, 2008). The challenge remains then as to how to ensure that the knowledges and experiences student teachers receive in their preparation enable them to not simply be more accepting and respectful of diversity, but educated in SJP. It is with these aims in mind that we make the following suggestions for action.

First, and most obviously, the field needs more research. To be sure, research on teacher education and teaching is a small and young field, but, as this review shows, it is also a somewhat disorganized one. In an era of accountability and mandates, it is necessary that teacher educators come together and develop a program of research to not just describe their practices, but also show the impact of those practices quantitatively and qualitatively. To be able to do this, teacher educators need to be explicit about the theoretical ideas that shape their understanding of diversity and difference. At the moment, the limited scholarship available in this area is more about what people do or do not do in practice, and not clearly focused on how they are theorizing their work around diversity preparation. The explication of theory and concepts being used to address diversity in the teacher education curriculum is necessary if we are to demonstrate the links between teacher education, teachers' practices, and student outcomes. At the moment, we do not really know what works and does not work, or which theoretical frames produce what results.

The absence of diversity content in teacher preparation programs would suggest that teacher educators are not necessarily knowledgeable in this area. Studies have shown that teacher educators are like their student populations: mostly White, middle class, and female (Lobman, Ryan, & McLaughlin, 2005; Maxwell et al., 2006), and are, therefore, often unaware of how their own position of privilege impacts how they view issues of equity and teacher preparation. While some teacher educators have begun to use the kinds of critical theory advocated by a social justice orientation (e.g., Lobman, 2005; Ryan & Grieshaber, 2005), most of this work remains marginal to the field. Therefore, a second pathway for action would seem to be the retooling of teacher educators around issues of diversity and social justice. This will require teacher educators to work across some of their differences and to admit that they may not be as knowledgeable in this area as they need to be. However, it is by coming together that we might be able to both learn in ways that best serve children and also develop a strategic agenda for research that leads to a relevant teacher education curriculum for the 21st century in which we all teach.

REFERENCES

American Association of Colleges of Teacher Education. (2004). The early childhood challenge: Preparing high-quality teachers for a changing society. Retrieved September 25, 2006, from www.aecte.org

Apple, M. (2000). Can critical pedagogies interrupt rightist policies? *Educational Theory* 50(2): 229–254.

Au, K. H., & Jordan, C. (1981). Teaching reading to Hawaiian children: Finding a culturally appropriate solution. In H. T. Trueba, G. P. Guthrie & K. H.-P. Au (Eds.), *Culture and the bi-lingual classroom: Studies in classroom ethnography* (pp. 139–152). Rowley, MA: Newbury House Publishers.

Ayers, W., J. A. Hunt, & Quinn, T. (Eds.) (1998). *Teaching for social justice.* New York: Teachers College Press.

Banks, J. A. (1993). Multicultural education: Historical development, dimensions, and practice. In M. Apple (Ed.), *Review of research in education Volume 19* (pp. 3–49). Washington, DC. : American Educational Research Association.

Banks, J. A., & Banks, C. A. M (Eds). (1997). *Multicultural Education: Issues and Perspectives.* Needham Heights, MA: Allyn & Bacon.

Banks, J.A., & Banks C. A. M. (Eds.) (2004.) *Handbook of Research on Multicultural Education* (2nd ed.). San Francisco, CA: Jossey Bass.

Beauboeuf-Lafontant, T. (1999). A movement against and beyond boundaries: Politically relevant teaching among African American teachers. *Teachers College Record* 100(4): 702–723.

Bowman, B. T., Donovan, M. S., & Burns, M. S. (Eds.). (2001). *Eager to learn: Educating our preschoolers.* Washington, DC: National Academy Press.

Cochran-Smih, M., Feiman-Nemser, S., McInyre, D. J., & Demers, K. E. (Eds.). (2008). *The handbook of research on teacher education: Enduring questions in changing contexts* (3rd ed.). New York & London: Routledge Taylor Francis Group.

Cochran- Smith, M., & Zeichner, K. (Eds.). (2005). *Studying teacher education: the report of the AERA panel on research and teacher education.* Washington, D. C.: American Educational Research Association.

Early, D. M., & Winton, P. J. (2001). Preparing the workforce: Early childhood teacher preparation at 2- and 4-year institutions of higher education. *Early Childhood Research Quarterly, 16,* 285–306.

Gay, G. (2000). *Culturally responsive teaching: Theory, research and practice.* New York: Teachers College Press.

Goodwin, A. L., Cheruvu, R., & Genishi, C. (2008). Responding to multiple diversities in early childhood education: How far have we come? In C. Genishi, & A. L. Goodwin, (eds.). *Diversities in early childhood education* (pp. 3–12). New York: Routledge.

Heath, S. B. (1982). Questioning at home and at school: A comparative study. In G. Spindler (Ed.), *Doing the ethnography of schooling: Educational anthropology in action* (pp. 102–131). New York: Holt, Rinehart, & Winston.

Hooks, L. M. (2008). Help! They don't speak English: Partnering preservice teachers with adult English language learners. *Journal of Early Childhood Teacher Eduation, 29*(2), 97–107.

Hyland, N., & Heuschkel, K. (2009). *Fostering understanding of institutional oppression among pre-service teachers through inquiry assignments.* Manuscript submitted for publication.

Hyson, M. (Ed.). (2003). *Preparing early childhood professionals: NAEYC's standards for programs.* Washington, DC: National Association for the Education of Young Children.

Isenberg, J. (2000). The state of the art in early childhood professional preparation. In National Institute of Early Childhood Development and Education & U.S. Department of education & Office of Educational Research and Improvements (Eds.), *New Teacher for a new century: The future of early childhood professional preparation* (pp. 17– 58). Washington, DC: U.S. Department of Education.

Kidd, J. K., Sanchez, S. Y., & Thorp, E. K. (2008). Defining moments: developing culturally responsive dispositions and teaching practices in early childhood preservice teachers. *Teaching and Teacher Education, 4,* 316–329.

Klug, B. J., & Whitfield, P.T. (2003). *Widening the circle: Culturally relevant pedagogy for American Indian children.* San Francisco: Jossey-Bass.

Ladson-Billings, G. (1994). *The dreamkeepers: Successful teachers of African American children.* San Francisco: Jossey-Bass.

Lobman, C. (2005). Improvisation: Postmodern play for early childhood teachers. In S. Ryan, & S. Grieshaber (Eds.), *Practical transformations and transformational practices: Globalization, postmodernism and early childhood education* (pp. 243–272). Stamford, CT: JAI/Elsevier Science.

Lobman, C., Ryan, S., & McLaughlin, J. (2005). Reconstructing teacher education to prepare qualified preschool teachers: Lessons from New Jersey. *Journal of Early Childhood Research and Practice,* 7(2).

MacNaughton, G., & Hughes, P. (2007). Tecahing respect for cultural diversity in Australian early childhood programs: A challenge for professional learning. *Journal of Early Childhood Research, 5,* 189–204.

Maxwell, K. L., Lim, C-I., & Early, D. M. (2006). *Early childhood teacher preparation programs in the United States: National report.* Chapel Hill, NC: The University of North Carolina, FPG Child Development Institute.

McCarthy, C. (1993). Multicultural approaches to racial inequality in the United States. In L. A. Catenell & W. F. Pinar (Eds.), *Understanding curriculum as racial text: Represntations of identity and difference in education* (pp. 225–246). Albany, NY: SUNY.

Miller, K.J., & Fuller, D.P. (2006) Developing cultural competency in early childhood preservice educators though a cultural self-analysis project. *Journal of Early Childhood Teacher Education.* 27(1), 35–45.

Moll, L., Amanti, C., Neff, D., & Gonzalez, N. (1992). "Funds of knowledge for teaching: Using a qualitative approach to connect homes and classrooms." *Theory into Practice* 31(2): 132–141.

Moll, L. C., & Gonzalez, N. (1994). "Lessons from research with language minority children." *Journal of Reading Behavior* 26: 439–456.

Ramsey, P. G. (2006). Early childhood multicultural education. In B. Spodek, & O. Saracho (Eds.), *Handbook of research on the education of young children* (2nd ed., pp. 279–301). Mahwah, NJ: Lawrence Erlbaum.

Ray, A., Bowman, B., & Robbins, J. (2006). *Preparing early childhood teachers to successfully educate all children: The contribution of four-year undergraduate teacher preparation programs.* Chicago: Erikson Institute.

Robinson, K. H. 2002. Making the invisible visible: Gay and lesbian issues in early childhood education. *Contemporary Issues in Early Childhood, 3,* 415–434.

Ryan, S., & Ackerman, D.J. (2005, March 30). Using pressure and support to create a qualified workforce. *Education Policy Analysis Archives, 13*(23), 1–17.

Ryan, S., & Goffin. S. G. (2008). Missing in action: Teaching in Early Care and Education. *Early Education and Development. 19*(3), 385–395.

Ryan, S., & Grieshaber, S. (2005). Shifting from developmental to postmodern practices in early childhood teacher education. *Journal of Teacher Education, 56,* 34–45.

Sleeter, C. E., & Grant, C. A. (2002). *Making choices for Multicultural Education: Five approaches to race, class, and gender* (4th ed.). New York: Wiley and Sons.

Spodek, B., & Saracho, O. (2006). *Handbook of research on the education of young children.* Mahwah, NJ: Lawrence Earlbaum.

Szente, J. (2008). Preparing preservice teachers to work with culturally and linguistically diverse children. A service learning experience. *Journal of Early Childhood Teacher Education.* 29(2), 140–145.

Wineburg, L.P. (1999). Lessons learned in four urban early childhood programs and the Implications for teacher education. *Journal of Early Childhood Teacher Education.* 20(3), 231–243.

Wolfe, R.B. (2006). Choosing to include gay issues in early childhood teacher preparation coursework: One professor's journey. *Journal of Early Childhood Teacher Education.* 27, 195–204.

PART IV

CONCLUSION

CHAPTER 12

CLASSROOM DIVERSIFICATION

A Strategic Future Perspective for Equal Rights

Olivia N. Saracho and Bernard Spodek

The enduring challenge to education that grows out of Americans' belief that "all are created equal and that all children deserve an equal chance to learn, to work, to contribute, and to prosper" (Raudenbush, 2009, p. 169) continues to be a major issue in the United States. The children of poverty have been euphemistically referred to as "culturally deprived," "disadvantaged," "disaffected," "alienated," and "socially unready." These children have been served by the public schools of America, the American "common" schools that were developed to prepare people "to live adequately in a republican society and to exercise effectively the prerogatives of citizenship..." (Cremin, 1951, pp. 213–214). In the course of action, these schools have been confronted by numerous problems. The major problem has been their treatment of the "minority children." The cultural, ethnic, religious, and linguistic differences among Americans have had an impact

Language and Cultural Diversity in Early Childhood Education, pages 253–264

on these children's social status, and they too often have been subjected to severe socioeconomic deprivation.

The issue of inequality continues to plague us, although many changes have transpired to reduce this inequality. Raudenbush (2009) points out that the disparity between Blacks and Whites in education has diminished dramatically over the past six decades. For example:

> Consider two men, one White, one Black, born... in the early 1920s. At the age of 30, right around the time of *Brown*,[1] we would expect the White man to have attained almost 2.5 years more of schooling than the Black man. Now consider two men born in 1965, after *Brown* had begun to take effect and 1 year after the historic Civil Rights Act of 1964. By the time these men were 30, in 1995, we would expect the gap between them to be 0.8 years—still intolerably large but one third of what it had been. For women, the story is similar. The Black–White gap was almost 2 years. For women born in 1965, the average gap was just over half a year. A somewhat similar story emerges when we look at college graduation rates. In 1960, White males were almost 4 times more likely to receive a 4-year college degree than were Black males. By 1990, White males were about twice as likely to do so. So, although a large gap in college graduation rates persisted from 1960 to 1990, the gap was dramatically reduced. The gap in college graduation for females was never as large as for males, but it too became narrower during those years. (Raudenbush, 2009, p. 170)

In this democratic society, all students have the right to succeed in school. Verkuyten (2009) suggests that the right to live in a multicultural and minority society remains important. In three studies, he examined how national identification relates to perceived realistic and symbolic threats, and to levels of support. His three studies indicate a *group identity lens* model that shows that the relationship between national identification and multiculturalism is interceded by perceived threat. Verkuyten's (2009) third study on authoritarianism independently suggests that the concern for immigrant and minority rights is perceived as a threat to national identification. Results across the three studies support the stability and the usefulness of the group identity lens model to understand the responses toward multiculturalism and minority rights.

The interpretations of rights and individual independence are usually considered to be the basic cornerstones for democratic social and political systems, where individuals make decisions that have an impact on them (Neff & Helwig, 2002). In Europe and North America, children's rights have been the focus of essential social policy issues for the last century. Western societies have been interested in children's rights and their child caregivers' responsibilities to insure that those rights are maintained (Peterson-Badali, Morine, Ruck, & Slonin, 2004). Many problems have emerged in maintaining children's rights, especially determining whether these rights are universal or cultural.

Cultural differences need to be considered in both maintaining the essential rights and appropriately implementing the educational process equitably. Cultural differences lead to different interpretations of *children's rights.* Several cultures have difficulty understanding that children have rights other than their parents' rights (Murphy-Berman, Levesque, & Berman, 1996). In some highly industrialized countries, adults believe that policies should stress the children's autonomy and uniqueness. In contrast, traditional societies consider that the family and the local community context, the children's rights, because they believe they have "the best interest of the children" as well as the family and the extended family's interests. There are also discrepancies in the basic definition and boundaries of childhood. It is evident that the differences focus on an independent versus an interdependent attitude (Markus & Kitayama, 1991). Cherney, Greteman, and Travers (2008) examined American, Swiss, and British adults' perceptions of children's rights, and explored whether the need for autonomy was integrated with cultural norms. Their study indicated that Swiss and British adults advocated autonomy and self-determination rights more often than adults from the United States. These differences consisted of seven of ten kinds of rights pertaining to family, political participation, sexual conduct, media access, appearance, privacy, and religion. The three cultural groups had similar views concerning conflict decisions, in relation to economics, social participation, or educational decision making. Since the United States is considered to be the most individualistic culture (e.g., Hofstede, 2001), it was expected that adults from the United States would advocate more strongly for self-determination and autonomy than British and Swiss adults, but the results from the study did not support this assumption. Other cross-cultural studies where children were interviewed about their rights support these results (e.g., Cherney & Perry, 1996; Cherney & Shing, 2008; Ruck, Abramovitch, & Keating, 1998). This demonstrates that judgments about personal domains may be endorsed, depending on the cultural context and specific kinds of rights, including the rights of immigrants.

IMMIGRATION

The United States has always been a nation of immigrants, but during the last decades, its immigrant population has drastically grown. The population in the United States has increased at the rate of two million people annually, and approximately half of that expansion is credited to immigration (Gollnick & Chinn, 2008). Immigrants and minorities oppose the country's social and cultural order. The major issue in the debate about immigrants is whether they are a threat to contemporary society and national identity. In three studies, Eccleston and Major (2006) examined immigrant rights as a result of perceived out-group threat and national identification. In the 1970s, Barker (1981) found that many people in England were afraid that foreign cultures would overwhelm the nation and overthrow the British way of life, which is used as the main argument against immigration.

Current research indicates that European countries express the same public discourse regarding the threat and fear of immigration, multiculturalism, and minority rights (e.g., Triandafyllidou, 2000). Presently, there is concern in Britain for citizenship and national identity (Lynn & Lea, 2003). Fear and perceptions of threat tend to generate prejudice toward minority groups, and especially immigrant groups (e.g., Esses, Dovidio, Jackson, & Armstrong, 2001). Perceptions of *realistic threats* (Stephan & Stephan, 1996) contribute to negative attitudes toward immigrants and minorities (Verkuyten, 2009). *Realistic threats* are considered to be physical, economic, and political. Ethnic minority groups are considered to be a *safety threat*, and struggles between groups and negative group responses are usually based in a debate about political and material interests. In an attempt to protect their interests, national majorities develop negative attitudes and discriminatory behavior toward immigrants and minorities (e.g., Bizman & Yinon, 2001; Esses et al., 2001). Verkuyten (2009) believes that authoritarianism independently assists in the acknowledgment of multicultural and minority rights. Indirectly, authoritarianism has an effect on national identification. Thus, issues discussed above on threat and fear of immigration, multiculturalism, and minority rights include:

- *National Identification.* National identity and national identification are fundamental issues in debates on immigration and the integration of ethnic minority groups in pioneer countries, such as Australia and the United States (Huntington, 2004), and nonpioneer European countries that have historically created a majority group (Joppke, 2004).
- *Authoritarianism.* Authoritarianism and social dominance are ideological beliefs (Duckitt, 2001) that influence the negative reactions toward immigrants, multiculturalism, and minority rights (e.g., Danso, Sedlovskaya, & Suanda, 2007).
- *Social Identity Perspectives.* Social identity perspective refers to group memberships and intergroup relations (Reynolds & Turner, 2006). It indicates that, in an intergroup environment, social identity creates intergroup behavior separate from personality or individual differences in ideological beliefs. For instance, Verkuyten and Hagendoorn (1988) found that, in an intergroup context, in-group stereotypes and not authoritarianism influenced out-group attitudes.

The terms *multiculturalism* and *minority rights* are widely used, but there is a lack of a single point of view or policy. In one view, multiculturalism presents a positive perspective of cultural and identity preservation for ethnic minority groups. Multiculturalism can be improved when diversity is adjusted to an equitable style. European multiculturalism has continuously aimed at immigrants and minorities, instead of the majority group (Joppke, 2004), which introduces minority groups to the possibility of cultivating their own culture and acquiring equal rights and status in society (Verkuyten, 2009). The participants in Verkuyten's (2009) study who had higher levels of education endorsed multiculturalism and minority rights, which suggest that the educational system can provide a culturally receptive education that can promote equal rights for all. Raudenbush (2009) assumes that schooling can decrease racial inequality, but only excellent instruction in school settings for minority children can diminish this inequality.

CULTURALLY RECEPTIVE EDUCATION

Researchers, scholars, and policy makers have focused their attention on the importance of young children's learning experiences to their cognitive development. Interest has focused on early childhood policy and practices that can help improve the academic paths of children in poverty, who are considered to be at high risk for early school drop out, poor academic performance, and behavior problems (Lima, Maxwell, Able-Booneb, & Zimmer, 2009). An extensive amount of literature on schools and poor children has emerged.[2]

During the last two decades, researchers have shown that schools have a strong impact on learning and that improving the quality of schooling can be particularly advantageous to low-income minority students (Raudenbush, 2009). A significant majority of low-income African American and Latino students are below average in academic achievement or continue to be at a basic performance levels on standardized achievement tests (Meece & Kurtz-Costes, 2001). Among all students in public school settings, Native American students have the highest dropout rates (Garrett, Bellon- Harn, Torres-Rivera, Garrett, & Roberts, 2003). Numerous Asian American students perform well academically, but they encounter problems with their school experiences and social interactions, leading to the development of anxiety and depression (Lee, Okazaki, & Yoo, 2006; Yoo & Lee, 2005). The United States Department of Education (2007) predicts that more than two thirds of the students in the public schools will soon be African American, Asian American, Latino, or Native American. This makes it critical that the public schools understand the sources of their learning problems.

In its struggles to meet its responsibilities, the public school infringes on the children's cultural identity and ancestral language. Saracho (1986) found that children, who had a different culture and language from the school, perceived a rejection of their language, culture, ethnicity, and personal approval. The school expected these children to simulate the characteristics of stereotypical middle-class, White, English-speaking children, who represented the nature of what American children should be. The schools' expectations of linguistically and culturally diverse children cause them to become confused, reject their identity, and fail to succeed in school. Traditionally, major institutions of the dominant society disapproved of these children's ancestors' lifestyles, languages, and cultures (Saracho & Spodek, 1995).

ENGLISH LANGUAGE LEARNERS

Many young English Language Learners (ELLs) from immigrant families arrived in the United States in search of a better quality of life. More than 400 different languages are spoken by young ELLs. Almost 80% of the ELLs in the United States live in poverty and are Spanish-speaking. The next largest clusters of ELLs in the United States are Vietnamese, Hmong, Cantonese, and Korean (Kindler, 2002). Consequently, the 10 million ELLs in the United States are highly diverse, in relation to their national origins, the quantity of experience and practice with the English language, their socioeconomic situations, and their family members' educational levels (Federal Interagency Forum, 2009). Many of these children are from culturally and linguistically diverse families who need to be provided with a high-quality education. Unfortunately, in the 21st century, many ethnic minority students continue to do poorly in the public schools. According to Tyler et al. (2008), linguistically and culturally diverse students encounter academic challenges when they perceive a cultural discontinuity between their home and school experiences.

The quality of the education children receive at home usually relates to the family's social background. Since the education children of low socioeconomic status (SES) receive at home is less than the one children from high-SES children receive, low SES children may benefit more from school instruction than do high-SES children. Nevertheless, both low and high SES children are able to benefit equally from school instruction (defined as a given contrast between instructional quality in school and at home). According to Carneiro and Heckman (2005), children's ability to learn and benefit from instruction develops early in life. They recommend that the government use their resources to provide young children with programs such as Head Start. They also recommend that very young low SES children be provided with better quantity and quality of school instruction. However, these children should continue to receive high-quality instruction during their K–12 years. This interpretation presents the foundation for educational policy to focus on an improvement in the quantity and quality of schooling for low SES children, in order to decrease the inequality in academic skills between low and high SES students. Several scholars have suggested several improvements to society and its educational system.

Raudenbush (2009) concludes from studies that an increase in the quantity and quality of schooling can make an important contribution to reducing racial inequality. He justifies this conclusion with his belief that knowledge of best instructional practice can guide teachers' work, teachers' expertise, school leadership, and parent involvement. He recommends a research agenda that integrates instructional practice and school organization, and a partnership between practitioners and researchers who have a firm commitment to provide high-quality educational opportunities to children who depend on a good education for their future success.

RECOMMENDATIONS FOR EDUCATIONAL RESEARCH AND PRACTICE

In evaluating the results of the studies that were reviewed, the following educational and research recommendations may be considered:

- *Educate the public.* Researchers suggest that educating the electorate about national identity and the immigrant groups that seem to present threats is important in encouraging multiculturalism and social justice. Public debates on immigrants and ethnic minorities usually concentrate on the alleged threat to national identity and culture. High national identifiers believe that newcomers and minorities threaten their national interests, beliefs, and values; therefore, high national identifiers oppose multiculturalism and minority rights. However, high national identifiers who have higher levels of education tend to support multiculturalism and minority rights (Verkuyten, 2009). Raudenbush (2009) believes that education can diminish racial inequality. Public hearings, workshops, or some type of communication can be used to educate those who oppose equal rights for all. In addition, studies can be conducted to examine the types and effects of communication that are used to educate high national identifiers.
- *Provide high-quality instruction.* Raudenbush (2009) proposes that minority children be provided with excellent instruction in school settings to reduce inequality. Instruction for minority children goes

beyond using superior teaching aids and improved textbooks. Teachers need to learn to respect individual differences in their communicative strategies. They need to know how to use instruction in both the linguistic and ethnographic facets of speech behavior. They need to become knowledgeable about the code selection rules in formal and informal settings, as well as the themes of folk literature and folk art that reinforce such rules (Saracho & Spodek, 1995). Studies can be conducted to examine the effects of high-quality instruction and the variables that were used in this instruction.

- *Understand cultural values.* Immigrant children are from different parts of the world. Their countries of origins have different languages and cultures. The languages and cultures of different ethnic groups need to be appreciated and respected. Teachers need to use the children's languages and cultural heritages as a basis for learning. They also need to help children develop flexibility and competence to perform in both the home and school language and culture, which will enrich the children's lives (Saracho & Spodek, 1995). Studies can examine the various cultural values that result from the immigrant children's language and cultural heritages from different parts of the world.
- *Support socialization.* Children need to develop flexibility in their socialization practices, based on the context. Young children need to be able to socialize into the larger society. Their family is their primary socializer, while the school is responsible for teaching children socialization procedures that usually differ from those learned at home. The children's socialization requires them to behave differently in home and school. They need to learn to use appropriate (1) behaviors in responding to others, (2) linguistic codes, (3) different behavioral repertoires, and (4) ways to obtain satisfaction (Saracho & Spodek, 1983). Studies can examine the types of socialization practices that children take to school and compare their reactions to those socialization practices in the school.
- *Identify determinants.* Emerging evidence suggests that minority groups judge their personal jurisdiction based on various perceptions of self, cultural factors, and universal principles. Since labels that have been attributed to them lack empirical support, it is important both to identify the predicting factors that influence minority groups to judge themselves (Cherney, Greteman, & Travers, 2008) and influence the groups' reactions to the different labels.
- *Shrink home–school cultural discontinuity.* Linguistically and culturally diverse students face academic conflicts when they perceive a cultural discontinuity between their home and school experiences (Tyler et al., 2008). The discontinuity between home- and school-

based behavioral communications of ethnic minority students has been theoretically related to their academic problems (Garrett et al., 2003; Gay, 2000). Nevertheless, research studies are needed to empirically support the presence and/or effects of cultural discontinuity in these children's lives. Current research studies are mostly based on anecdotal or qualitative data to provide evidence of cultural discontinuity (Gay, 2000). It seems apparent that studies that use other research methodologies in a variety of contexts are needed.

- *Provide for home–school transition.* Many children are able to make the transition from home to school with ease. They are cognizant of the incongruities in the situations; they accommodate their previous knowledge to the new environment. They discover that the (1) teachers' language differs from that of their parents, (2) the school's values are much more controlled than the ones in their home, and (3) those values vary from their home-held values. A partnership between the home and school can help make the children's transition from home to school easier. Such partnership can make it possible for children to make the transition from one social environment to another with relative ease and little feeling of dislocation (Saracho & Spodek, 1995). Research studies can be conducted to examine children's adjustment to school.
- *Identify the critical separation.* Linguistically and culturally diverse children encounter a critical separation when they make the transition from home to school. They find unknown language patterns, social interactions, values, and culture. For instance, they are required to use (1) a language that is different from their native language and (2) social patterns and interactions that differ from the ones at home (Saracho, 1986; Saracho & Spodek, 1995). Linguistically and culturally diverse children may perceive that they need to reject their own language and culture to conform to those of the school, which can make them experience bewilderment, rejection, and a loss of ethnic identity (Saracho, 1986). Children need more than minor behavior changes to do well in school. Teachers need to accept the children's language and cultural differences and use these differences as a basis for their instruction. Research can examine how children respond to their critical separation when they enroll in school. Studies can also include the different reactions that teachers have toward these children.
- *Support parentalism.* Parentalism indicates an existence of a hierarchy of power. The extent of parentalism in a culture can be used to predict the adults' understanding of children's rights. In addition, individuals who are high in the hierarchy of power (such as those with authority) are able to restrict the personal freedoms of those

who are at the bottom of the hierarchy of power (such as those without authority). Giving freedom to those without authority can assist society in making an improvement for most of the people (Tyler et al., 2008). Studies that examine the hierarchy of power can provide evidence that supports allocation of equal rights for those without authority.

The recommendations suggested here can guide researchers to conduct studies that can contribute to knowledge that can promote the equal rights of linguistically and culturally different children. In addition, these recommendations can help educators improve the ways they relate to children from linguistically and culturally diverse backgrounds. They can also improve the way that social justice is provided in the schools.

REFERENCES

Barker, M. (1981). *The new racism.* London: Junction Books.

Bizman, A., & Yinon, Y. (2001). Intergroup and interpersonal threats as determinants of prejudice: The moderating role of in-group identification. *Basic and Applied Social Psychology, 23,* 191–196.

Carneiro, P, Heckman, J, Krueger, A, & Heckman, J. (2005). Human capital policy. In P. Carneiro, J. Heckman, A. Krueger, & J. Heckman (Eds.) *Human capital policy. Inequality in America: What role for human capital policies?* (pp. 77–239). Cambridge, MA: MIT Press.

Cherney, I. D, Greteman, A. J., & Travers, B. G. (2008). A cross-cultural view of adults' perceptions of children's rights. *Social Justice Research, 21*(4), 432–456.

Cherney, I., & Perry, N. (1996). Children's attitudes toward their rights: An international perspective. In E. Verhellen (Ed.), *Monitoring children's rights* (pp. 241–250). Boston: Martinus Nijhoff Publishers.

Cherney, I. D., and Shing, Y. L. (2008). Children's nurturance and self-determination rights: A cross-cultural perspective. *Journal of Social Issues, 64*(4), 835–856.

Cremin, L. A. (1951). *The American common school: An historic conception.* New York: Bureau of Publications, Teachers College, Columbia University.

Danso, H. A., Sedlovskaya, A., & Suanda, S. H. (2007). Perceptions of immigrants: Modifying the attitudes of individuals higher in social dominance orientation. *Personality and Social Psychology Bulletin, 33,* 1113–1123.

Duckitt, J. (2001). A dual-process cognitive-motivational theory of ideology and prejudice. In M. P. Zanna (Ed.), *Advances in experimental social psychology* (*33,* 41–113). San Diego: Academic Press.

Eccleston, C. P., & Major, B. N. (2006). Attributions to discrimination and self-esteem: The role of group identification and appraisal. *Group Processes and Intergroup relations, 9,* 147–162.

Esses, V. M., Dovidio, J. F., Jackson, L. M., & Armstrong, T. L. (2001). The immigration dilemma: The role of perceived group competition, ethnic prejudice, and national identity. *Journal of Social Issues, 57,* 389–412.

Federal Interagency Forum on Child and Family Statistics (July, 2009). America's children: Key indicators of child well-being, 2009. Retrieved on August 23, 2009, from http://childstats.gov/

Garrett, M. T., Bellon-Harn, M. L., Torres-Rivera, E., Garrett, J. T., & Roberts, L. C. (2003). Open hands, open hearts: Working with Native youth in the schools. *Intervention in School and Clinic, 38,* 225–236.

Gay, G., & Howard, T. C. (2000). Multicultural teacher education for the 21st century. *The Teacher Educator, 36,* 1–16.

Gollnick, D. M., & Chinn, P. C. (2008). *Multicultural education in a pluralistic society* (8th ed.). Upper Saddle River, NJ: Merrill Prentice Hall.

Hofstede, G. (2001). *Culture's consequences: Comparing values, behaviors, institutions, and organizations across nations* (2nd ed.). Thousand Oaks, CA: Sage.

Huntington, S. (2004). *Who we are: The challenges to American national identity.* New York: Simon and Schuster.

Joppke, C. (2004). The retreat of multiculturalism in the liberal state: Theory and policy. *British Journal of Sociology, 55,* 237–257.

Kindler, A. (2002). Survey of the states' limited English proficient students and available educational programs and services 2000–2001 summary report. National Clearinghouse for English Language Acquisition & Language Institution Educational Programs, Washington, D.C.

Lee, M. R., Okazaki, S., & Yoo, H. C. (2006). Frequency and intensity of social anxiety in Asian Americans and European Americans. *Cultural Diversity and Ethnic Minority Psychology, 12,* 291–305.

Lima, C., Maxwell, K. L., Able-Booneb, H., & Zimmer, C. R. (2009). Cultural and linguistic diversity in early childhood teacher preparation: The impact of contextual characteristics on coursework and practica. *Early Childhood Research Quarterly, 24*(3) 64–76.

Lynn, N., & Lea, S. (2003). A phantom menace and the new apartheid: The social construction of asylum-seekers in the United Kingdom. *Discourse and Society, 14,* 425–452.

Markus, H. R., & Kitayama, S. (1991). Culture and the self: Implications for cognition, emotion, and motivation. *Psychological Review, 98,* 224–253.

Meece, J. L., & Kurtz-Costes, B. (2001). Introduction: The schooling of ethnic minority children and youth. *Educational Psychologist, 36,* 1–7.

Murphy-Berman, V., Levesque, H. L., & Berman, J. (1996). U.N. convention on the rights of the child: A cross-cultural view. *The American Psychologist, 51,* 1231–1233.

Neff, K. D., & Helwig, C. C. (2002). A constructivist approach to understanding the development of reasoning about rights and authority within cultural contexts. *Cognitive Development, 17,* 1429–1450.

Peterson-Badali, M., Ruck, M. D., Morine, S., & Slonim, N. (2004). Predictors of maternal and child attitudes towards children's nurturance and self-determination rights. *Journal of Early Adolescence, 24*(2), 159–179.

Raudenbush, S. W. (2009). The *Brown* legacy and the O'Connor challenge: Transforming schools in the images of children's potential. *Educational Researcher, 38,* 169–180.

Reynolds, K. J., & Turner, J. C. (2006). Individuality and the prejudiced personality. In W. Stroebe & M. Hewstone (Eds.), *European review of social psychology* (Vol. 17, pp. 233–270). New York: Psychology Press.

Ruck, M. D., Abramovitch, R., & Keating, D. P. (1998). Children's and adolescents' understanding of rights: Balancing nurturance and self-determination. *Child Development, 69*, 404–417.

Sáracho, O. N. (1986). Teaching second language literacy with computers. In D. Hainline (Ed.) *New developments in language CAI* (pp. 53–68). Beckenham, Kent (London): Croom Helm.

Saracho, O. N., & Spodek, B. (1983). The preparation of teachers for bilingual bicultural early childhood classes. In O. N. Saracho & B. Spodek (Eds.) *Understanding the multicultural experience in early childhood education.* (pp. 125–146). Washington, DC: National Association for the Education of Young Children.

Saracho, O.N., & Spodek, B. (1995). The future challenge of linguistic and cultural diversity in the schools. In E. E. García, B. McLaughlin, B. Spodek, & O. N. Saracho, O. N. (Eds). *Meeting the challenge and Cultural diversity in early childhood education: Yearbook of early childhood education:* (pp. 170–173). New York: Teachers College Press.

Stephan, W. G., & Stephan, C. W. (1996). Predicting prejudice. *International Journal of Intercultural Relations, 20*, 409–426.

Triandafyllidou, A. (2000). The political discourse on immigration in Southern Europe: An analysis. *Journal of Community and Applied Social Psychology, 10*, 373–389.

Tyler, K. M., Uqdah, A. L., Dillihunt, M. L., Beatty-Hazelbaker, R., Conner, T., Gadson, N., et al. (2008). Cultural discontinuity: Toward a quantitative investigation of a major hypothesis in education. *Educational Researcher, 37*, 280–297.

United States Census Bureau. (1990). *U.S. Census 1990.* Retrieved on August 1, 2009, from http://www.census.gov

United States Census Bureau. (2000). *U.S. Census 2000.* Retrieved on August 1, 2009, from http://www.census.gov

United States Department of Education (2007). *The condition of education.* Washington, DC: National Center for Education Statistics.

Verkuyten M. (2009). Support for multiculturalism and minority rights: The role of national identification and out-group threat. *Social Justice Research, 22*(1), 31–52.

Yoo, H. C., & Lee, R. M. (2005). Ethnic identity and approach-type coping as moderators of the racial discrimination/well-being relation in Asian Americans. *Journal of Counseling Psychology, 52*,497–506.

NOTES

1 Refers to the 1954 *Brown v. Board of Education* Supreme Court case that desegregated America's public schools, even though most minority students continued to attend schools where they were the majority.

2. An abundance of scholarly work (mostly an array of current research articles) is available on the schools and the children of the poor.

ABOUT THE CONTRIBUTORS

Kathryn H. Au is Chief Executive Officer of SchoolRise, LLC. She began her career in education at the Kamehameha Elementary Education Program (KEEP) in Hawai'i as a teacher in grades K–2, and then researcher and teacher educator. Kathy was the first person to hold an endowed chair in education at the University of Hawai'i. Her research interests are school change and the literacy achievement of students of diverse cultural and linguistic backgrounds. She has published widely on issues of literacy and diversity, and her latest book is *Multicultural Issues and Literacy Achievement* (Erlbaum, 2006). A member of the Reading Hall of Fame, Kathy received the Causey Award for outstanding contributions to reading research. She has served as president of the International Reading Association, president of the National Reading Conference, and vice president of the American Educational Research Association.

Judith K. Bernhard is a Professor in the School of Early Childhood Education at Ryerson University and Director of its MA program. Her research program focuses on the social determinants of migrant and refugee children's performance in the educational systems of U.S. and Canada. Dr. Bernhard has investigated structural alterations of such families as they affect the children's social functioning. She has studied and proposed innovative practices tailored to meeting the needs of immigrant children and their families. She has published articles in refereed journals including *International Migration, Journal of Early Childhood Literacy, Refuge, Educational Policy Analysis, Canadian Ethnic Studies Journal, The Early Years Journal, Intercultural Education, Canadian Journal of Research in Early Childhood Education, Collectif*

Language and Cultural Diversity in Early Childhood Education, pages 265–272

Interculturel, Journal of Regional Studies, Journal of Early Childhood Teacher Education, Teachers College Record, and the *Canadian Journal of Education.* Recent publications include: *Using teachers' volunteer experiences in the Dominican Republic to develop social responsibility in Canadian middle-school students: An Authors in the Classroom approach* (2009), *Affirming plural belonging: Building on students' family-based plural and linguistic capital through a multiliteracies curriculum* (2009), *The institutional production and social reproduction of transnational families* (2009), *Living with uncertain legal status in Canada: Implications for the wellbeing of children and families* (2008), *Read my story: Promoting early literacy among diverse, urban, preschool children in poverty with the Early Authors Program* (2008), *Identity texts and literacy development among preschool English Language Learners* (2006), *The school 'misbehavior' of Latino children in a time of Zero Tolerance: Parents' views* (2004) and *Toward a 21st century developmental theory: Principles to account for diversity in children's lives* (2003).

Virginia Buysse is Senior Scientist at the FPG Child Development Institute at the University of North Carolina at Chapel Hill. She is co-directing a program of research to develop and validate *Recognition & Response (R&R),* a school-age model of Response to Intervention (RTI) for use in pre-kindergarten programs that is funded by the U.S. Department of Education, Institute of Education Sciences. She also serves as Co-PI on three other projects: the Center for Early Care and Education Research: Dual Language Learners funded by the U.S. Department of Health and Human Services (Administration for Children and Families, Office of Planning, Research, and Evaluation), and the National Professional Development Center on Inclusion and CONNECT (Center to Mobilize Early Childhood Knowledge), both funded by the U.S. Department of Education (Office of Special Education Programs). She is president of the *Division of Early Childhood* (DEC) of the *Council for Exceptional Children* (CEC) and Associate Editor of the *Journal of Early Intervention.*

Molly Cain is a new preschool teacher in New York City and is looking forward to incorporating storytelling into the classroom. She received her Master's degree in Early Childhood Education in 2009 from the Department of Curriculum and Teaching, Teachers College, Columbia University.

Dina C. Castro is a Scientist at the FPG Child Development Institute at the University of North Carolina at Chapel Hill. Her research program focuses on improving the quality of early care and education practices to promote development and learning among young children who are dual language learners, children of immigrants, children from diverse cultural and ethnic backgrounds, and those living in poverty. She serves as director of the Center for Early Care and Education Research: Dual Language Learners funded by the U.S. Department of Health and Human Services

(Administration for Children and Families, Office of Planning, Research, and Evaluation). She also serves as PI on the study *Nuestros Niños* Program: Promoting School Readiness for English Language Learners funded by the National Institute for Child Health and Human Development (NICHD), and on a study of child care utilization patterns for Latino families funded by the U.S. Department of Health and Human Services (Administration for Children and Families, Child Care Bureau). Her previous research includes a national study of early childhood programs' policies and practices to address the needs of Latino children and their families, a randomized controlled intervention study to promote early language and literacy among Latino Spanish-speaking children, the evaluation of an Early Head Start initiative to support dual language learner infants and toddlers, as well as studies of language and literacy development in young children, factors affecting the well-being of Latino immigrant families, and family involvement in Head Start. Dr. Castro is the lead author in the book *New Voices ~ Nuevas Voces Guide on Cultural and Linguistic Diversity in Early Childhood* and has published numerous articles and reports.

Anne Haas Dyson is a former teacher of young children and, currently, a professor of education at the University of Illinois at Urbana-Champaign. Previously she was on the faculty of the University of Georgia, Michigan State University, and the University of California, Berkeley, where she was a recipient of the campus Distinguished Teaching Award. She studies the childhood cultures and literacy learning of young schoolchildren. Among her publications are *Social Worlds of Children Learning to Write in an Urban Primary School*, which was awarded NCTE's David Russell Award for Distinguished Research, *Writing Superheroes*, and *The Brothers and Sisters Learn to Write: Popular Literacies in Childhood and School Cultures.* She recently co-authored two books with Celia Genishi, *On the Case*, on interpretive case studies, and *Children, Language, and Literacy: Diverse Learners in Diverse Times.*

Cara Furman is a doctoral student in Philosophy and Education at Teachers College Columbia University. Prior to that, she worked as an elementary school teacher in a New York City public school. She is interested in the role of imagination in identity formation and empowerment and classroom communities that foster the inclusion and successful participation of all students.

Eugene García is a Professor of Education and Vice President for Education Partnerships at Arizona State University. He is a regular contributor to the research and scholarships related to ELL and Hispanic students.

Celia Genishi is professor of education and chair of the Department of Curriculum and Teaching at Teachers College, Columbia University. She is a former secondary Spanish and preschool teacher and now teaches courses related to early childhood education and qualitative research methods. She is co-author (with Anne Haas Dyson) of *Children, Language, and Literacy: Diverse Learners in Diverse Times*. Her research interests include collaborative research and assessment with teachers, childhood bilingualism, and children's language use in classrooms.

Cristina Gillanders is an investigator at FPG Child Development Institute at the University of North Carolina at Chapel Hill. She served as an investigator in the *Nuestros Niños* Early Language and Literacy Program, a study that developed and evaluated an intervention to support language and literacy learning among Latino children who are dual language learners funded by the U.S. Department of Education, Institute for Education Sciences. She currently serves as Co-PI in the study *Nuestros Niños* Program: Promoting School Readiness for English Language Learners funded by the National Institute for Child Health and Human Development (NICHD). She has been a principal investigator in a pilot study for the development of the ASLA (Assessment of Second Language Acquisition in Young English Language Learners). She has conducted research in early childhood teaching practices for Latino English language learners, young Latinos emergent literacy, and Latino parents' beliefs about their children's literacy development and schooling. She has also worked as a bilingual teacher and director in early childhood settings in both the U.S. and her home country, Venezuela, and is the author of a Spanish emergent literacy manual for early childhood teachers.

Susan Grieshaber is Professor of Early Years Education at the School of Early Childhood, Queensland University of Technology, Brisbane, Australia. She taught for 14 years in before school and the early years of compulsory schooling contexts before teaching and researching in the university sector. She has published widely and her research interests include early childhood curriculum, policy, gender and families, with a focus on equity and diversity.

Nora E. Hyland is an assistant professor of Elementary Education at Rutgers, the State University of New Jersey. Using ethnographic and action research methodology, she examines the ways that race, class, gender, and sexuality position individuals within the sociocultural context of schools. She is particularly interested in the role of teachers in disrupting oppressive discourses and practices and working toward emancipatory teaching. Her work has appeared in numerous journals including: *The Journal of Teacher Education, Curriculum Inquiry, The New Educator,* and *Theory into Practice.*

Mary Renck Jalongo is a professor at Indiana University of Pennsylvania where she earned the university-wide outstanding professor award and co-ordinates the Doctoral Program in Curriculum and Instruction. As a class-room teacher, she worked with children of Mexican migrant farm workers in a federally funded bilingual preschool program. She has written, co-authored, or edited more than 25 books, including *Early Childhood Language Arts* (5th ed. Allyn & Bacon), *Creative Thinking and Arts-Based Learning* (4th ed. Merrill/Prentice Hall), *Exploring Your Role: An Introduction to Early Childhood Education* (3rd ed., Merrill/Prentice Hall), and *Major Trends and Issues in Early Childhood Education: Challenges, Controversies, and Insights* (2nd ed. Teachers College Press). In addition, she has written two books for NAEYC (*Learning to Listen, Listening to Learn; Young Children and Picture Books*) and two for ACEI. Dr. Jalongo is the recipient of seven national awards for excellence in scholarly writing that include two EDPRESS awards for Position Papers published by the Association for Childhood Education International. Since 1995, she has served as editor-in-chief of the Springer international publication, *Early Childhood Education Journal* and, since 2006, she has served as series editor for Springer's edited book series, *Educating the Young Child: Advances in Theory and Research, Implications for Practice.* Dr. Jalongo has made presentations throughout the world on various aspects of early childhood education.

Bryant Jensen is an Assistant Professor in Cognition and Learning at Bard College. He earned a Ph.D. in Educational Psychology from Arizona State University, and currently teaches courses in cognition and learning in a Masters of Arts in Teaching (MAT) program in California's San Joaquin Valley. His scholarly interests include the intersection of culture and cognition, early education, immigration, literacy development, home–school collaborations in student learning, and mixed methodological approaches in educational research. Bryant has worked as a school psychologist in urban schools in the Southwest, and studies literacy learning across diverse communities and school types in Mexico. Awards include the CIES New Scholars Award and the Fulbright-García Robles Fellowship. His work appears in the *Journal of Latinos and Education, The New Educator, Current Issues in Education, Journal of Immigrant and Refugees Studies, Social Policy Report, Educational Leadership,* and the *Harvard Journal for Hispanic Policy,* among other sources.

Nan Li is an Assistant Professor of Education at Claflin University. She received her doctoral degree in Curriculum and Instruction from Indiana University of Pennsylvania in 2004 and began teaching at Claflin University in 2005, where she earned the Exemplary Teacher Award in 2008-2009. Her teaching and research interests include the academic success of minority students, qualitative research, second language education, educational equality, and multicultural education. In 2007, Dr. Li received a million-dollar research grant from United States Department of Education. The title of this federal grant project is English Language Acquisition: National Professional Development Program. This grant program won The Rose-Duhon-Sells Multicultural Program Award in 2008 due to the contributions of the grant program participants in supporting the disadvantage school students in four low-income school districts in South Carolina. Dr. Li has presented at over twenty international and national conferences, including 2007, 2008, and 2009 AERA (American Educational Research Association) Annual Meetings. Her recent publications include several journal articles and two book chapters that advocate promoting quality education for all minority students.

Melinda Miller is a Doctoral student at the School of Early Childhood, Queensland University of Technology, Brisbane, Australia. Her research interests focus on cultural diversity and professional development for teachers in early childhood settings.

Laura Osterman recently earned her Master of Arts degree in Early Childhood General and Special Education at Teachers College, Columbia. She is teaching kindergarten at Growing Up Green, a new charter school in Queens, New York. She looks forward to continuing her work with storytelling as she embarks on this new endeavor.

C. Kanoelani Nāone is the CEO of the Institute for Native Pacific Education and Culture (INPEACE). She received a Ph.D. in Political Science from the University of Hawai‘i. Nāone is a speaker of the Hawaiian language with a deep interest in perpetuating Hawaiian language and culture. She has served as a teacher in Hawaiian immersion classrooms at the elementary level, and she has extensive experience as a leader of early childhood programs designed for Native Hawaiian and other children of diverse cultural backgrounds.

Veronica Pacini-Ketchabaw is an Associate Professor at the School of Child and Youth Care, University of Victoria, Victoria, British Columbia, Canada. Dr. Pacini-Ketchabaw is the co-director of the Investigating Quality Project and the Implementation of the British Columbia Early Learning Framework Project. These initiatives promote the active engagement of early childhood educators in discussions and actions that can lead to the formation of sustainable and positive early learning environments in B.C. She has also taken the lead at the University of Victoria, School of Child and Youth Care in developing an Early Years Specialization offered at the 3rd and 4th years of the Bachelors degree in CYC. In addition, Veronica is an executive for Research in Early Childhood Care, Education and Health (REACH). REACH is a consortium of early childhood researchers at the University of

Victoria. REACH advances collaborative and inter- disciplinary approaches, through university and community partnerships, to enhance the well- being of children. REACH is an affiliate of the Human Early Learning Partnership (HELP), a network of researcher at BC's six major universities (UVic, UBC, SFU, UNBC, TRU and UBC-O).

Ellen Peisner-Feinberg is a Senior Scientist at the Frank Porter Graham Child Development Institute and Research Associate Professor in the School of Education at the University of North Carolina at Chapel Hill. She has conducted numerous statewide and national research studies focused on the quality of early care and education programs and the effects on children, especially dual language learners and children at risk. Current efforts include the Recognition & Response (R&R) Project, which is developing and evaluating amodel of Response to Intervention (RTI) specifically designed for pre-k children (funded by the U.S. Department of Education, Institute for Education Sciences); the Center for Early Care and Education Research: Dual Language Learners (CECER-DLL), a national research center funded by the U.S. Department of Health and Human Services (Administration for Youth and Families, Office of Planning, Research, and Evaluation); the Child Care Choices Project, a study of child care utilization patterns for Latino families (funded by the U.S. Department of Health and Human Services, Administration for Children and Families, Child Care Bureau); and the Evaluation of the North Carolina More at Four Prekindergarten Program, a publicly funded early education program designed to serve at-risk children, for which she has directed the statewide evaluation for the past 9 years.

Sharon Ryan is Associate Professor of Early Childhood Education at Rutgers, the State University of New Jersey. Her research interests include early childhood curriculum and policy, early childhood teacher education, and the potential of critical theories for rethinking early childhood practices. She has published a number of articles, book chapters, and reports in these areas including the recently themed issue of *Early Education and Development* on Teachers and Teaching in Early Education and Care (Goffin & Ryan, 2008).

Aya Takemura is originally from Japan and graduated from Teachers College, Columbia University in 2009 majoring in child development and special education (Intellectual Disability and Autism). Currently she is living in San Diego, CA working as a therapist for children with autism. Her future plans include publishing her own children's books and establishing an agency or school for children with disabilities in Japan.

Wei-Yee (Angela) Tsang is originally from Taiwan and recently graduated from Teachers College, Columbia University with a Master of Education degree in

Intellectual Disability/Autism and Early Childhood Education. Currently a special education itinerant teacher in New York City, she thinks observation and reflection are crucial components of education and thoroughly enjoyed incorporating both into the storytelling project and chapter.

Julianne P. Wurm is the author of *Working in the Reggio Way: A Beginner's Guide for American Teachers,* drawn from work she conducted as a participant-observer in the schools of Reggio Emilia, Italy. Julianne began her career in education as a member of Teach for America, earned her M.A. and Ed.M. at Teachers College, Columbia University, and is currently working as an instructor in the Department of Curriculum and Teaching as she writes her dissertation. Julianne's work continues to focus on teacher education, documentation, and teacher inquiry.